Shakespeare's
Troilus and Cressida

Shakespeare's
Troilus and Cressida

Textual Problems and Performance Solutions

Roger Apfelbaum

Newark: University of Delaware Press

Associated University Presses
2010 Eastpark Boulevard
Cranbury, NJ 08512

The paper used in this publication meets the requirements of the American National Standard for Permanence of Paper for Printed Library Materials
Z39.48-1984

Library of Congress Cataloging-in-Publication Date

Apfelbaum, Roger, 1962–
    Shakespeare's Troilus and Cressida : textual problems and performance solutions / Roger Apfelbaum.
        p.   cm.
    Includes bibliographical references (p.) and index.
    ISBN 0-87413-813-2 (alk. paper)
    1. Shakespeare, William, 1564–1616. Troilus and Cressida—Criticism, Textual.   2. Shakespeare, William, 1564–1616—Dramatic Production.
3. Troilus (Legendary character) in literature.   4. Troy (Extinct city)—In literature.   5. Trojan War—Literature and the war.   6. Cressida (Fictitious character) I. Title.
PR2836.A858 2004
822.3′3—dc21
                                                                    2003007717

PRINTED IN THE UNITED STATES OF AMERICA

I dedicate this book
to my parents for their boundless love and support.

Contents

Illustrations

Acknowledgments

THERE HAVE BEEN MANY TEACHERS, COLLEAGUES, STUDENTS, ACTORS, directors, editors, friends, and family that have helped make this book possible. Work on the topic began at the Shakespeare Institute of the University of Birmingham, and nearly everyone associated with that marvelous place was involved in my work. Stanley Wells and Tom Matheson directed my research and offered continual encouragement and extensive commentary and discussion about my writing. Susan Brock is a researcher's ideal librarian; one who teaches and supports as well as knows where to find everything. Robert Smallwood was the first to provide encouragement that my interest in bringing performance and bibliographical studies together would be a suitable book project. Peter Holland, John Jowett, and David Bevington provided valuable suggestions and a continued interest in helping to turn it into a book.

I have been particularly fortunate in having friends that have taken an interest in my work. Barbara Hodgdon provided both a scholarly ideal and an extremely insightful, detailed, and encouraging reading of my work. She continues to help me raise the critical stakes in my thinking and writing. Her extensive suggestions offered a learning experience I have only begun to absorb. Thomas Berger ran a *Troilus and Cressida* seminar at a Shakespeare Association of America conference that provided my first opportunity to present this work to a group of scholars. The warm reception by Tom and others in the group also helped support the idea that the project would yield worthwhile insights.

The archive of the Royal Shakespeare Company was the primary resource for book's theatre history. The librarians there, especially Silvia Morris, have helped make the research and publication process enjoyable and efficient. I want to gratefully acknowledge a grant from the Shakespeare Birthplace Trust and their assistance in obtaining permission rights for most of the photographs in this book. I thank the Huntington Library for the permission to reproduce images of early editions. I also want to thank staff at the British National Sound

11

Archives, the Players Club of New York, the Library for the Performing Arts of the New York Public Library, the Birmingham (U.K.) Central Library, the Shakespeare Institute Library, the British Library, the University of London Library (Senate House), the Folger Shakespeare Library, and the Library of Congress.

I am very grateful to the actors and directors (listed in the appendix) who agreed to be interviewed. As described in the conclusion, Ian Judge provided me with the valuable opportunity to observe and contribute to rehearsals for his Royal Shakespeare Company production and the actors and stage managers made me feel very welcome. My colleagues and students at Seton Hall University provide a wonderful community for writing. I would particularly like to thank Chrys Grieco and Martha Carpentier for their support in helping me complete additions and revisions. Publication of the book has been assisted in various and valuable ways by Kathryn Lee, Jeff Lee, Sarah Lyons, Donald Mell, and Christine Retz.

Shakespeare's
Troilus and Cressida

Introduction: "Shall I Not Lie in Publishing a Truth?"

Dᴜʀɪɴɢ ʀᴇʜᴇᴀʀsᴀʟs ꜰᴏʀ ʜɪs ʀᴏʏᴀʟ sʜᴀᴋᴇsᴘᴇᴀʀᴇ ᴄᴏᴍᴘᴀɴʏ (ʀsᴄ) ᴘʀᴏ-duction of *Troilus and Cressida,* Sam Mendes was photographed sitting at a table with three different editions of the play (edited by Kenneth Muir, R. A. Foakes, and Peter Alexander) on his left, his promptbook (made from enlarged photocopies of Foakes's edition) on his right, and some props behind him (see illustration).[1] The photograph sets up a number of relationships between Shakespearean texts and performances, and between the divisions and convergences of academic and theatrical interpretations. The editions laid out in front of Mendes are evidence of the play's textual uncertainty and of the debate among scholars that produces editions with differences in the dialogue and stage directions. In this study I will explore how directors like Mendes make use of this textual ambiguity and how the activity of producing the play for the theater comments on editorial debates.

The photograph of Mendes was taken at the Shakespeare Institute in Stratford-upon-Avon, in a large room normally used for academic lectures, forums with actors and students, and also, on occasion, rented as a rehearsal space by the RSC. Two years after he rehearsed *Troilus and Cressida,* Mendes returned to the same room at the Shakespeare Institute to discuss his RSC productions (of *Troilus and Cressida, The Alchemist,* and *Richard III*) with a gathering of scholars at the International Shakespeare Conference.[2] He was introduced by his former Cambridge tutor Peter Holland, who told the members of the conference that Mendes had telephoned him to discuss which play Mendes might choose to direct as his first play for the RSC. In both the photograph and the talk, the room became the site of an exchange between scholarly and theatrical approaches to *Troilus and Cressida.* How did Mendes use the different editions during rehearsals, and how did his encounters with academics (at university and as editors) influence his theatrical choices? What are the benefits for academics that not only see Mendes' productions but also

1. Sam Mendes rehearsing at the Shakespeare Institute, *Observer Magazine,* **22 April 1990. Reproduced by permission of The Image Works, Inc.**

hear the director speak about his methods and choices? However wary they may be of each other, there are many influences and exchanges between theater practitioners and academics, and in this study I hope to show the value of juxtaposing editorial and theatrical treatments of bibliographical problems.

The editions on Mendes' desk during rehearsals were not only used for their glosses and explanatory notes, but were also referred to for their differences in dialogue and stage directions. Before rehearsals began, Mendes consulted promptbooks of previous RSC productions of *Troilus and Cressida;* in doing so he reshaped the play not only with an awareness of some editorial alternatives but also with some knowledge about textual choices made for the theater. These printed and performed texts raise many questions about what the text of a play can be and how editors, directors, and performers are special kinds of readers and shapers of the text.

There are nearly five hundred substantive differences between the 1609 Quarto (Q) and 1623 Folio (F) versions of *Troilus and Cressida* and many more instances where editors have emended the dialogue and stage directions.[3] The goals of editors and directors are certainly different, if not completely contradictory, but both need to make choices in creating a unique version of the play. While editors may attempt to gain historical accuracy by striving, however vainly, to present the most authoritative text, directors need only cite their dramatic judgment or pragmatic constraints in defense of an attempt to create a version of the play that will work for their audience. The different rationales with which editors and theater practitioners devise a version of the play need not, however, preclude a meaningful dialogue about what the text can be, the meaning and significance of variants and emendations, and the performance possibilities for moments of textual ambiguity. The discrepancies between different editions of *Troilus and Cressida* and the dissimilarity between productions of the play signal the inability to fix a stable text in either theory or practice, in print, or in the theater. Moments in the play that are open not only theoretically, critically, and dramatically, but also in the more concrete sense of not having an agreed content, offer an ideal site for expanding and conflating the usual domains of theater history and bibliographical studies.

While it may be unique to base a study on the juxtaposition of editorial and theatrical history, and unusual to establish such an extended dialogue between the concerns of bibliographers and theater historians, there are certainly precedents for cross references between the two fields.[4] Most influential for the present study, however, is the way that poststructuralist theory and criticism has established a theoretical basis and vocabulary for expanding the notions of text, encouraging the sort of intertextual approach that brings together seemingly disparate histories.

The most radical rethinking and debate about the text of a Shakespeare play in recent years must surely be the controversy surrounding the texts of *King Lear*. Although the bibliographers who argued against conflating *King Lear* may not have been directly influenced by trends in critical theory, their arguments for a changing view of the texts have led to what Russ MacDonald calls "post-structuralist editing."[5] Margreta de Grazia and Peter Stallybrass poignantly opened their important essay on "The Materiality of the Shakespearean Text" by describing the influence of the *King Lear* controversy:

For over two hundred years, *King Lear* was one text; in 1986, with the Oxford Shakespeare, it became two; in 1989, with *The Complete "King Lear" 1608–1623,* it became four (at least). As a result of this multiplication, Shakespeare studies will never be the same . . . because something long taken for granted has been cast into doubt: the self-identity of the work. We are no longer agreed on the fundamental status of the textual object before us. Is it one or more? The significance of this uncertainty cannot be overestimated. Identity and difference are, after all, the basis of perception itself, the way we tell one thing from another. The possibility of multiple texts, then, constitutes a radical change indeed: not just an enlargement of Shakespeare's works but a need to reconceptualize the fundamental category of a *work* by Shakespeare.[6]

The statement makes clear, with both its language and argument, that the bibliographical and editorial division of *King Lear* has had an impact on many aspects of critical work. The revisionist theories not only argued for preserving the individual integrity of the Q and F versions of *King Lear* and against the editorial practice of conflation, but they also undermined the ideal of a single, recoverable, authorial text. If Shakespeare revised his plays and was involved in their performances, and if the changes to the text that occurred during the first rehearsals and performances are not corruptions but part of the process of a play's composition, then the project of identifying an authorial text must be questioned. Rather than simply divide the search for an authorial text into the task of uncovering two authorial texts, the *King Lear* debate contributed to a destabilizing of the notion of textual authority.[7]

The rethinking about the *King Lear* texts was accompanied by other shifts in bibliographical and editorial theory that compounded the case against many of the goals and methods of the New Bibliography.[8] Jerome McGann's concept of a socialized text, and critics such as D. F. Mackenzie and Paul Werstine who expressed skepticism about what can be recovered by bibliographical research, encouraged a reconsideration of the way we think about the first editions of Shakespeare's plays.[9] Where once there was a general consensus about the attempt to identify and rid Shakespeare's play from the influence of bad quartos, foul papers, and theatrical interpolations, the usefulness of these categories and the marginalization of such bastard texts have been dramatically reconsidered.[10] Leah Marcus, considering the relationship between *The Taming of the Shrew* and *The Taming of a Shrew,* suggested that

we start thinking of the different versions of *The Taming of the Shrew* intertextually—as a cluster of related texts which can be fruitfully read together and against each other as "Shakespeare." To do that, of course, is to give up the idea that either Shakespeare or the canon of his works is a single determinate thing. It is to carry Shakespearean textual studies out of the filiative search for a single "authentic" point of origin and into the purview of poststructuralist criticism, where the authority of the author loses its élan and the text becomes a multiple, shifting process rather than an artifact set permanently in print.[11]

A critical meditation on textual ambiguity need not be guided by an attempt to solve a problem. Perceiving the text as a "multiple shifting process" can foreground the cultural and critical prejudices involved in preparing an edition of a play by highlighting the motives and significance of editorial choices and theories. Modern productions can offer an especially rich source of commentary for widening the study of textual cruxes, presenting a theatrical history of the text and textual choices that can interrogate editorial history. Within a poststructuralist framework, the conflict between editorial and theatrical choices cannot be dismissed as irrelevant because of the different aims of the productions and editions, but the conflict is particularly relevant because it emphasizes the subjectivity involved in reshaping the text.

In his introduction to *The Division of the Kingdoms,* the seminal collection of essays subtitled "Shakespeare's Two Versions of *King Lear,*" Stanley Wells expressed a

> hope that the new attitudes [against conflating the different versions of *King Lear*] will be represented in theatre practice. It would probably be over-optimistic to expect professional directors to give us either the Quarto or the Folio text uncut, but it would be perfectly easy for a director to base his production on one or the other text, not admitting any degree of conflation. And it would be especially valuable to have such a production based on the Folio as a way of testing, in the only way that is ultimately valid, the belief that the revisions are theatrically justified, and that *King Lear* is a better drama in its latter state. A director who took this course would be following Granville-Barker's recommendation: "On the whole then—and if he show a courageous discretion—I recommend a producer to found himself on the Folio. For that it does show some at least of Shakespeare's own reshapings I feel sure."[12]

Theater practice cannot only be influenced by editorial theories, but it can also serve as a testing ground for these theories. Wells looks not only to future performances, but with his citation of Granville-Barker, he also shows how past considerations by theater professionals can be incorporated into editorial debate. In the same way that productions can help clarify the overall distinctions between the two texts of *King*

Lear, theater history can also offer commentary on different versions of specific passages. One of the essays that Wells introduced was Roger Warren's "The Folio Omission of the Mock Trial," which cites modern productions of *King Lear* to support conjectures about the meaning and significance of the differences between Q and F.[13] Although he welcomes the commentary that theater history can provide, Warren also cautions that "although theatre evidence is inconclusive since no major modern production has used the Quarto or Folio exclusively, it does confirm the interdependence of 3.6 and 4.6."[14] Even without strictly adhering to the bibliographical theory that separates Q and F versions of *King Lear,* and perhaps even without knowing of the textual ambiguity of the passages, productions can contradict, support, and supplement a critic's understanding of the passage.

The year before *The Division of the Kingdoms* was published, an article appeared by Gary Taylor entitled "*Troilus and Cressida:* Bibliography, Performance and Criticism."[15] While the title might seem to promise a fusion of theatrical and scholarly approaches to textual problems, the reference to performance is not to theater history, but to performance possibilities. Only once, in a parenthetical comment, does Taylor refer to a production to illustrate a possible reading.[16] The "Performance" in his title refers to the performance alternatives that arise from textual ambiguity, but it is in the imaginary theater of the critic's mind and in conjectures about the theater of Shakespeare's time that Taylor, and most bibliographers and editors, seek to stage their theories.

Taylor's essay is crucial to this study in many respects, and is referred to often because of his innovative ideas about many of the play's bibliographical cruxes. Most importantly, however, it is what Taylor's essay does not do that helped suggest the idea of using theater history to interrogate bibliographical theories and editorial choices. Renaissance scholars have a specialized knowledge of the printing and performance conditions of plays, but their judgments about variants and the need for emendations in the dialogue and stage directions often go beyond what can be known about the printing or performance of plays four hundred years ago. Editorial decisions are commonly made with little more than a sense of what is most effective according to a particular editor's dramatic and literary tastes.

Instead of looking for the solution to a bibliographical problem, moments of textual uncertainty can be explored for the ways that variants and conjectures can provide meaningful alternatives. Rather than only defending their choices in textual notes, editors could more frequently encourage considerations of different readings.

Such humility would serve to remind readers that editorial choices are constantly being made. Michael Warren forcefully points out that

> to make an edition is to make a book; to make an edition of a Shakespeare play is to make a text over, and in many cases to create the play anew. Even the most sparing editor of Shakespeare is an alterer. Such editorial activity has a particular irritation in relation to dramatic texts, for the pursuit of clarity in editions leads to special problems; theatrical possibility being various, the establishment of a text may involve the restriction of the potentialities of the original text as dramatic script.[17]

A comparison of different editors' decisions and their bibliographical and critical justifications for those decisions clearly shows that if any specialized knowledge privileges the scholarly quest for an authorial text, it is of a kind that leads to as many disagreements as agreements. What is most disconcerting is that the theories and notes arguing for readings are all too often given in dogmatic terms that seek to narrow choices rather than celebrate options. While editors must make decisions about variants and emendations, it does not follow that other readings need to be dismissed as inferior. Certainly some editors and bibliographers do point readers in a positive way to alternatives in the dialogue and stage directions, but the passages examined in this study will repeatedly provide examples of editors attempting to convince readers that one choice is better than another or that only one reading has any claim to authority or dramatic viability. Theater history can show the effectiveness of different variants and emendations, and can contribute in a positive way to exploring moments of textual ambiguity.

Bringing together theatrical and editorial history for a discussion of a single moment creates a number of problems, perhaps the most glaring being that editorial arguments and performances are taken somewhat out of context. Choosing to write only about the textual problems that have appropriate and interesting theatrical commentary means that some major textual cruxes are not discussed, and some of the most important and insightful moments of the play's theater history are excluded. This study does not attempt to offer new theories about the texts of *Troilus and Cressida*, nor does it provide an overview of the play's performance history. Each chapter discusses in some depth the editorial and performance history of a single passage, and therefore glimpses into the editorial and theatrical history of the play, but the focus remains on the method of interrogating textual problems with performance decisions.

Broader issues of performance and editing are occasionally addressed but only when they are related to the study of the passage.

The search for the provenance of the Q and F texts and theories that attempt to connect one text more directly to Shakespeare, Shakespeare's final thoughts, or Shakespeare's theater (with such categories as foul and fair papers, promptbooks, and notions of revision) are largely irrelevant to the exploration of how different readings might work, and how they have been made to work onstage.[18] The limited space of this study is devoted to the analysis of individual passages, and no attempt is made to provide the kind of textual introduction found in a scholarly edition.[19] The theater history in the discussion of the Prologue is somewhat less selective than in other chapters in order to introduce most of the productions that are discussed, but the reader is referred elsewhere for a more general theater history.[20]

Passages were chosen for discussion after the editorial history of the play had been extensively researched and the main points of textual debate identified. Promptbooks, reviews, and other archives were then mined for evidence of how productions treated the moments of textual ambiguity. This research produced a variorum-like set of notes cataloguing the editorial and theatrical history of many variants and emendations. Although these notes may be used for an edition of the play, or a detailed commentary on the play's editorial and theatrical history, for the present study they provide the raw material for a critical analysis of selected passages.[21] Rather than briefly presenting the many instances where theater history can comment on editorial issues, the study is divided into chapters that study one moment, or a group of related moments, in some depth. Developing a critical narrative around such moments allows for an investigation of matters surrounding the editorial and theatrical issues. Most chapters discuss Elizabethan stage practice and the rich tradition of literary, historic, and dramatic versions of the Trojan legend, but not with a desire to recover a stage event or establish a source. Literary and dramatic connections, like the play's theater history, expand the scope with which bibliographical and editorial cruxes are considered.

It is probably not surprising that the richest source for theatrical comment on editorial issues is the debates about the wording and placing of stage directions. The analysis of stage directions in Q and F has been used as a vital clue in signaling the copytext used by the printers, but the editorial choice in fixing the point of an entrance or exit is also one of the most theatrical decisions editors must make. In placing directions editors are, in effect, staging the play, and their interpretative decisions can significantly alter the stage images and dialogue. Adding to the ambiguity of the play's many staging questions is the debate over where the play was performed, and whether it was performed, during Shakespeare's life. Peter Alexander's influential Inns of Court theory is discussed in the chapter about the play's ending, but throughout the study there are references to the way in which different theaters might have provided alternative staging opportunities and various stage spaces.

Using modern productions in the discussion of Elizabethan staging is an approach extensively championed by Alan Dessen.[22] The influence and importance of Dessen's work will be reiterated throughout this study, both for his analysis of stage conventions, and for the way he utilizes modern productions and the views of theater professionals.

> An intelligent and well-realized production of *any* play will provide a variety of insights not available even to the most imaginative reader, for the skilled actors and directors can probe a script through and beyond the rehearsal process in ways that go far beyond the resources of even the most careful explicator. Especially when such a process is brought to bear upon a play not regularly produced, insights, answers, and even new questions can emerge. Admittedly, many productions do not achieve this level of insight or do so only fitfully, but the opportunity *is* there *if* (and this is a very big *if*) the academic playgoer approaches the theatrical experience with a mind open to new meanings and juxtapositions rather than a mind fixed upon the "right" interpretation.[23]

Modern productions are not only valuable as interpretations of a play or as a reflection of the culture that revives the play, but they can also contribute to an investigation of Elizabethan stage practice. In questioning, for example, how tents might have been used in a performance of *Troilus and Cressida* at the Globe, Dessen encourages an approach that would only begin with an examination of the use of tents by Shakespeare and his contemporaries. Productions of the play since Shakespeare's time also provide a valuable exploration of the issues that cannot be answered fully by any historian. The process of rehearsing a play for any theater or any stage, such as proscenium arch, thrust, in-the-round, studio space, or amphitheater, usually requires a close scrutiny of the relationship between dialogue and movement. The experience and experiments of theater professionals, especially concerning the physical space of the stage, should not be dismissed simply because they are not attempting to recreate Elizabethan staging. When the early texts are unclear about when a character enters or exits, whether or not characters hear or are deaf to certain lines, the play's theater history can offer a valuable source of options that moves the inquiry from asking how a moment should be done, to exploring the dramatic consequences if it is done in different ways.

Troilus and Cressida fits neatly into Dessen's remarks about the value of productions of rarely performed plays, although Dessen refers to plays far less often performed than even the most neglected plays by Shakespeare. Between 1609, when the first state of the Quarto title page asserted that the play was "acted by the Kings Maiesties seruants at the Globe," and 1907, when Charles Fry offered a staged reading of the play, there is no evidence of the play being performed in English. During the nearly three hundred years that *Troilus and Cressida* was absent from the stage, there were several performance considerations that can offer relevant editorial and theatrical interpretations. Dryden's adaptation (in 1679) came thirty years before Rowe's first edition (1709). In "correcting" the play, the changes Dryden made can be seen as both theatrical and editorial, anticipating many of the emendations and dramatic choices made in editions and productions.

The acting editions that appeared in the eighteenth and nineteenth centuries did not have productions of *Troilus and Cressida* to base their cuts and comments upon, but a kind of performance tradition was nevertheless established.[24] Bell's acting edition made some reference to Dryden's play for its suggestions on cuts and rearrangements, and John Philip Kemble may have consulted the Bell edition when he prepared a promptbook for a production that never made it to the stage.[25] The editors of the Henry Irving edition referred to Kemble's promptbook for its suggestions on how the play should be cut if it were to be performed. Dryden's adaptation, Kemble's promptbook, and the acting editions can substitute for an early theater history for the purposes of this study, but they also highlight the lack of real stage performances that might have influenced editorial and critical interpretations. What Dessen's comment about rarely performed plays makes clear is that when *Troilus and Cressida* finally began to be regularly performed, the long history of editorial debate was for the first time subjected to theatrical experimentation.

The twentieth century theater history of *Troilus and Cressida* provides many ways of commenting upon editorial problems. The acceptance and rejection of editorial decisions during rehearsals and the changes made during the life of a production are at least as important as what happens onstage at any given performance. Both the reception of a production and the decision-making process of rehearsals can offer theatrical insights into a moment, but not without enormous logistical and theoretical problems. The raw materials of theater history, namely rehearsal notes, promptbooks, photographs, journalistic and scholarly reviews, archive tapes, and interviews, all give selective views of the production and can be extremely ambiguous (and sometimes contradictory) when used to clarify what actually happened, what was the rationale for a choice, and what was the re-action to a choice.[26] The inability to answer these questions can be both frustrating and liberating, provoking alternatives that are relevant for a debate about the textual possibilities, but which may not have taken place in rehearsals or performances. For the purposes of this study, an ambiguously placed promptbook note or a partially erased cut can be just as useful as a review or a videotape in suggesting a range of dramatic potential for a textual crux.

Much of the theater history for this study relies on promptbooks, and almost every opportunity to check a promptbook against another performance archive (such as stage manager's scripts, other prompt-books, and audio- and videotapes) revealed major differences. Discussions with actors, directors, and stage managers confirm that the promptbooks are rarely kept up to date with the variety of changes that occur during the life of a production. When moments in a production are referred to, the production record that describes the moment is usually noted, but it can never be confidently asserted that promptbook notes, or photographs, for example, provide conclusive evidence about the staging of that moment. Rehearsal notes or interviews can help recover the decision-making process, but much more common is the inability to identify when or by whom a staging choice was made. Even when the handwriting of promptbook notes can be identified, as in Kemble's and Poel's, the decisions may not be entirely instigated by the director. For purposes of convenience, however, all productions, and their cuts and staging choices, are referred to by the name or names of the directors.

Productions are discussed not necessarily because they are considered the most successful or important, but rather because they had accessible archives or were productions that I attended.[27] Reviews are often unhelpful in determining how a particular moment was performed, and therefore many productions are left out of this study because of lack of appropriate evidence. Some productions that have left sufficient evidence, and even some personally attended, were also left out because they did not offer useful commentary on the particular moments chosen for discussion. There is not an attempt to argue for the primacy of British productions or RSC productions over either American, translated, or other productions, but access to archives and to individuals involved in British productions, particularly by the RSC, have led to their receiving the majority of attention.

At the risk of presenting a somewhat disjointed description of production decisions, the theater history of each passage is arranged chronologically. It is hoped that a narrative thread is created by the way that productions interrogate textual issues from a number of dramatic perspectives, but there is no attempt to group productions together or to present the theater history as part of a broader critical argument. Production choices that have not found editorial support are more extensively considered than widely accepted readings, but not with the desire to replace one reading with another. By arguing for the dramatic viability of variants that are often rejected, each chapter will hopefully expand the range of options for a particular passage.

Productions can provide not only contradictory views on how to play a moment, but they also reveal a variety of approaches to the text. This introduction began with the image of Sam Mendes surrounded by editions, making dramatic decisions with some reference to editorial differences. Such an image is important for defining the subject of this study as the exchange between editions and productions, but the photograph represents only one of the many ways that directors use editions. When I interviewed John Barton about his involvement in three productions of *Troilus and Cressida,* I asked him if, like Mendes, he consulted different editions. He replied that he sometimes would look to other editions for glosses but did not often seek out textual differences. His decision to use Alice Walker's edition of *Troilus and Cressida* was part of a larger decision to use the editions in the New (Cambridge) Shakespeare series. For practical reasons, he did not like using editions in rehearsal that cluttered the page with notes (such as the Arden), but he also particularly liked working with the Cambridge series (The New Shakespeare) because he found their decisions, especially those of the general editor John Dover Wilson, to be "quite eccentric."[28] Barton was therefore eager for some textual instability, and found it useful to mistrust his edition as a way of provoking reactions against editorial choices.

I pursued the matter with John Barton by asking him about his treatment of stage directions. I mentioned that Donald Sinden once said, "the first thing I do is go through my text and cross out all stage directions,"[29] and I asked if this was a common practice among actors and directors. Although Barton does not take such drastic steps, he emphasized the need to discover what was right for each production, each theater, and each set. Rehearsals often brought into question the placement of stage directions, the characters included in stage directions, and the actions described in stage directions, but he stressed that decisions to depart from an edition were often initiated by pragmatic considerations specific to a production, and were only sometimes the result of questioning an editorial decision.

The photograph of Mendes and the comments by Barton provide two examples of the many different ways that productions use editions. Throughout this study there are instances where production decisions can be shown to have been made with an awareness of editorial issues, instances where it is not known whether the editorial issues were considered, and instances where it is almost certain that a decision was made without knowledge or concern for the textual debate. All of these cases can provide relevant commentary, for even the most pragmatically made decisions can inadvertently support or contradict an editorial or a bibliographical theory.

The methodology employed in this study can be used to study the editorial and performance history of almost any play, and among Shakespeare's plays, perhaps most resonantly for those plays with particularly complex editorial problems arising from the existence of two or more early editions. *Troilus and Cressida* provides a relatively brief and recent theater history and means that while being selective, many of the major productions can be discussed in each chapter. *Troilus and Cressida* also creates the opportunity to study the textual instability of a play that is obsessively concerned with issues that directly relate to this study's method of inquiry. When de Grazia and Stallybrass write about doubting the "self-identity of the work," or when Marcus states that we must "give up the idea that either Shakespeare or the canon of his works is a single determinate thing," few plays can complement such views with repeated explorations into the complex questions of having and communicating personal identity.[30] Similarly, the ambiguity about characters' movements and the staging issues often are related to the repeated actions and dialogue that raise profound questions about the nature of observation.[31] The relevance of the play's thematic content to its editorial and theatrical history often expands the discussion into areas of critical concerns, and it is hoped that throughout this work the textual and performance questions can provide significant insight into many aspects of this challenging and extraordinary play.

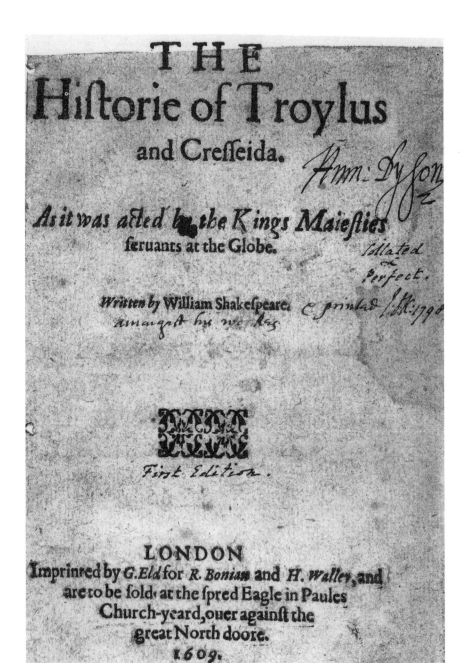

THE
Hiſtorie of Troylus
and Creſſeida.

As it was acted by the Kings Maieſties
ſeruants at the Globe.

Written by William Shakeſpeare.

LONDON
Imprinted by *G. Eld* for *R. Bonian* and *H. Walley*, and
are to be ſold at the ſpred Eagle in Paules
Church-yeard, ouer againſt the
great North doore.
1609.

2. Qa and Qb title pages. Reproduced by permission of The Huntington Library,
San Marino, California.

THE
Famous Historie of
Troylus *and* Cresseid.

Excellently expressing the beginning
of their loues, with the conceited wooing
of *Pandarus* Prince of *Licia.*

Written by William Shakespeare.

LONDON
Imprinted by *G. Eld* for *R. Bonian* and *H. Walley,* and
are to be sold at the spred Eagle in Paules
Church-yeard, ouer against the
great North doore.
1609.

A neuer writer, to an euer reader. Newes.

Ternall reader, you haue heere a new
play, neuer stal'd with the Stage,
neuer clapper-clawd with the palmes
of the vulger, and yet passing full of
the palme comicall; for it is a birth of
your braine, that neuer vnder-tooke
any thing commicall, vainely: And
were but the vaine names of commedies changde for the
titles of Commodities, or of Playes for Pleas; you should
see all those grand censors, that now stile them such
vanities, flock to them for the maine grace of their
grauities: especially this authors Commedies, that are
so fram'd to the life, that they serue for the most common Commentaries, of all the actions of our liues. shew-
ing such a dexteritie, and power of witte, that the most
displeased with Playes, are pleasd with his Commedies.
And all such dull and heauy-witted worldlings, as were
neuer capable of the witte of a Commedie, comming by
report of them to his representations, haue found that
witte there, that they neuer found in them-selues, and
haue parted better wittied then they came: feeling an
edge of witte set vpon them, more then euer they
dreamd they had braine to grinde it on. So much and
such sauored salt of witte is in his Commedies, that they
seeme (for their height of pleasure) to be borne in that
sea that brought forth Venus. Amongst all there is
none more witty then this: And had I time I would
comment vpon it, though I know it needs not, (for so

¶ 2   much

3. Qb, Epistle. Reproduced by permission of The Huntington Library, San Marino,
California.

much as will make you thinke your cesterne well be-
stowd) but for so much worth, as euen poore I know to be
stuft in it. It deserues such a labour, as well as the best
Commedy in Terence or Plautus. And beleeue this,
that when hee is gon, and his Commedies out of sale,
you will scramble for them, and set up a new English
Inquisition. Take this for a warning, and at the perrill
of your pleasures losse, and ludgements, refuse not, nor
like this the lesse, for not being sullied, with the smoaky
breath of the multitude; but thinke fortune for the
scape it hath made amongst you. Since by the grand
possessors wills I beleeue you should haue prayd for them
rather then beene prayd. And so I leaue all such to bee
prayd for (for the states of their wits healths)
that will not praise it

Vale.

1
"The Vaunt and Firstlings"

How is the fictional world of a play introduced, and how are the first moments of the experience uniquely important? What types of literary, theatrical, and cultural preconceptions are fed by an advertisement, the purchase of a ticket, a review, a program, a confrontation with an open set, or the list and description of characters, a book's cover, title page, introduction, and format? These peripheral factors inform a dramatic experience before the dialogue begins, but what of prologues, choruses, and inductions that exist somewhere between the real and fictional worlds of the theater? It is the journey from outside the framework of the fiction, and the crossing into drama that I want to focus on in considering the opening of *Troilus and Cressida*.

The earliest editions of *Troilus and Cressida* present many aspects of the often conflicting aims of preparing a reader and an audience for a play. Even the differences between the two states of the 1609 quarto (Q) offer very different introductions to the play.[1] What is believed to be the first state (Qa) has a title page advertising the play "As it was acted by the King's Majesties servants at the Globe," sanctioning the play as performed at the popular theater by the royally approved players. The second state (Qb) cancelled the mention of a performance, inserting in its place the assessment of *Troilus and Cressida* as a play "excellently expressing the beginning of their loves, with the conceited wooing of Pandarus Prince of Licia." Along with the different title page, the second state adds what can be considered the first critical introduction attached to a Shakespeare play. In an epistle to the reader, a device Shakespeare's contemporaries (or printers of Shakespeare's contemporaries) often used to introduce their plays, a "Never writer" addresses an "ever reader" with particular interest in what is now labeled reader response.[2]

Whether or not Q's two states were devised to attract different types of readers, they appeal to different reasons for owning and reading the play. The sales pitch of the second state shifts the value of the play from the historical performance (Qa's "King's Majesties servants at the Globe") to what the play is (Qb's "beginning of their loves"), and what it can do for the readers (in the epistle's claim that they will become "better witted").[3] Actually praising the play for not having been "clapper-clawed by the palms of the vulgar," the epistle splits and judges the different formats for appreciating the text. The "scape" the epistle claims the play has made from its "grand possessors" dramatizes the separation of the text from the theater, dividing the play into a text to be possessed by the theater or the reader.

The epistle's preoccupation with wit provides an intriguing analysis of the benefits of reading Shakespeare's comedies.

> This author's comedies, that are so framed to the life that they serve for the most common commentaries of all the actions of our lives, showing such a dexterity and power of wit that the most displeased with plays, are pleased with his comedies, and all such dull and heavy-witted worldlings as were never capable of the wit of a comedy, coming by report of them to his representations, have found that wit there that they never found in themselves, and have parted better witted than they came, feeling an edge of wit set upon them more than ever they dreamed they had brain to grind it on.

The "never writer" is confident that the truth of the comedy will overwhelm even those who dislike plays. Representing life within a frame, Shakespeare's comedies reveal more than was thought to exist. The readers discover more about themselves, both increasing their wit and leading to their enjoyment of plays. Falstaff's reflections on wit are quite close to those of the "never writer" when he notices, "I am not only witty in myself, but the cause that wit is in other men" (2 *Henry IV*, 1.2.9). The epistle challenges the reader to use the play, much as Falstaff sees other men use him, for both the appreciation and acquisition of wit. The reader is enticed to begin the play with the anticipation of enjoyment and enrichment.

Twenty years after the 1603 Stationers' Register entry claimed that *Troilus and Cressida* was acted by the Lord Chamberlain's men, and fourteen years after Q was printed, the First Folio (F) reader, a different consumer at least for having paid more for the volume, was introduced to the play quite differently. The circumstances of the publication, readership, prefatory material, and collection of plays in F have been extensively explored by scholars, most recently within the context of New Historicist criticism.[4] These larger concerns, along with a fuller discussion of the concept of wit, are too broad to be discussed fully here, but it is worth taking a brief look at the contrasting ways the readers of Q and F are addressed.

In F's address "To the great Variety of Readers," Heminges and Condell

> hope, to your diverse capacities, you will find enough to draw and hold you; for his [Shakespeare's] wit can no more lie hid than it could be lost. Read him, therefore, and again, and again, and if then you do not like him, surely you are in some manifest danger not to understand him.[5]

Shakespeare is identified with his collected works, and the reader who fails to enjoy the contents is in danger of not seeing the obvious wit of the author. While Qb's epistle claims that the undiscovered wit of the reader will be revealed by the comedy, F's "Address" dismisses the reader's wit.

> And though you be a magistrate of wit, and sit on the stage at Blackfriars or the Cockpit to arraign plays daily, know, these plays have had their trial already, and stood out all appeals.[6]

Even when the reader's wit is that of a privileged frequenter of private theaters, an individual's judgment cannot outweigh the popular approval of the play. This is in direct contrast to the epistle's exhortation not to "like this the less for not being sullied with the smoky breath of the multitude." Heminges and Condell, as men of the theater, situate the proving ground for the play with the medium for which it was devised. Its appearance in print only supplements, and cannot overturn, the theatrical experience. In the relatively new medium of printed plays, the innate contradiction of setting a performance-text into print is defined. Introducing and justifying an edition as a Shakespearean work, a performed play, or a literary text influences how it will be experienced. The modern appropriation of the play into theaters, editions, and scholarship, and the conflicting claims for the authority and benefits of these appropriations are foreshadowed by the prefatory material in the first two editions of *Troilus and Cressida*.

The mysterious circumstances surrounding a disruption in the printing of *Troilus and Cressida* for F seem to explain the play's exclusion from the "Catalogue" at the front of the volume.[7] When printing resumed, F's compositors had access to a text with "about five hundred substantive differences"[8] from Q, including the addition of the Prologue that F's readers encounter before the title of the play is announced anywhere in the volume. The Prologue's description of the play's action as "beginning in the middle" of the Trojan War creates a very different first impression than Q. Without the Prologue, Q's readers are immediately presented with two scenes fulfilling the promise on Qb's title page that the play presented "the conceited wooing of Pandarus."

F's addition of the Prologue raises many questions about the play's bibliographical and performance history. Was the Prologue always, sometimes, or never performed? Was Q's omission of the Prologue, or F's inclusion, a result of circumstances relating to printing, performance, or revision? Do the different beginnings relate to other differences between Q and F, such as the possibility of different endings? How is the play changed by the inclusion or exclusion of the Prologue, and how does the play's theater history comment on the differences between the Q and F openings? Starting with an examination of the clues about the first performances and concluding with an analysis of modern productions, this chapter addresses these critical, textual, and theatrical questions about the different ways of beginning *Troilus and Cressida*.

A brief look at some prologues written in the decades surrounding 1600 reveals that many playwrights composed specific prologues for private performances, often paying tribute to an important member of the audience. These prologues would be omitted, or perhaps a different one inserted, for performances in public theaters. A revival, or some other reason for revision, might also have occasioned the writing of a prologue. Jonson, for example, added a prologue in his revision of *Everyman in his Humour,* and for a revival of Marlowe's *The Jew of Malta,* Heywood added a prologue and epilogue for court, and a different pair for the public stage.

The metatheatrical nature of prologues often extends beyond speaking of the play and players, to rationalizing the need for a prologue. The *Troilus and Cressida* Prologue somewhat unusually goes further by explaining his costume, wanting to justify being armed, probably in place of the prologue's "traditional long black velvet cloak."[9] During the War of the Theatres, Jonson presented an armed prologue (in *Poetaster*) and Marston an armed epilogue (in *Antonio and Mellida*), both describing their armor as a potentially threatening gesture to the audience. Somewhat like Snug the joiner, who suggested that a "prologue must tell he is not a lion" (*A Midsummer's Night Dream*, 2.2.31) to diffuse any fearful misinterpretation, the *Troilus and Cressida* Prologue explains that the armor is to be understood as part of the fictional representation and is not meant to intimidate the audience. Shakespeare may have included the armed Prologue when a reference to the *Poetaster* Prologue was topical, and he or the company may have cut it when the reference was out of date; however, the armed figure of the *Troilus and Cressida* Prologue is always appropriate as an introduction to the wealth of allusions to

The Prologue.

IN Troy there lyes the Scene: From Iles of Greece
The Princes Orgillous, their high blood chaf'd
Haue to the Port of Athens sent their shippes
Fraught with the ministers and instruments
Of cruell Warre: Sixty and nine that wore
Their Crownets Regall, from th' Athenian bay
Put forth toward Phrygia, and their vow is made
To ransacke Troy, within whose strong emures
The rauish'd Helen, Menelaus Queene,
With wanton Paris sleepes, and that's the Quarrell.
To Tenedos they come,
And the deepe-drawing Barke do there disgorge
Their warlike frautage: now on Dardan Plaines
The fresh and yet vnbruised Greekes do pitch
Their braue Pauillions. Priams six=gated City,
Dardan and Timbria, Helias, Chetas, Troien,
And Antenonidus with massie Staples
And corresponsiue and fulfilling Bolts
Stirre vp the Sonnes of Troy.
Now Expectation tickling skittish spirits,
On one and other side, Troian and Greeke,
Sets all on hazard. And hither am I come,
A Prologue arm'd, but not in confidence
Of Authors pen, or Actors voyce; but suited
In like conditions, as our Argument;
To tell you (faire Beholders) that our Play
Leapes ore the vaunt and firstlings of those broyles,
Beginning in the middle: starting thence away,
To what may be digested in a Play:
Like, or finde fault, do as your pleasures are,
Now good, or bad, 'tis but the chance of Warre.

4. F's Prologue. Reproduced by permission of The Huntington Library, San Marino, California.

armor throughout the play. The way helmets obscure and help constitute the identity of characters, most notably the Trojan warriors passing before Cressida and Pandarus (1.2) and the Greeks being introduced to Hector (4.7), contain more than the practical excuse of identifying the long list of characters.[10] The dialogue creates the possibility for the costumes to add to the play's interrogation of the search for, and the source of, personal identity and value. Hector's pursuit of "one in Armour" (5.6.26.1), and his unarming before Achilles orders his murder, also show how the warrior's costume contributes to the play's climactic examination of the hollowness of chivalric honor. The Prologue can add to this visual, rhetorical, and thematic motif if presented in armor, but this chapter will also trace how modern productions differently utilize the image of an armed Prologue.

To help imagine the Prologue as performed by Shakespeare's company, it is perhaps not too pedantic to ask about the style of armor worn. Heywood's *The Second Part of The Iron Age* has several relevant stage directions that provide some insight into the costumes for a Trojan War play, although probably for a different company. After an entrance of Prince Choerebus with other "Troians in Greekish Habits," Aeneas enters, and "taking Choerebus for a Grecian by reason of his habite, fights with him and kills him."[11] Without demanding too much realism, these directions make obvious what seems the dramatic necessity of having Greeks and Trojans wearing discernibly different armor. Was there an attempt to portray "Greekish habits" with classical costume or armor? Were both sides wearing armor from the same period, or were the Greeks in an ancient costume and the Trojans in Elizabethan? The Peacham drawing of *Titus Andronicus,* with characters in a mixture of Elizabethan and classical costume, adds to the possibility that something other than contemporary armor was worn.[12] The use of royal armor, often bought by acting companies, might have had a particular resonance if the armor was recognized as a symbol of the dying or recently deceased Queen.[13] In a play that deals with decaying values and, in Hector's case, naïve and idealistic codes of honor, identifiable armor could have visual associations with contemporary questions about the end of an era or the end of a connection to chivalry.

Whether the Prologue's armor was Elizabethan or "Greekish," the armor and the rhetoric set up expectations that are immediately overthrown by Troilus's opening line, "Call here my varlet, I'll unarm again" (1.1.1). Troilus cannot bear to be inwardly "weaker than a woman's tear" (9) when he wears the trappings of masculine pride. Without the Prologue, Troilus's unarming is the first action of the play, and when he says that the "argument is too starved a subject for my sword" (93), the concern is initially with his personal dilemma. When preceded by an armed Prologue, suited in like condition as the play's argument, Troilus is unarming against that which his society and the play expect from him. Such distinctions between beginning the play with or without the Prologue lead to generalizations, and within each way of opening the play can be seen the elements made more obvious by the other. Audience anticipation of a Trojan War play, and the entrance of a character armed who immediately unarms can achieve with Q some of the effects of the Prologue. The Prologue does, of course, introduce an air of cynicism into the epic war and its wanton cause, and prepares for Troilus's struggle between private and public duty. Troilus's unarming contributes to the debate that extends throughout the play and provides both a visual and verbal instance of the debate that asks whether Helen, or what she represents, is worth fighting and dying for.

The Prologue's placement in F, with a page to itself preceding the title page, might easily be explained bibliographically, but it is still important to ask about the dramatic relationship of the Prologue to the play. Does the Prologue describe the conflict from a dramatically or historically neutral viewpoint, as a character involved in the war, or as an actor in the production? Many editions before the twentieth century placed the Prologue before the *dramatis personae,* causing it to stand outside the play in a similar way to F's placement of the Prologue before the title.[14] Editors' insertion of the title or the list of characters after the Prologue intrudes on a direct connection between the Prologue and the entrance of Troilus and Pandarus. The Prologue becomes involved in the framework of introductory material, existing outside the play and presenting information relating to the drama rather than beginning and being a part of the play. The Prologue was only first included in the dramatis personae by Alice Walker in her 1957 New [Cambridge] Shakespeare, and since then it is normally included in the variously titled list of characters. If the Prologue is suited to the argument, is it part of the argument or merely its presenter? By beginning with "In Troy there lies the scene," the Prologue sets the scene before the characters enter, and when speaking of "our play," the author, and other actors, as is common in prologues, the Prologue speaks as one of a group who perform the play, rather than a character who exists within the fiction. But when speaking of his armor and himself as "Prologue," the actor also claims a part within the play. One of the main issues to emerge from the following performance history of the play's beginning is how the Prologue is divorced from or incorporated into the play.

When John Dryden adapted *Troilus and Cressida* into *Truth Found Too Late,* he wrote a prologue specifically for Betterton, who rose "Representing the Ghost of Shakespear."[15] When the play was published, Dryden wrote the famous preface detailing the failures of Shakespeare's play and presenting his neoclassical theories of drama and tragedy. Dryden's frames for the publication and performance of his adaptation manifest a preoccupation with similar concerns to the introductory material in QF. Expounding dramatic theory in an introduction, as in Dryden's sophisticated preface or Qb's cruder epistle, the reader begins the play not with an idea of what will happen in the drama, but what will happen to the reader. The evocation of Shakespeare's ghost to speak Dryden's Prologue both sanctions and qualifies the adaptation, exalting and fictionalizing the dead author in a manner not very different from the portrayal of Shakespeare's image and character in the portrait and commendatory verses of F. Seventy years after the 1609 quarto appeared, Shakespeare was a dead playwright whose obsolete language, chaotic scene ordering, and indecisive conclusion needed radical revision before conforming to the different agenda of Dryden's theater.

Early editors believed that the omission of the Prologue from Q, combined with its unusual style, created some doubt about its authorship. George Steevens printed the Prologue in his 1793 edition but argued influentially against its authority. Bell's acting edition (1774) was published with suggestions by Francis Gentleman (the Dramatic Censor) on adapting the play for the stage.[16] Gentleman suggested that the play should begin either with the second or third scenes but admitted the objection that "we should, in that case, be less acquainted with the disposition of Troilus."[17] While cutting or transposing the first two scenes might leave the audience less acquainted with the love story, other cuts and comments make it obvious that what the 1609 quarto called "the excellent wooings of Pandarus" were often deemed either distasteful or not dramatic. The first true footnote of praise is in the third scene, where it is noted that "all the sentiments in *Agamemnon's* mouth are pleasingly and strongly expressed."[18]

Around 1795 John Philip Kemble prepared a promptbook of *Troilus and Cressida* that was partially cast, and some parts were perhaps distributed; however it remained one of the few Shakespeare plays Kemble did not produce.[19] The edition Kemble marked up was one of the few that did not even print the Prologue, and there is no indication that he would have included it. Other changes to his copy indicate that he did consult other editions and was therefore probably aware of the Prologue. He owned a copy of the quarto, which he marked "Collated & Perfect. 1798," and may have preferred its opening on dramatic or bibliographical grounds.[20] Kemble's knowledge of Dryden's adaptation or the Bell edition is difficult to determine, but he also began the play with the first part of the Greek council scene. A combination of the first and second scenes followed, and the first act concluded with the final part of the Greek council scene (beginning with Aeneas bringing Hector's challenge). This opening is much as the play would develop for Kemble. His cuts and rearrangements show an interest in the tragedy of Hector and the Greek political intrigues, while much of the love story, Thersites' railing, and the entire Helen scene were pruned.

The 1889 Henry Irving Edition, which like the Bell edition aimed to mark cuts usually made in performance, had only Dryden's adaptation and Kemble's unperformed prompt-book as practical considerations of arranging the play for the stage. Editorial commentary was also influential, and the judgments of Steevens, Ritson, and Fleay that the Prologue was not written by Shakespeare are cited as the reason for recommending its omission from performance. Frank Marshall, co-editor and annotator with A. W. Verity for the Irving edition, agreed with "Mr. Kemble's arrangement" of the opening, and noted that starting with the Greek council scene

> is certainly a better arrangement from a dramatic point of view, as it places a comparatively dull Scene at the beginning instead of the end of the Act, which by that means is made to conclude with a Scene in which the hero and heroine, Troilus and Cressida, are both considered, and which marks a distinct step in the progress of the story.[21]

There is much to be doubted in Marshall's assessment of Kemble's motives. Kemble clearly marked a split in the Greek council scene, ending the first scene with four lines Kemble himself seems to have written where Agamemnon tells Ulysses and Nestor that they "Must find some stop to these increasing evils."[22] As mentioned above, the remainder of the scene, beginning with the trumpet announcing Aeneas's presence in the Greek camp (1.3.212) was moved to follow Cressida's soliloquy, and Ulysses and Nestor's discussion of the solution to the "increasing evils" ended the first act. The significance of Marshall's misreading is that it betrays an important shift of interest in the play. While Francis Gentleman praised the verse of the Greek council scene and railed against the feebleness of the love story, Marshall's note, quoted above, and Verity's introduction to the play, took pains to highlight the title characters. Verity cites Troilus and Cressida as the keys to understanding the play but revealed his Victorian values in judging Pandarus completely distasteful. Opening with the Greeks had a different purpose for the Irving editors, giving an audience the long and "dull" speeches first, building to a climatic conclusion for the first act. Kemble's rearrangement quite differently allowed the first act curtain to rise and fall on his primary interest.

A production has many ways to convey its vision of the play and to prepare the audience for that vision. While the first moments of the play can be crucial in establishing the setting and tone of the interpretation, audiences can be prepared for a production with advertisements, programs, or preconceptions about the kinds of productions put on by a director, actors, acting company, or a theater. The booking slips for William Poel's 1912 Elizabethan Stage Society production contained quotes from Arthur Acheson, enticing potential customers with the notion that "Shakespeare was, no doubt, moved in the first place to this satire by personal considerations incidental . . . to English life."[23] Anyone who came to the play wanting to find out more about Acheson's statement could purchase from the program sellers copies of Poel's essay which explained and elaborated on Acheson's theory.[24] The less inquisitive were still confronted in the program with "Notes by the Producer," where Poel stated that Shakespeare probably wrote the play

> with the object of satirizing Chapman's extravagant claims for the ethical teaching of Homer's *Iliad,* and also to voice the public disapproval of the withdrawal of the Earl of Essex from Court in that year.

Poel had flooded the audience with an elaborate contextualization of the play, attempting to influence both the presentation and its reception with an understanding of the play's composition and original staging.

Poel's program notes also included his rationale for the costumes:

> There is nothing in the text of the play that justifies its production as a picture of Greek or Trojan life of the Homeric period. In this representation, therefore, the Greeks are dressed as Elizabethan soldiers, and the Trojans, "courtiers as free, as debonair, unarmed as bending angels," are in masque costume of Elizabethan flamboyant design.
> Thersites, the "Chorus" of the play, wears the costume of a clown, as worn on the public stages by the jesters of the theatres. Prologue is in full armor—a satirical device adopted by Marston and Ben Jonson to ward off the attacks of hostile critics.

The logic and historical justification for Poel's decisions may raise expectations, supported by Poel's reputation, that his Elizabethan Stage

Society production would strive to achieve some kind of Shakespearean authenticity. While the use of an inner stage and the costumes would confirm such expectations, several curious decisions
were made. Actresses played not only women's parts, but women also
played Aeneas, Paris, Helenus, and Alexander. Poel's desire to highlight the parallel between Achilles and Essex seems to have influenced the cuts he made, especially to the scenes involving the title
characters, in order to emphasize Achilles' role.[25]

Although the Prologue was also dressed as Poel believed he would
have been on Shakespeare's stage, only about half the speech was delivered. The cuts (lines 5–7, "sixty and Nine . . . Phrygia," 11–22, "To
Tenedos . . . on hazard") eliminated the description of the Greeks'
departure and arrival, the Trojan gates arousing Troy's sons, and the
anticipation of hostilities. The long second cut brought together the
Prologue's abrupt "and that's the quarrel" with the self-referential
"and hither am I come." The Cassell's National Library edition that
Poel used followed Pope in emending "and hither" to "hither," trimming the line of its extra syllable. Poel reinstated "and," creating a
line which read, "And that's the quarrel. And hither am I come," disregarding the editorial concern over an extra syllable. The created
line allows the reductive description of the war's cause to be immediately connected to the Prologue's purpose.

In 1936, Ben Iden Payne presented his Stratford-upon-Avon audience with a program note similar to Poel's, offering what he felt was
vital information to understanding the play.

> It is highly probable that *Troilus and Cressida* was written in part to voice
> the public disapproval at the withdrawal of the Earl of Essex from the
> court in 1598, and also as a counterblast to the pretentious claims for the
> superiority of Greek ethics made by the poet Chapman, who was then en-
> gaged on his translation of Homer's *Iliad.*

As Poel had done, Payne also tried to stage the play as he believed it
would have been performed on an Elizabethan stage. Poel's and
Payne's audiences, both close to world wars, were introduced to a
rarely performed play with notes emphasizing the relevance of the
play to its original audience and with a staging that aspired to look
like the original production. The 1936 Prologue appeared before the
inner stage curtains and retreated to the sounds of cheers as the inner stage curtains opened to reveal Troilus and Pandarus. Standing
between frames, with the audience on one side of the proscenium
and the play's characters within the inner stage, the Prologue func-

tioned as intermediary between audience and drama, real and fictional worlds, playhouse and play. The frame within a frame was given another layer by the pseudo-Elizabethan Prologue addressing what the director had hoped would be a pseudo-Elizabethan audience, carefully trained in their part by Payne's historical notes.

Payne's Elizabethan setting was criticized by several reviewers.[26] Sidney Charteris lamented the lack of "graceful garments in the classic style" and concluded that the production provided "final proof, if proof were needed, that this Elizabethan business can be carried too far."[27] Writing before the production opened, an anonymous *Evening Dispatch* critic indicated that despite Payne's efforts, some of the audience would not enter the theater thinking about Essex or Chapman.

> The history of Europe has been largely a succession of wars with even as trifling a reason [as the abduction of Helen]. And to-day, when anything or nothing is likely to set the armament dumps ablaze, it will be found that Shakespeare's satirical treatment of the Trojan War has a singular topicality.[28]

Was this writer or his readers disappointed when the production failed to make explicit reference to current events? Perhaps they could be satisfied that, by emphasizing the circumstances of the play for Shakespeare's audience, the production offered the 1936 audience a further instance in history when similar issues were topical. This was not, however, the opinion of the *Morning Post's* dramatic critic, who confessed,

> with all reverence for William Poel's memory, that for me—and I fancy, for a good many in tonight's audience—the Elizabethan side-issues counted for practically nothing at all. . . . With Agamemnon in doublet and hose, wearing a kind of combined hat and crown, the thing is made for the most part mildly laughable where it is not meaningless and dull. Even modern dress would have been more logical and less confusing.[29]

The appropriateness of classical, Elizabethan, or modern dress will always produce heated debate, but the relevant point for the present discussion is the way an audience is led into the world of the play, and how the discovery of costumes and sets contributes to the first impressions of the play and the production. The Prologue's first words, "In Troy there lies the scene," elicit questions about how the stage will represent Troy, and Troilus's first words, "Call here my varlet, I'll unarm again," like the Prologue's description of himself as "armed," calls immediate attention to how the actors are dressed. The way a production decides to represent Troy, the Trojans, and the Greeks significantly determines how the audience will relate the play to epic, historic, and current events.

While Payne's production attempted to simulate Troy as it was presented on Shakespeare's stage, a German production of the same year produced a version of Troy with implications far more modern. A correspondent for the *Times* described his surprise upon discovering in Munich a small cinema advertising a theatrical production of *Troilus und Cressida* illuminated in electric lights.

> It seemed incongruous to find among the café and shop signs of this busy street of a city in modern Germany a reference in electric lights to this play of Elizabethan England. But this sense of incongruity was quickly dispelled.... The prologue was spoken by a helmeted, robot-like figure who declaimed his lines with an unvarying hoarse loudness in the manner of one of the Nazi speakers on the wireless with whom the shortest residence in Germany renders one familiar.[30]

The reviewer gives a chilling example of how the Prologue can immediately create a dialogue between events in the play and outside the theater. Instead of a museum piece that alluded to squabbles of the past, the Munich production announced itself in electric lights and began in the recognizable voice of the present, introducing a frightening image of impending war that must have truly "set all on hazard."

On the eve of Neville Chamberlain's second peace mission to Germany in 1938, Michael Macowan staged a modern dress production in London's Westminster Theatre. In defiance of Poel and Payne, Macowan stated in the program that "much of what Shakespeare wanted to say can only be clearly seen by relating it to contemporary experience."[31] Macowan may have been the first director to assign the Prologue to a specific character. Thersites, who was played as a left-wing journalist, delivered the Prologue "leaning against the proscenium in his trench coat, with a cigarette hanging from his lips."[32] It was thought inappropriate for Thersites to speak the three lines referring to the Prologue as armed (lines 23–25), resulting in the reading: "and hither am I come / To tell you, fair beholders." Leaving out the threatening armor and the apology for it, Macowan used the Prologue to introduce Thersites' function as a reporter soliciting the sympathy of the "fair beholders."

In their program notes, Poel and Payne established the historical basis for their interpretation and staging. Macowan, however, used his program note to defend his alterations, feeling the need to plead guilty to considerable cutting and a little editing. The excuse for the former is the play's tremendous length and my desire to keep the main issue as clear as possible. The editing consists chiefly in the use of Thersites as a commentator, which I think is justified by Shakespeare's having made him the mouthpiece for his own bitterness and torment of spirit.

The interest of Poel and Payne in the political and literary issues of the years surrounding 1600 were replaced in Macowan's production by an interest in Shakespeare's personal psychology and philosophy. Spoken by Thersites, the Prologue was incorporated into the play to a degree not sanctioned by the text but justified by the Shakespearean authority with which Macowan felt Thersites speaks. Equating Thersites' opinions with Shakespeare's mood, Macowan followed Dryden in having Shakespeare's ghost rise to deliver the Prologue. As he leaned against the proscenium, Thersites stood at the very point of theatrical exchange, presenting the past as the present.

In 1948, the Stratford-upon-Avon audience was once again brought into the play through an Elizabethan frame, but Anthony Quayle's production did not resort to the historical scholarship of Poel or Payne. The curtain opened on a scene that created the atmosphere of an Elizabethan London street, with a street crier, a flower seller, a water carrier, and several citizens. The image was broken when an actor, described in the promptbook as representing Mars, stepped forward to deliver the Prologue. Introducing the play through an image of Shakespeare's world presented multiple levels of time, myth, and social class. The device was not noted in the reviews and perhaps did not make a significant impact. The juxtaposition of the Roman god of war disturbing a busy Elizabethan street in a 1948 Stratford-upon-Avon production of a Trojan War play, however, may have at least raised some expectations about the dramatic depiction of epic war and the impact of heroic rhetoric on civilian life.

Glen Byam Shaw's 1954 Stratford-upon-Avon production began with the Prologue entering through the gates of Troy. The Trojan Wall was set at the back of the stage, and through the open gates, tented fields could be seen in the distance. The Prologue wore a helmet and was armed with a spear, but over his armor he wore a black cloak, allowing the conventional Elizabethan costume of the Prologue to coexist with the armor. The production photograph gives the impression of an imposing figure, and several reviewers remarked that the speech was particularly well spoken; one stated that it gave the play "a magnificent start,"[33] and another reported that "the audience warmly responded."[34] A reviewer noticed that the ac-

5. James Grout as Prologue, SMT 1954, Byam Shaw. Photographer Angus McBean, Shakespeare Centre Library. Copyright Royal Shakespeare Company.

tor (James Grout) also played Ajax but did not say whether it was as Ajax that he spoke the prologue.[35] The association in the reviewer's mind is enough to provoke speculation on the appropriateness of having this "beef-witted lord" (2.1.13), whom Thersites describes as having grown "languageless" (3.3.256), speak the vaulted verse of the prologue. The reviewer's comment can also highlight the possibilities that arise from the actor not speaking the Prologue in character, not including the speech as an addition to Ajax's role, and not setting up an agenda that will be developed as part of the character. In contrast to Macowan's decision to give the speech to Thersites, Shaw's Prologue appears to have provided a more heroic opening, but one that may not have been able to achieve a similar level of cynicism. The applause the speech received offers another way in which the speech can be separated from the action of the play.

The ability to situate Shakespeare in a production was again an issue when Tyrone Guthrie presented the play in twentieth-century dress. When the Old Vic production moved to New York in 1956, Guthrie wrote an article for the *New York Herald Tribune* entitled "This is Shakespeare?" He explained that he set the play just before 1914 because that was the last time when war could be considered a "sport, a gallant and delightful employment . . . for young men of the upper class."[36] Many of the reviews answered Guthrie's question by claiming that it was not Shakespeare's play but Guthrie's staging they enjoyed. The production did, however, provide a unique authenticity by following the opening of Q. It seemed appropriate to one reviewer that there was

> no prologue, and it would certainly be odd to have it. The curtain rises on an elderly exquisite, straight from a Maugham comedy and clearly just back from a Trojan idea of Ascot, in talk with a young man whose mirror-winking breastplate seems to have been worn on a ceremonial parade. These prove to be Pandarus and Troilus.[37]

In a production that foregrounded the love story and often cut the political intrigues or reduced them to farce, it was fitting to begin immediately with the "excellent wooing of Pandarus." Guthrie's version paralleled the Quarto not only in the opening but also in treating the play as a comedy, which Q's epistle calls it. As will be discussed in the chapter on the play's conclusion, Guthrie also ended the play as some critics believe only Q should end, with Pandarus's address to the audience. Guthrie's production thus began and ended with Pandarus onstage and can be seen to give a theatrical argument for understanding how Q's text, and not only Qb's title-page, may emphasize the role of Pandarus.

The often debated question about the play's genre seemed to receive a firm answer in Guthrie's comic production, and during the inaugural 1960 Royal Shakespeare Company season, Peter Hall and John Barton directed *Troilus and Cressida* in a season of comedies.[38] The audience was, however, immediately aware that this was a very unusual kind of comedy. There was an "almost savage enunciation of the prologue, each word a blow,"[39] "warning that this production will pull no punches."[40] A tall, robust, helmeted figure appeared as the Prologue in the armor later worn by the Myrmidons and stood in the center of the sand-pit that was the main feature of the set. The Prologue became a soldier's arrogantly boastful speech, which had "an

6. Paul Hardwick as Prologue, RST 1960, Hall/Barton. Photographer Angus McBean, Shakespeare Centre Library. Copyright Royal Shakespeare Company.

effect of disturbing comedy, or comic aggression,"[41] immediately qualifying any pretence to heroism or epic grandeur by the overzealousness of military fanaticism.

Joseph Papp, in his 1965 New York production, introduced a comic element into the Prologue by assigning it to a character from the love story.

> The director used the Prologue to set the tone of the play. Clad in armor, he was fat, jolly, and bearded. Good natured and pleasant, he doubled as Cressida's man, Alexander; serving as her confidant as well as a court gossip. Although beginning the opening speech at a heroic level, he gradually lowered the tone through a suggestive and lascivious manner of delivery.[42]

Papp introduced both the war and lechery in the Prologue with an armed but lewdly suggestive Prologue who both stood within the play and encapsulated it. Alexander's function can be equated with the Prologue's in several respects. The Prologue tells the audience about the armies' preparations for the battle and that Helen sleeps with

Paris, just as Alexander gossips about who is hurt, who is angry, and where Helen is going. Instead of merely juxtaposing an armed Prologue with Troilus unarming, Papp showed how both the Prologue and the first scene can expound and undermine within themselves the heroic ideals of love and war. The Prologue's exalted description of the war and the deflated rendering of its cause are immediately echoed by Troilus's ambiguous attitude toward fighting, first calling the war "too starved a subject for my sword" (1.1.93) while later going off with Aeneas "to the sport abroad" (1.1.115). Papp's armed Prologue, who spoke convincingly of both the "crownets regal" and "wanton Paris," began the play as an example and a guide to the plague of contradictions that follow.

John Barton's 1968 RSC production began with a very different kind of armed but lascivious Prologue. Unlike Papp's "fat, jolly, and bearded" Trojan, Barton had "a Greek prologue, posed as on a painted vase, masked, cloaked and helmeted in scarlet"[43] opening the production that is often remembered for its shaved and oiled bodies and its overt homosexuality. In a production punctuated with extra appearances by the "camping" Myrmidons, it seems fitting that they took turns speaking the Prologue, which was used as a kind of audition speech for the young actors.[44] This democratization of the Prologue illustrates what Ralph Berry described as "the transference of interest away from the lovers to the rest of the dramatis personae."[45] These Myrmidons did not, however, appear as the "mangled Myrmidons" that Ulysses describes as "noseless, handless, hacked and chipped" (5.5.33–34). They were instead scantily dressed actors who were made to train with weights during the rehearsals and displayed their well-toned bodies as an appropriate introduction into the obsessions of a warrior society.

The Prologue's armor in the 1976 RSC production (directed by John Barton and Barry Kyle) was the find of an archaeological dig, and the play opened with the Prologue emerging from a trap carrying a dust covered bag filled with two swords and a helmet. The excavation brought onstage the relics of the past. Blowing dust off the armor, the Prologue began with the discovery of an ancient story and its dated artifacts. Several critics noted that one of the Prologue's lines was given special emphasis.

(John Nettles, who doubles as Thersites) is properly sardonic, mocking the "fair beholders" with the inevitably limited amount that may be "digested in a *play*": the last word spat out.[46]

If there is one passage that sums up the show it is the Prologue's reference to "What may be digested in a play." John Nettles spits out the word "play" with brutal derision, implying the absurdity of the theater's pretension to do any justice to real life.[47]

Hamlet's description of a Trojan war play as "an excellent play, well digested in the scenes, set down with as much honesty as cunning" (2.2.442–43) provides another example of Shakespeare's use of "digested" as "the usual word for reducing material into dramatic form."[48] It is the author who has digested the material into a play rather than the audience who will digest it. Like the Chorus of *Henry V* apologizing for the physical limits of the stage, the Prologue indicates the dramatic necessity for reduction. While apparently referring to the temporal impracticality of dramatizing the entire Trojan War, the implications are far reaching, raising questions about the author's adaptation of an epic story and the actors' depiction of love and war. In condensing material into drama, the author makes choices, like beginning in the middle of the war, manipulating sources, and inventing and reinventing characters, motives, speeches, and actions. The actors must similarly make choices with the play's text, and their physical, emotional, and verbal decisions can eliminate some of the ambiguity, and simplify some of the complexity. The Prologue emphasizes the dramatic necessity and invention involved in these choices, disclaiming any attempt at completeness in favor of what will serve the play.

Although the Barton/Kyle Prologue was spoken by the actor playing Thersites,[49] the speech was not delivered in character, but when the RSC next produced the play, the Prologue was spoken by Thersites. Robert Cushman began his review of Terry Hands's 1981 RSC production by stressing the importance of the opening speech.

> There are two ways of delivering the Prologue to *Troilus and Cressida*, and they determine the tone of a production. One is to ring out the polysyllabic proper names. The other is to undercut the heroics by stressing the absurdity of the entire Trojan War: "The ravish'd Helen, Menelaus' Queen / With wanton Paris sleeps, *and that's the quarrel?*"
> Terry Hands at the Aldwych takes the second course, though he takes the rough irony rather than the smooth: inevitably, since he gives the prologue to Thersites [played by Joe Melia]. Melia's summary of the action ("all wars and lechery") would convince any audience.[50]

Thersites' ability to convince the audience has been a point of contention between directors and critics. Since Michael Macowan's 1938 production, Thersites' stature has continued to grow. Even when he did not speak the prologue, Thersites' reductive vision was sometimes used to introduce the play. The Barton/Kyle (1976) program, for example, had "All wars and lechery" scrawled across the cover in large letters, and in the 1968 program, Barton is quoted in the "director's notes to the company at rehearsal" as saying that Thersites' "philosophy achieves a monstrous domination." Thersites' choric role has also been stressed and reinforced with extra-textual appearances, and he often accompanied Pandarus at the end of the play (as discussed in chapter 8, in productions at the Birmingham Repertory Theatre in 1963, the RSC in 1968, 1976, and 1981, Nunn in 1999, where Thersites is also given lines, and Hall in 2001). Kenneth Muir warns that "it would not, however, be legitimate, in the interests of contemporary 'relevance', to offer Thersites as the fount of truth and wisdom."[51] Increasing Thersites' choric role does not necessarily ordain his views as truth, but a production might feel that the half-truths Thersites expresses come close to the half of truth with which a modern audience will sympathize (with perhaps the significant exception of his judgment of Cressida as a whore). If a production's vision of the play merges too closely with Thersites, the production is then surely in danger of presenting a reductive view of characters and events, but in the theater, a critical simplification can produce a dramatic revelation. Having Thersites speak the Prologue can also be merely a comment on his dramatic function in the play, and Macowan's decision to play him as a left-wing journalist shows how Thersites' unsolicited opinions can be contextualized in a way that tempers his views with a modicum of doubt.

If Terry Hands took the course of rough irony by having Thersites deliver the Prologue, Jonathan Miller opts for soft irony, appropriately beginning the televised BBC *Troilus and Cressida* with a voice-over. As the camera moved through the brightly lit rooms of a palace, no Prologue appeared. Instead, a casual, emotionless, and unheroic voice accompanied the camera's journey, seeming somewhat absurd for the self-referential "hither am I come . . . armed," but suited to the production's medium.

The voice of the Prologue was the last speech to be taped for the production, and Miller contemplated several different options. Susan Willis, who was present at rehearsals, recorded that

> when asked who would do the voice-over of the prologue, Miller said he might, though what he had wanted, he jested with a wicked sparkle in his eye, was to get a famous British newscaster to be seen in Renaissance clothes wandering about Troy with a microphone doing the prologue, then handing the mike to a passing courtier who would look at it dumbfounded, while someone would be heard muttering, "I didn't think those things had been invented yet."[52]

Perhaps such absurd, if not silly, toying with the Prologue is indicative of a difficulty Miller had in finding an adequate solution for a television Prologue. Once editing began, four days after the production left the studio, Miller

> had still not decided whether to include the prologue or not, mainly because he had not yet decided who should deliver the lines, but since the titles were not ready, he could postpone the decision a while longer. (He ultimately did include the prologue, with Ben Whitrow [who played Ulysses] delivering it.)[53]

The first lines of the play were the last taped. Unlike a reader or observer, who takes initial information and presentation of the Prologue as a guide into the play, Miller's last decision was to create a Prologue suitable for his production.

Stanley Wells began his review of Miller's production by comparing it to the "interpretative excess" of Terry Hands's RSC production at the Aldwych Theatre, London.

> The difference in approach is typified in the treatment of the Prologue. At the Aldwych it was spoken, in character, by Thersites, thus setting the tone for a production which took a generally satirical view of the play's characters and events. On television it is delivered by an unseen speaker, courteously, anonymously, with neither rhetoric nor passion.... Jonathan Miller's whole production is similarly dispassionate.[54]

Hands's and Miller's Prologues, performed and broadcast in the same year, present two extremes of interpretation. The device of having a character speak the lines has become as much a part of the Prologue as the Prologue's description of itself as armed. Miller's rejection of both traditions suggests a very different use for the Prologue, whose nonconfrontational delivery gave the informative nature of the speech primary importance. As the Prologue could not be seen, its identity was only as a voice, and the detached and nonchalant delivery was reminiscent of a newscaster or documentary narrator. The voice was not assigned a place in the conflict but can be associated with the medium of presentation, sounding not very different from the BBC announcer who informed the television audience that a Shakespeare play was about to begin.

Without assigning the Prologue to a specific character, Howard Davies found a way to present a Prologue that was very much involved in the war. Walking into the Royal Shakespeare Theatre in 1985, the audience was presented with a decayed mansion and a prominent staircase at the back of the open set. When the audience was allowed into the theater, Pandarus was already onstage, sitting at a café-style table smoking a cigarette and reading a newspaper. After the audience took their seats and the house lights were dimmed, shouts and screams were heard, and several soldiers carried a dying man onto the stage, causing Pandarus only a slight interruption in his reading. While some of the soldiers examined and covered the face of the now dead soldier, one of them stepped forward to deliver the Prologue. The double image of Pandarus casually reading (downstage left) and a soldier dying (downstage right) provided a brutal first impression. The Prologue told the audience about the war, perhaps in terms not much different from those Pandarus read in his newspaper, but the grim reality of war was brought onstage in the soldier's death. As the Prologue finished, and the corpse was carried offstage, Troilus appeared on the balcony and ran downstairs to deliver his first line, "Call here my varlet, I'll unarm again" to the exiting Prologue. Troilus then crossed to Pandarus and slammed his sword down on the table for the line "I'll fight no more against Troy." The wooing game that followed was in disturbing contrast to the surrounding war, especially after Troilus had told the bloody, mourning soldier playing the Prologue to call a servant to help him unarm.

The soldier dying during the Prologue's heroical rhetoric and spiteful explanation of the war's cause created a striking illustration of a view expressed by Hector, Thersites, and Diomedes. Hector compares the loss of souls with the value of keeping Helen (2.2.18), Thersites characteristically judges that "All the argument is a whore and a cuckold. A good quarrel to draw emulous factions and bleed to death upon" (2.3.72), and Diomedes numbers the deaths of Greeks and Trojans in terms of false drops of blood in Helen's bawdy veins, and measures of her "contaminated carrion weight" (4.1.71). Davies' Prologue showed immediately that love and honor were played for at the cost of human life. While Pandarus's description of the unnamed soldiers as "chaff and bran" (1.2.238) invites laughter, the audience entered this production with an image of the common soldier that qualified the laughter.

Pandarus's presence during the delivery of the Prologue was taken one step further by Sam Mendes for his 1990 production at the RSC's Swan Theatre. Pandarus, played by Norman Rodway, appeared through the back curtain into a single spotlight to deliver the Prologue, reminding one reviewer of Olivier's sleazy *Entertainer*.[55] Irving Wardle was impressed by this opening, and noted that

> what he presents is a simultaneously official and private view of the war. As he itemizes the massive preparations of the Grecian fleet his voice swells to a majestically brazen climax, and then collapses into a wheezing giggle on revealing their squalid cause. Rodway rolls out a red carpet for

the Homeric top-brass and then pulls it from under their feet. He then does the same thing to us, the "fair beholders," to whom he opens his arms in mocking courtesy, promising to show us—in the crowning irony of the speech—"what may be digested in a play." Zilch, in other words.[56]

As a lone figure on a virtually empty thrust stage, Pandarus drew the audience in from all sides, seducing them, as he later enticed Troilus and Cressida, with a mixture of romance and bawdiness. Pandarus

7. Norman Rodway as Pandarus, delivering the Prologue, Swan Theatre 1990, Mendes. Joe Cocks Studio Collection, Shakespeare Centre Library. Copyright Shakespeare Birthplace Trust.

relished describing for the audience the "six-gated city" just as he enjoyed showing Cressida the soldiers as they pass along. As he grinned and mischievously rubbed his fingers, it seemed particularly appropriate for Pandarus to speak of "expectation tickling skittish spirits" as an image for setting "all on hazard." His descriptions of the cruel war and its wanton cause foreshadowed the voyeurism that he later displayed watching the Trojans come home, Helen being displayed (as she was seductively unwrapped, in Mendes' production), and the lovers' first meeting. While Thersites often speaks to the audience, only Pandarus actually addresses them directly as a theater audience, setting up the symmetry of stepping outside the play, in character, at the beginning, middle (3.2.207), and end.

There is obviously some difficulty with presenting Pandarus as the armed Prologue, since he is the only male civilian in the play (except for Alexander and the servants). In previews, Rodway used a newspaper to mimic a sword, taking it from his pocket and thrusting the rolled-up paper into the air to show that he was "a prologue armed." He was armed with the news of the war, reciting what the journalists wrote. On press night and thereafter, Pandarus wore a medallion on the breast pocket of his blazer, and showed it to the audience as a different indication that he was armed. The awkwardness of having Pandarus refer to himself as being suited in like condition as the argument was at first resolved by the director cutting the words, "but suited / In like condition as our argument." During the production's run, however, Rodway himself made the decision to reinstate the words. He felt that people coming to the play for the first time might be confused by the dress and action of the first two scenes, "more like a Noel Coward light comedy than the epic war play they might have expected," or that the Prologue leads them to expect. He wanted to explain that "all the jargon about the war merely provides the setting, but the play leaps over that to tell of a love story happening in the middle of the war."[57] Norman Rodway, as Pandarus, in agreement with Qb's title-page, saw the argument of the play as the love story, for which he was perfectly suited.

For the Prologue's parting remark, "now good or bad, 'tis but the chance of war," Rodway took the newspaper out of his pocket and waved it at the audience. This use of the newspaper was not cut, but its implications may have changed throughout the season. On press night, the newspaper might refer to the good or bad of the reviewers' opinion. On the night during the International Shakespeare Conference, the scholars might have connected the line and gesture to the play's interrogation of the dependence on public opinion for identity and value. On the production's last night in Stratford-upon-

Avon, the line might set the Swan Theatre audience thinking about the unpredictability of events outside the theater, and the newspaper might remind them of reports about day nine of the Gulf War.

Ian Judge's 1996 RSC production brought *Troilus and Cressida* to the company's main Stratford and London theaters for the first time in over a decade. The production, however, was treated with trepidation by many critics. Some reviews, including positive ones, expressed qualms about having a director who was noted for his comedies and his sentimentality deal with such a dark play. How would the RSC's "feel good" "cheeky chappie" director deal with the play's cynicism and nihilism?[58] Would a director who told the cast at the opening of rehearsals (and included excerpts of the talk in the production's program) that the play was "very very funny" look for jokes at the expense of the play's dark cynicism, emotional tragedy, or philosophical explorations?

While there were a number of positive reviews of the production, some that found fault with Judge's approach began by disapproving of the decision to have Thersites open the play. Russell Jackson believed that the "framing function of Thersites was enhanced, perhaps wrongly, by having him speak the prologue (not "armed" at all, and holding the very word up with amusement at its inappropriateness)."[59] Nightingale, however, was more positive about the decision.

> The ravished Helen, Menelaus's queen, with wanton Paris sleeps—"*and that's the quarrel!*", wails Richard McCabe's Thersites in his best believe-it-or-not voice at the opening of Ian Judge's production. A glance at the text confirms that the words actually belong to the Prologue; but it would be ungrateful to complain of their hijacking when the speaker is in every sense giving the performance of the evening. With his pale, bloated face, lank hair and awful ingratiating smirk, his Thersites is part depraved clown, part gloating chorus, and, when he assures us that all is lechery, very much the voice of Shakespeare's most cynically modern play.[60]

While some agreed with Nightingale that the "hijacking" was justified, Gross sided with Jackson, calling it a "mistake" and "much too clownish to start with."[61] The clownishness and comedic manner of McCabe's Prologue was noted in many reviews. He was described as "outrageously gossipy," "less a malicious observer, more of a stand-up comedian," and likened him to a "TV warm-up man."[62] Peter remarked that Thersites "is almost a send-up of what is to follow," preparing the audience for a show of "enjoyable sleaze," and Hewison described how, in delivering the Prologue, the "clown Thersites . . . sends it up for all it is worth. Judge is saying: 'Don't worry, Shakespeare can be fun.'"[63]

While some critics dismissed McCabe's portrayal of Thersites as too trifling an introduction to the play, several relevant issues emerged, particularly concerning the advantages of adding to the choric and carnivalesque potential of Thersites' role. Likening Thersites' delivery of the Prologue to a stand-up comedian's routine presents the image of a lone figure on the stage observing the world, particularly sexual and political icons, through a bitingly ironic lens. Perhaps in the late twentieth century the metatheatricality of the image was also suitably postmodern, mixing high and low culture (a stand-up comedian in a Shakespeare play; Thersites introducing the classical epic) in a self-referential performance that seems to match some of the debunking of legendary and heroic characters throughout the play.

Michael Boyd's RSC touring production (1998–99) again had Thersites (Lloyd Hutchinson) opening the play, presenting a slide show during the Prologue to illustrate his introduction of the conflict. With the use of a handheld clicker to move from slide to slide, Thersites offered a kind of illustrated lecture of scenes and characters, mostly "sepia photographs of soldiers,"[64] as a way to introduce the production's eclectic modern setting (with references to conflict in the Balkans, Ireland, and elsewhere). For the reference to Helen, he displayed a close-up photograph of her and waited for the audience to laugh at her image and at his incredulous tone that this woman represented, in the Prologue's words, "the quarrel." When he spoke of being "armed," Thersites indicated the old-fashioned flashbulb camera that he carried. The audience was here introduced to Thersites' role as a kind of war correspondent, and he would later make an extratextual appearance to take photographs during the first part of the Greek council scene (1.3), staged as a political rally with characters coming to the microphone to give propaganda speeches.

Like Macowan, who also had a journalist Thersites speak the prologue, Boyd gave Thersites the role of a social commentator and chronicler. While Boyd's Prologue, with Thersites as a kind of war correspondent, might seem more sophisticated and knowing than the depiction of Judge's comedian, both are similarly choric and metatheatrical. As presenters of the play, and commentators to and for the audience, they provided mediation between spectator and performance in a way that raises questions about how such mediation works in the play and in society. A comedian's use of irony and laughter involves an audience in social criticism and invites them to share a satiric view. A journalist too can offer insight and reassessment of complacently held value judgments, just as Thersites constantly offers reductive views of characters and events.

Trevor Nunn's Royal National Theatre production, staged in the vast amphitheater of the Olivier Theatre in 1999, began with most of the cast entering through the many doors that formed a wall near the back of the stage. With white actors, dressed in black leather and classically styled helmets, playing Greeks and nearly all black actors, dressed in flowing white robes (described by critics as vaguely African or Arabian), playing Trojans, the large cast circled around the stage in mixed groups until they divided, with Trojans and Greeks on separate sides of the stage. Between the divided armies emerged a warrior dressed in elaborate armor, neither Trojan nor Greek, walking downstage forcefully delivering the Prologue.

Where Boyd's Prologue had Thersites introduce Helen with the slide show, Nunn brought the cause of the quarrel onstage. At the line "The ravished Helen, Menelaus' Queen," the Prologue waved Helen downstage toward the outstretched arms of Menelaus, but she quickly glided past her husband to embrace Paris as the Prologue described that she now "With wanton Paris sleeps." Menelaus immediately looked to Agamemnon as if to ask for some help in retrieving Helen, and all the kneeling Greeks drew their swords and assumed an aggressive stance towards the Trojans, while the Prologue continued, "and that's the quarrel."

When the Prologue described the Greeks "pitch[ing] their brave pavilions," the Greeks moved downstage and the Trojans began to move upstage, filling up the doorways near the back of the stage. With the naming of each of the six gates, another door was slammed shut (accompanied by a dramatic drumbeat), closing the Trojans in and leaving the Greeks onstage. But as the "expectation" was described, a single Trojan snuck through a door and scampered across the stage to join the Greeks. This staging of Calchas's defection suggests a desire, also seen in the Helen dumb show and the other action during the prologue, to tell a story and reinforce the background that the Prologue supplies. Such a populated stage for the Prologue presented an image of storytelling and cast involvement that is unusual in the stage history of the speech, but the ensemble accompaniment to the speech especially suited a production that was part of Nunn's efforts as artistic director to create an ensemble company, or a mini company within his National Theatre.

The Prologue walked further downstage to address the audience more directly for "Hither am I come." He had finished with the background of the legend and shifted to preparing the audience for what would be in the play. But as he finished, the Trojans came storming through the doors to confront the Greeks in the first of several extra battle scenes. Rather than juxtaposing the armed Prologue that introduces the conflict with Troilus unarming, Nunn had a skirmish not only add to the audiences' expectations, but partially fulfill them with a staged battle, something which the play postpones until the final act.

In one of the many rearrangements Nunn made, it was not Troilus and Pandarus but Cressida alone who came onstage after the warriors exited. In an image that would be repeated at the end of the play, again with some rearrangement of text, Cressida's isolation became a defining visual motif for this production. She wandered the stage alone for a few moments before Pandarus entered down one of the aisles through the audience, beginning the dialogue for the play in the middle of the second scene, where Pandarus and Cressida watch the soldiers return from battle (1.2.173). If Q and F present different ways of opening the play, either emphasizing the war setting or the love story, Nunn's fighting did not simply emphasize the war but created a setting for love in the midst of a more threatening (and staged) warfare.

Sir Peter Hall directed his first off-Broadway production in 2001, staging *Troilus and Cressida* for Theatre for a New Audience with a combination of a few veteran British actors (including Tony Church playing Pandarus as he had in the Barton/Kyle RSC production of 1976) and mostly American actors. An actor, who the audience can either guess or will later learn is Thersites, began the production by coming onstage to view several skeletons, including one pair of skeletons in a copulating position, that occupied the stage's central sand pit. From a dusty bag he pulled out bones that made up other skeletons, and also distributed a helmet and various pieces of armor around the stage. He also took out of the bag a fairly new copy of David Bevington's Arden Shakespeare Third Series edition of the play (first published in 1998). Before speaking the Prologue, Thersites took a long drag on his cigarette and began reading from Bevington's text a cut version of Qb's Epistle.

By conflating the Q's Epistle and F's Prologue, Hall also conflated textuality with performance. When Thersites read from Bevington's text, rather than simply learning the Epistle as an additional speech, he is using the Arden edition as a prop, one that he held and read with a strong sense of irony. He interrupted his reading at one point, when the epistle described the play as a comedy, and looked at the book's cover as if to question the authority of the statement.

Throughout these preliminary actions the house lights were still on, and only after Thersites finished his reading did the audience move into darkness and the spotlights created a more usual distinction (at least in the modern theater) between actor and audience. As the house lights dimmed ominous music started to swell, and Thersites began performing the prologue in a different, more serious voice, at least in the beginning. This opening was theatrically self-aware in a number of ways, and would connect with the ending of the production, where Thersites was present during Pandarus's final speech (and gave a signal as if to turn out the stage lights and end the production, as discussed in chapter 8). By putting the props out and reading from the Arden text, Thersites was also exploring the theatrical space and the complex relationship of text and performance.[65]

In interviews with actors and directors, and in Susan Willis's account of Miller's production, it emerged that a fairly common practice is to decide last about the Prologue.[66] A production must ask how the Prologue will introduce its specific interpretation, and might reasonably want the production to be in a finished state before knowing how to introduce it. The success of these decisions is determined using often contradictory criteria. A production can be extremely illuminating while working against critically accepted parameters of the text, or can render a relatively safe, or conservative performance of the text that falls completely flat. Without delving too deeply into a discussion of what is or should be sacred, I want to conclude by briefly considering some ways theatrical history can contribute to literary criticism.

In 1967 a debate was carried out in "Letters to the Editor" of the *Times Literary Supplement* that endeavored to make sense of the *Troilus and Cressida* Stationers' Register entries, Q's title-pages and epistle, F's delayed inclusion of the Prologue, and the possibility of alternative endings. The discussion, initially between Peter Alexander and Nevill Coghill, was joined by William Empson, Fredson Bowers, and others.[67] The dispute centered on the different theories Coghill and Alexander proposed about "the purpose of the Prologue arm'd." *The Return from Parnassus* reports a "purge" that Shakespeare gave Ben Jonson, and Alexander restated and supported the argument that the "purge" was the Prologue of *Troilus and Cressida*. Coghill objected to Alexander's "evidence that Shakespeare is having his fun at Jonson's expense" with the Prologue. Coghill, who once directed the play (at Exeter College, Oxford, in 1938) and witnessed five productions, asked:

> what is so funny about an armed Prologue? Where is the note of parody or mockery or even mention of Jonson? In the theater the effect of this Prologue is invariably awe-striking. It creates an unusually tense silence of startled anticipation when the menacing armor-clad figure, spear in hand, appears and dominates visual imagination, while the splendid and ironical lines he is given to say are uttered with commanding force. Who

is going to think of Ben Jonson at such a moment? Not even Ben Jonson himself.[68]

Both critics attempted to recreate the experience of the original audience, but Coghill disputed Alexander's historical explanation in favor of his particular experience in the modern theater. The debate poses some crucial questions about the relationship between theater history, literary criticism, and textual scholarship. Can a play's effect in the theater tell us something useful about Shakespeare's theater, or merely provide new performance possibilities? Opening up the text to the subjective imagination of a theater production renews the play and challenges the audience to think about a production's relationship to the text, other productions, and current and historical events. Modern theater's usefulness to the Renaissance scholar comes at a cost, often gaining insight into the text, but also changing the play to suit its particular vision and version.

A lesson to be learned from the instability of the early texts is that the play never seems to have existed in a stable format, and as a play-text, it includes variables that produce meanings in a variety of ways. "What is the purpose of the armed Prologue?" is a question that should only be answered by destroying the limits the question attempts to impose. There is not one purpose to be discovered but a multiplicity of purposes to be explored. The problem with opening up the question in such a way is that it leads to a relativism that can run amok, and no simple rule can determine the fine line between meaning based on the text and interpretations and adaptations widely divergent from it. The Prologue's customary declaration, "Like or find fault, do as your pleasures are," anticipates the diversity of opinions, and provides an invitation to trust personal judgment not only as a criterion for valuing the presentation, but also for presenting and interpreting the play.

2

"Who Were Those Went By?"

CRESSIDA'S FIRST LINE, "WHO WERE THOSE WENT BY?" (1.2.1), IS A QUES-
tion that is repeated in different ways throughout a scene whose main
action is the observation of characters. She asks "Who comes here?"
(1.2.35) for Pandarus's entrance, "Who's that?" (1.2.185, 214) for the
entrances of Antenor and Helenus, and "What sneaking fellow comes
yonder?" (1.2.223) for Troilus's entrance. Barbara Hodgdon believes
that some of these questions may show Cressida as a controlling force,
with Cressida bringing into focus the subject of dramatic conversation and representation.[1] Conversely, Cressida's questions might suggest a naïveté or a desire for others to provide possible modes of behavior and value. More practically, Cressida is allowing characters to
be announced and identified for the audience, but conflicting conclusions about the stage actions implied by her questions result in
some significantly diverse interpretations of the characters and actions in the scene. Editors and directors variously interpret clues in
the dialogue to supply and locate stage directions. The dialogue and
dramatic impact of a moment, both in print and in performance, can
be vastly different depending on when characters enter and exit,
what they should do while onstage, and whether or not stage structures or props specifically locate a scene. Cressida's opening question
and the scene's central action of watching the soldiers "as they pass
toward Ilium" (1.2.174) provide two excellent examples of how different editorial and performance interpretations alter the focus and
significance of the dialogue.

Kenneth Muir's Oxford edition includes a note suggesting that
"perhaps Hecuba and Helen should pass over the stage before Cressida's entrance."[2] Janet Adelman, however, specifically stresses the
importance of Hecuba's absence:

In *Hamlet*, Hecuba serves as reassurance, as the model of the beneficent
mother Hamlet hopes to find—or to make—in Gertrude. But this potentially restorative figure is strikingly missing from *Troilus and Cressida*'s
version of the matter of Troy. In fact Hecuba herself never appears on

stage; and insofar as she is present by allusion, her presence is sexualized and trivialized by her association with Helen (1.2.1), her laughter at Helen's sexual banter (1.2.144–45), and her promotion of her daughter's sexual relation with Achilles, where she is emblematically reduced to the function of bawd, trading tokens between the illicit lovers (5.1.38). This mother could not restore paternal presence or make milch the eyes of heaven (*Hamlet*, 2.2.513); she herself is corrupted by her association with—not her differentiation from— . . . Helen.[3]

Cressida's concern with the identity and destination of the passersby shows her interest in courtly life, but more importantly, she is immediately confronted with two powerful female role models. Helen, as the object of beauty and desire which incited war, and Hecuba, as mother of nineteen and a potential mother-in-law for Cressida, present two women whose epic resonance epitomizes the female roles of lover and mother. Naming Helen and Hecuba is enough to circumscribe the limitations of the female world in which Cressida lives, a world where the chaste and fruitful wife and mother watches the battle with a woman who was conceived in a rape and whose marriage was severed by abduction and "fair rape" (as Paris himself describes it at 2.2.147). Each of Cressida's decisions—in courting, in desiring, or even in observing the etiquette of the captive—stands in some relationship to Helen, Hecuba, and a society where patriarchal dominance in marriage is portrayed as a destructive force.[4] If, as Adelman suggests, Helen and Hecuba do not present a pure dichotomy of chaste woman and whore, the male desire which objectifies Helen— especially in the debate of whether she is "a worthy (Q) / noble (F) prize" (2.2.85)—degrades all women and gender relationships. Just as Helen can corrupt the image of Hecuba, Cressida's association with Helen constantly cheapens desire and romance. Carol Rutter considers Helen to be

> framed as Cressida's *alter ego*. To begin with, it merely seems odd that they happen to keep turning up in the same conversations together. Later, it looks less like accident than policy. They're constantly compared, troped with the same metaphors ("pearl"; "merchant"), crossed in identities, and, most bizarrely, fantasized as rivals. . . . At significant moments Helen's narrative inserts itself into Cressida's. . . . It's as though Helen constitutes the primary narrative that keeps surfacing through the palimpsest of individual women's histories—grounding, contaminating and over-determining them.[5]

When Cressida loosely follows Helen's example by being exchanged and desired by both Trojan and Greek men, Troilus evokes the maternal image of Hecuba ("Think we had mothers," 5.2.132). Perhaps

Troilus is beginning to doubt his own identity when the potential for promiscuity is observed in women, but also, like Helen, Cressida's duplicity is generalized to the point where it "can soil (F) / spoil (Q) our mothers" (5.2.136) and therefore condemn the entire gender.

Without the editorial prompting supplied by Muir, directors had Helen and Hecuba cross the stage in some major British and American productions before 1960.[6] Bringing Helen and Hecuba onstage introduces a brief gathering of women, something Shakespeare avoids until Andromache and Cassandra appear onstage together to plead with Hector to stay at home (5.3.7–30 and 61–81). Presenting Helen and Hecuba could dramatize the fact that while living in their shadow, Cressida is without women to converse with. Unlike many of the female protagonists in Shakespeare's plays who have female companions or servants, Cressida is isolated from her gender. Directors could highlight her isolation by having her enter moments too late to meet a passing Helen and Hecuba, or their passing could be a device to create a female community that Shakespeare denied his title character. It is worth noting that some directors provided additional women in other ways. Kemble, for example, had Alexander accompanied by two "virgins," Payne had a group of "virgins" greet the Trojans returning from battle, Shaw included four "ladies in waiting" for Cressida, and Macowan had Alexander played as a woman. More recently, Boyd had Andromache take Alexander's place as Cressida's companion at the start of the scene. The restaging and regendering of the scene, particularly Kemble's and Payne's indication of the purity of the additional women, and Boyd's giving Alexander's part to Hector's wife, reveals a desire by directors to surround Cressida with female companions conspicuously absent from the text.[7]

While it is easy to understand the directors' desire to bring Helen and Hecuba onstage, Muir's suggestion highlights the different agenda of editors, directors, and critics. An appearance by Helen and Hecuba may be theatrically effective, but it may be calling for too much realism to warrant editorial intervention in the form of a stage direction. The dramatic impact of constantly referring to Helen throughout the play while limiting her to one scene might be diminished, and her single appearance at the play's center may be preempted by bringing her onstage in the second scene.

A less literal treatment of the scene's opening lines has become more common in the theater. In Davies' production, for example, Cressida entered on the balcony enthusiastically observing all around her, though nothing actually was happening. As she descended the staircase she did a double take after looking out a window, finally catching sight of something of interest. Excitedly, she retreated a few steps and leaned over the banister in an attempt to gain the best view of an offstage event. After finishing her descent, she crossed to the piano and began to tinker with the melody from the Chopin etude as it faded from the loudspeakers, and without looking up she asked Alexander (who had entered from beneath the balcony) "Who were those went by?" While an appearance by Helen and Hecuba could strengthen the significance of the reference to the two queens, their absence allows the lines and the stage business of looking to become more of a comment on Cressida's inquisitiveness. Without a visual cause for her question, Cressida's first line tells the audience more about her character and what provokes her interest, rather than voicing the obvious question the audience would share with Cressida if two women did pass by.

Most productions that included Hecuba and Helen leave little trace of critical reaction to their crossing the stage, but Stephen Rathbun is one critic that did question if Henry Herbert had any authority for his use of Hecuba. Rathbun admitted that he did not have any "vast 'variorum' knowledge of Shakespeare" and wondered whether any edition supported the appearance of Hecuba. In praising Herbert as "a Benson veteran, [who] knows more about Shakespeare than does any other player in America," Rathbun acknowledged that the director's decision may have stemmed from an authoritative source. Rathbun went so far as to request that "somebody please page" Herbert at the Broadhurst Theater to inquire about his decision to improve "Shakespeare to the extent of introducing into the play an extra character?"[8] Herbert himself replied to Rathbun, and the following week, Rathbun quoted from the letter, where Herbert cited the exchange between Cressida and Alexander ("Who were those went by") as his "authority for introducing the figure" of Hecuba.[9] Herbert may have been aware that twenty years earlier Poel had Helen and Hecuba cross the stage, but a theatrical precedent may not have been the kind of justification that the critic sought. Perhaps Muir's note, coming from an editor (albeit fifty years later), would have helped convince Rathbun of the acceptability of the addition.

Miller's video production provides the opportunity to examine more closely an example of Helen and Hecuba's appearance. Miller began his second scene with Helen and Hecuba crossing through the palace before ascending a small set of stairs. Cressida entered the scene chasing quite quickly after them only to encounter Alexander descending the stairs, obviously having passed the queens on their way up to the eastern tower. It is up these same stairs that Pandarus will later lead Cressida to watch the soldiers pass, and in this way Miller made an explicit visual parallel between the two pairs of spectators who watch the soldiers.[10] Cressida's first question sets up one of the many parallels between herself and Helen and provides another instance of the play's recurring motif of watching and naming. The staging of such moments is particularly important in terms of foregrounding characters for the observation by both onstage and offstage spectators. While Cressida's question about the passing women sets up some editorial and performance possibilities, Cressida and Pandarus watching the soldiers "pass toward Ilium" raises much more complex questions about the interpretation of dialogue in order to determine the entrance, exit, and movement of characters.

~~~

Where, in theatrical or fictional terms, does Pandarus suggest watching the soldiers when he asks Cressida, "Shall we stand up here and see them as they pass toward Ilium? . . . Here, here, here's an excellent place, here we may see most bravely. I'll tell you them all by their names as they pass by, but mark Troilus above the rest" (1.2.173)? The repetition of "here" as the "excellent place" to "see them as they pass" provokes the question of whether Pandarus, Cressida, or both are already at the place or must go to it. Pandarus's "up here" certainly implies a raised location, but are they already aloft, do they go up, does a movement on a flat or raked stage somehow signify "up here," or is the phrase more decorative than literally descriptive? Editors who provide specific fictional (as opposed to theatrical) locations for scenes generally follow Theobald's somewhat absurd setting of the scene in "a street" as the most likely place for Cressida, Alexander, and Pandarus to meet and watch the soldiers come home. Most editors since Malone omit Theobald's further indication that the street was "near the Walls of Troy," but Kemble provided a contrary theatrical opinion by crossing out his edition's location of "A Street in Troy" and writing in its place "The Walls of Troy."[11] Kemble's elevating the scene to the walls has implications drifting back to Trojan legend and forward to the most recent productions. The descriptions throughout the different versions of the legend of events taking place with spectators on the walls is mirrored in many modern productions that construct walls onstage from which Cressida and Pandarus watch the soldiers. In Shakespeare's time, however, there are at least two significant examples of playwrights staging scenes on Troy's Walls.

Troy's Walls were somehow represented by the Admiral's company for their Trojan War play around 1600 (perhaps by Dekker and Chettle). In the final scene described in the damaged "plot," what would seem to be onstage fighting between Troilus and Diomedes, and then Hector and Achilles, is watched by Priam, Paris, Helen, Polyxena, and Cassandra from "on the walls." The final line of the "plot" is the revealing direction that "Priam & they on the wall desce."[12] Heywood's *The Iron Age* also contains two similar scenes upon Troy's walls. The scene containing the duel between Ajax and Hector begins with the direction, "Flourish. Enter above upon the wals, Priam, Hecuba, Hellena, Polixena, Astianax, Margareton, with attendants" (2.5.0.1).[13] Paris enters "below" and speaks to Priam before "Hector and Ajax appeare betwixt the two Armies" (2.5.21.1). The scene in which Achilles kills Margareton begins with the direction: "Alarum. Enter above Priam, Hector, Astianox, Hecuba, Hellen, etc. Below Achilles and Margareton" (4.3.0.1). While those above remain silent, Achilles and Margareton speak and fight, and although no direction is given, it would seem Achilles exits after he kills Margareton. Priam vainly attempts to persuade Hector not to avenge his brother's death on the day when Andromache had dreamt of Hector's death, but Hector vows he will kill Achilles "before the Sonne decline" (4.3.17). The stage directions then call for an "Exit from the wals," and immediately there is an "alarum," and Hector reenters "beating before him Achilles['] Mermidons" (4.4.0.1, Weiner's brackets).

The significance of the directions from another play by another author for a different theater must be limited, but several possibilities are suggested from contemporary theater practice. Both the "plot" and the two directions in *The Iron Age* direct a fairly large group to enter onto the Trojan Walls, implying that perhaps the walls supplied a larger space than is usually utilized for scenes above. The naming of the walls in the stage directions may indicate that the space above was somehow made to appear specifically like a wall. The direction for the descent in the "plot" and the sequence in *The Iron Age* requiring Hector to exit from the walls and immediately enter on the main stage, suggests that it was possible to go up to and come down from the walls quickly within a scene.[14]

The lack of specific and obvious use of walls in Shakespeare's play may relate to the theater for which the play was written or may simply indicate that staging particulars were to be taken up in rehearsals rather than in the text. Alexander describes Helen and Hecuba ascending the eastern tower to watch the battle, but no specific use of the Trojan Walls is evident in the dialogue. Shakespeare's frequent staging of scenes on walls (sixteen times[15]) usually has clear indications in both stage directions and dialogue that would seem to require something which, in Bottom's words, would "signify 'wall'" (*A Midsummer Night's Dream*, 3.1.64). Arguing that Pandarus's "up here" is meant to signify the Trojan Walls is therefore a very problematic assumption, while remaining an intriguing possibility.

Delius (in his edition of 1856) proposed a specific Shakespearean staging of the scene that has been both rejected and supported by editors and directors: "Pandarus and Cressida go up to an elevated point, in the Shakespearian theater to the balcony at the back of the stage, and from there watch . . . the homecoming Trojans pass over the stage, without themselves being seen."[16] J. Q. Adams objected to Delius's conjectured use of the balcony on the grounds that it "would involve an entrance and an exit" and suggested instead that the soldiers passed at the rear of the stage while Pandarus and Cressida were at the front.[17] Adams's rejection of the use of the balcony is cited with approval by Muir, who added the conjecture that "up here" may refer either to "'upstage' or a raised place on the stage."[18] Bevington offers an analysis of the phrase from several perspectives. While "stand up here" "seems to suggest that they find some elevated position—conceivably the 'window' position in the gallery," the dialogue also "seems continuous in a way that would make the ascent difficult." He tentatively suggests, similarly but in contrast to Muir's "upstage," that Pandarus and Cressida "simply move downstage."[19] Gary Taylor, however, argues that "the review parade of Trojan warriors is most easily staged with Pandarus and Cressida on the upper stage."[20] Cressida, Alexander, and Pandarus enter and exit "above" in Taylor's text, and the only action to take place on the main stage during the entire scene is the soldiers passing by. Taylor's staging both agrees with Delius's suggestion of the balcony, while also answering Adams's and Bevington's objection by eliminating the need for an ascent within the scene.[21]

Leslie Thomson disputed Taylor's stage directions, arguing that

> it would have been most unusual to have a long and important exchange above and none below. As well, there is no specific indication that Cressida and Pandarus are above, and given the probability that those above on the Renaissance stage were both less visible and less audible than those below, it is doubtful that Shakespeare would have arranged the scene as this modern editor suggests.[22]

Providing support for Thomson's objections are Hosley's statistics showing how most actions placed aloft have clear indications, usually in stage directions, which signify the use of a gallery.[23] Hosley has also shown that two-thirds of Shakespeare's actions aloft are under 100 lines, and only two are more than 200 lines (*The Two Noble Kinsmen* 2.2 is 282 lines, *King John* 2.1.201–561 is 360; Hosley does not include the 291 lines in 1.2 of *Troilus and Cressida*). Thomson's belief that those above were less visible and less audible carries the dubious implication that the important and poetic scenes of Juliet on her balcony or Richard II upon Flint Castle's Walls presented difficulties for the audience.

Briefly considering what is arguably Shakespeare's most problematic scene aloft provides some interesting possibilities. The Folio's stage direction, "Enter Cleopatra and her maids, with Charmian and Iras, aloft" opens the scene in which "They heave Antony aloft to Cleopatra" (*Antony and Cleopatra*, 4.16.0, 4.16.38). Peter Thompson judges it "lunacy" to "set one of the play's climactic moments at the back of the stage, behind at least a railing or bannister if not something more solid."[24] He suggests instead that the scene represents an instance when "a raised unit constructed on stage seems to be implied."[25] Peter Thompson's view is not endorsed by the New Variorum editor, who instead supports the more common view that the scene would have taken place on the Globe's balcony.[26]

The possibility that Cressida and Pandarus observe the soldiers from a construction easily accessible from the main stage would allow them easily to "go up" and perhaps come down within the scene. A wall could therefore be brought onstage, and Quince's worries that he must present "a wall in the great chamber" (*A Midsummer Night's Dream*, 3.1.64) could be a parody of a stage practice of bringing a wall onstage. While Bevington warns that "staging conventions in Elizabethan theater offer few precedents for a raised platform,"[27] it is worth noting that many modern productions actually do bring a raised space onstage, allowing Pandarus and Cressida to ascend for the parade and then descend back onto the main stage after the soldiers' exit. The modern practice is, however, a solution usually for a proscenium arch stage without a balcony, making clear the importance of establishing what theater an editor has in mind when inventing or interpreting stage directions. The conflicting claims and theories about whether the play was performed in Shakespeare's lifetime in public performances at the Globe or private performances at the Inns of Court or a university, at least brings into question the way stage directions should be worded or placed and the way dialogue is used to interpret movement on a general or specific Shakespearean stage.[28]

Wherever Pandarus and Cressida stand, the soldiers' entrances seem to be an example of the common occurrence of characters silently entering and exiting while "observed and commented upon by others."[29] Allardyce Nicoll concluded that the phrase that occurs in many plays, "passing over the stage," was a technical theatrical term. He suggests that the usual staging may have included "a movement from yard to platform to yard again,"[30] where actors would enter through the audience and cross the front of the stage before descending back into the yard to exit through the audience. While Bevington considers such action to be "probably unnecessarily elaborate,"[31] Michael Hattaway agrees with Nicoll's staging, noting that this

> movement neatly establishes the customary double perspective for the audience: the players enter the yard, making the audience feel they are "there," actually present for the show, but they then mount the playing space from which the audience is physically and aesthetically detached.[32]

Pandarus wants to watch the men as they "pass toward Ilium," telling Cressida "their names as they pass by" (1.2.178–79). If a procedure was common for passing over the stage, the dialogue and the stage directions for entrances could be enough to signal that the usual staging was to take place. A parade of warriors through the yard and over the stage provides a good example of how the character groups could be separated to allow Pandarus and Cressida to remain on the main stage, perhaps moving upstage to watch the soldiers pass over the front of the stage.[33]

The physical separation between the soldiers and observers has both a practical and thematic significance. Delius's note quoted above includes the assumption that Pandarus and Cressida are unseen by the soldiers, but this has not been the choice of many directors. Barbara Hodgdon, in her analysis of the scene's theater history, points out some of the implications in different stagings:

> Although Cressida's and Pandarus' dialogue suggests that the men may simply pass by, unaware of being seen by either onstage or offstage spectators, nothing in the playtext restricts their look. Moreover, although Cressida wishes to remain unnoticed (especially, it would seem, by Troilus [186; 233]), nothing specifically prevents the Trojans from looking her way or from acknowledging her presence as well as Pandar's. What is at issue here involves more than the obvious: the question of whether Cressida, already defined in relation to a male tableau, is further constructed by their gazes.[34]

Surely Cressida's insistence that Pandarus "speak not so loud" (1.2.181) and hold his "peace, for shame" (1.2.227) at least allows for the possibility of their being seen and heard by the soldiers. Productions fluctuate between including or excluding interactions between Pandarus and Cressida and the warriors, and vary the distance in height and length between the civilians and the warriors. Two extremes are the productions which entirely eliminated the warriors from the stage (Macowan, Guthrie, Hall, Harrison, and Davies) and productions that have the soldiers pass within arm's reach of the spectators. In Hands's production, Pandarus grabbed Troilus's hand and pulled "Cressida toward him, anticipating their later joining together (3.2)."[35] Hodgdon's thorough and intriguing commentary on the stage history of the action still leaves room to supplement her essay with an exploration of Miller's video and Mendes' and Judge's RSC productions which she did not write about.

Two similarities between the very different versions of the scene in Miller's and Mendes' productions are that both directors had Pandarus point to a space "above" for the question, "Shall we stand up here and see them as they pass toward Ilium?" and both directors changed "here" to "there."[36] This would seem to imply that they found difficulty with the word "here" to indicate a place at some distance, but such a theory cannot account for the productions that similarly altered or cut the line when Cressida and Pandarus remained on the main stage. Guthrie and Davies both had Pandarus and Cressida look through binoculars at the front of the stage as imaginary soldiers passed behind the audience, and both altered the text. Guthrie changed the line to "Shall we stay here,"[37] and Davies cut all references to "here," equally implying that the phrase is also problematic when the characters did not move.[38]

Miller's Pandarus spoke "here, here, here's an excellent place" as he climbed the stairs, leading Cressida to a balcony where they watched the warriors pass quite close by. All the soldiers, except Troilus, ignored Pandarus's waves and calls, but Susan Willis reports that Miller "built in a shy wave by Cressida trying to attract Hector's attention as Pandarus praised him, though on the best take, the one used, a banner carrier masked that lovely gesture."[39] What remained visible was a brief glance and smile between Hector and Cressida as she agreed with Pandarus: "O a brave man" (1.2.199). The proximity of the spectators to the soldiers adds to the anxiety of Cressida's girlish shyness but also increases Pandarus's potential for both embarrassing Cressida and being noticed by Troilus ("If he see me you shall see him nod at me," 1.2.190–91).

Pandarus's role as announcer and commentator on the warriors both to Cressida and the audience should not completely overshadow his own voyeuristic pleasure in the procession. Miller made this point by having some attendant soldiers disdainfully ignore Pandarus's obviously audible remarks, creating an onscreen comment on his exuberance. Like Cressida, the soldiers seemed to know Pandarus for the bawd he is, and their scorn of him foreshadowed the humili-

ation he is subjected to by Paris's servant, Paris, Helen, and of course at the end of the play by Troilus. Miller began the tragedy of Pandarus as early as the second scene, using the soldiers' looks and gestures to make the connection between the procession of the soldiers coming home in the second scene with the "free march to Troy" (5.11.30) at the end of the play.[40]

Miller's Troilus almost immediately spotted Pandarus and Cressida. As he looked up and walked backwards, there was perhaps a visual reference to Ophelia's description of how Hamlet

> seemed to find his way without his eyes
> For out o'doors he went without their help.
> And to the last bended their light on me.
>   (*Hamlet*, 2.1.99–101)[41]

After Troilus exited, Pandarus turned and walked down the stairs as he spoke "nere look, nere look." The camera returned to the interior of the palace as Pandarus continued with "the eagles are gone" (1.2.240), following Pandarus and Cressida as they descended the stairs into the area where the scene began.

In Mendes' production, Pandarus and Cressida exited to climb to the Swan Theater's side gallery after Cressida consented ("At your pleasure" 1.2.176) to Pandarus's request to "stand up there." While Pandarus and Cressida were offstage, the warriors formed a line across the rear of the stage with their backs to the audience (the same image they presented for the battle sequence). Mendes' business provided an interesting option of having Pandarus and Cressida's exit and ascent covered by the soldiers' appearance. In Hosley's study of Shakespeare's use of the gallery, he cites instances where action or dialogue would cover a descent from the gallery, and presumes that

> where dialogue is insufficient to "bridge" this period, stage business by players remaining on the stage was employed to help cover descents; and evidently a *Florish* of trumpets was also, where appropriate, occasionally used for this purpose.[42]

The stage direction, "sound a retreat" (after 1.2.170 in QF) could perhaps be the cue for an extended flourish, not only providing the signal for Pandarus's line "Hark, they are coming from the field" (1.2.173), but perhaps continuing until, and maybe throughout, the procession.[43] Mendes' staging can also be related to the possibility that the soldiers entered through the audience, where perhaps an early entrance into the yard or onto the stage could provide a distraction from a stage left otherwise empty if Cressida and Pandarus somehow go up.[44]

The often elaborate stage business that accompanies the soldiers' appearances in many productions suggests that the length of the commentary allows time for more than a short trip across the stage, and that the descriptions themselves invite such business. Mendes had the preoccupied soldiers pass without noticing their observers, stopping at the center stage pool to perform a cleansing ritual that had some specific connection to Pandarus's descriptions. Helenus, who can "fight indifferent well" (1.2.219), momentarily forgot his sword, and instead of majestically cleaning his sword as Hector, Paris used a bit of water to slick back his hair (as Pandarus remarked, "this will do Helen's heart good," 1.2.211).[45] After the soldiers knelt at the pool, they exited through the audience, half following Nicoll's suggestion of using the yard by presenting a ritualistic and stylized tableau which slowly dissolved as the soldiers exited through the auditorium.

After the "common soldiers" left, Cressida alone returned to the main stage, regaining her self-confidence as she undermined Pandarus's praise of Troilus with her own praise of Achilles. Pandarus exited from the balcony but made his descent slowly, leaving Cressida alone for the speech that reveals how she defends herself ("Upon my back to defend my belly, upon my wit to defend my wiles," 1.2.256). Pandarus re-entered for his line "Say one of your watches" (1.2.261). Many productions that used either a balcony or a raised structure on the stage similarly return the action to the main stage after the warriors' exit. The desire for both an ascent and a descent in the scene comments not only on its plausibility and practicality, but also attests to the effectiveness of the movement. The many different solutions for providing a raised place for the observers all agree that Pandarus and Cressida stand upon stairs, walls, chairs, and balconies only while watching the soldiers. Perhaps the image of Cressida stalking the main stage for her soliloquy is irresistible, or maybe there is a consensus on the need to present the dialogue between Cressida and Pandarus before and after the parade in a space that does not limit their movement or hamper their ability to communicate with the audience.

Commenting on Mendes' production, Terry Hands (then the RSC's artistic director) objected to the use of the balcony for part of Cressida's crucial first scene.[46] He felt the focus of the audience should be primarily on Pandarus and Cressida, and by putting them above while the soldiers passed below, he feared the main interest became the warriors rather than Pandarus and Cressida. Mendes did wrestle with the problem somewhat. In rehearsals and the very first preview, the top balcony (about 15 feet directly above the stage) was used by Cressida and Pandarus but was changed by the second preview to the lower side balcony (about 7 feet above and to the audience's right of the stage) because "the focus was too split."[47] While

Hands's desire to focus primarily on Pandarus and Cressida is certainly valid, Mendes' staging was still very effective. Certainly some of the audience had trouble seeing Pandarus and Cressida, but, and Hands might say this is a significant "but," a good seat provided a double focus that allowed the dialogue and actions of Pandarus and Cressida to control the procession.[48]

The impressive set for Judge's production, designed by John Gunter, had an imposing Trojan Wall running from beyond the proscenium to the back of the stage, roughly parallel to the stage right proscenium wall. The original set designs included a moving segment of the wall that rolled toward center stage, with a window and a small balcony for Pandarus and Cressida to watch the soldiers. The decision to have Pandarus and Cressida go up to a raised location was therefore made before the first rehearsal, when it was also decided that they would start and finish the scene on the main stage below. As Pandarus and Cressida exited to go up to the balcony, the warriors began to emerge from under the stage on the stairs at the front of the stage before they moved to a set of benches where they unarmed. When the last of the Trojans had entered and unarmed (and partially undressed), and when the dialogue about them concluded ("chaff and bran," 1.2.238), the soldiers exited in a mass of steam, as if into a shower room, while Pandarus and Cressida descended to the main stage to finish the scene.

The production offered another example of a literal interpretation of Pandarus's remark, "Shall we stand up here," using the above space only for the central part of the scene. The movements up to and down from the balcony were covered by the entrance and exit of the soldiers, and the time it took Pandarus and Cressida to go up and come down were not considered awkward, but welcome opportunities to develop the image of the soldiers returning from battle. In a critical essay unknown to Judge, René Girard describes the scene as "prestigious football players going back to their locker room after a hotly contested game,"[49] but in this production Cressida, Pandarus, and the audience were able to peer into the locker room.

Miller, Mendes, and Judge provided a frame for Pandarus and Cressida by placing them in a balcony, putting them on show as much as the soldiers who passed before them. Just as the rooms above the Globe's stage were probably both a place to watch and a place to be watched, modern directors have chosen to situate Pandarus and Cressida in a space where they were both observers and observed. While they played with the idea of knowing and judging by sight, they were also themselves objects of gaze and judgment, whether by the audience alone or by the characters as well. Cressida makes clear several times in the play that she knows she is being evaluated and judged,

but in her first scene she gets the chance to be the observer and eval-
uator. The degree to which she is either empowered by her looking
or demeaned as a spectacle will begin to determine a production's interpretation of the character.

The choices made in staging the scene, whether editorial, critical,
or theatrical, can shift the focus by inventing physical arrangements
and interactions of characters. Studying the many different opinions
about where Pandarus and Cressida are placed and how the warriors
pass by makes clear the effectiveness of various stagings, and reveals
the lack of any obvious single solution. Two reviews of different productions that excluded the soldiers' entrances provide an example of
very different assessments of directors' decisions. The reviewer for
the *Times* described Guthrie's production in relation to the moment's
stage history.

> The march back from the field of the Trojan heroes, before the ecstatic
> eyes of Pandarus and the lively interest of Cressida, is usually an ineffec-
> tive bore. Mr. Guthrie lets the heroes march invisibly over the heads of
> the stalls and leaves Mr. Paul Rogers with his grey topper and racing
> glasses to act the old fribble's ecstatic admirations. Mr. Rogers turns the
> scene into a few minutes of comic perfection; and Miss Rosemary Harris
> supports him with a beautiful show of mock naiveté.[50]

Robert Speaight wrote that in the Hall/Barton "sandpit" production,

> in only one scene did the decor seem to me deficient—where Pandarus
> and Cressida watch the Trojan warriors go forth to battle. The stage di-
> rections make it clear that they pass, singly, across the stage, and in Shake-
> speare's theater Pandarus and Cressida would have watched them from
> the balcony. But since there were no upper levels in Mr. Hurry's set, they
> had to imagine them in the audience. I thought this a serious loss, and if
> I had been producing the play, I should have lain awake at night until I
> had found a means of making it good.[51]

Speaight's review shows the often dubious assumptions made by both
theatrical and scholarly critics. Critics who find it useful to specify a
theatrical or fictional location to provide a visual dimension to their
arguments often risk offering a questionable interpretation of an action. For example, Ralph Berry, like Speaight, assumes that Pandarus
and Cressida watch the soldiers from "the upper stage," while Joel Altman firmly places the scene "on the wall of Ilium," apparently from
beginning to end.[52] These critics confirm the desire to locate the
scene both on Shakespeare's historic stage and within Troy's epic architecture, but just as Theobald's locating the scene in "a street before the walls" provides an unjustified specificity, many editors and

critics also answer staging questions in a way that imposes unnecessary limits on the visualization of the texts.

Another problem in editing and staging the warriors' parade is the placement and wording of the soldiers' entrances. QF supply separate directions for Aeneas, Antenor, Hector, Paris, Helenus, Troilus, and the "common soldiers"[53] to enter, without indicating where they exit. While nearly all editors substantially follow Rowe's rewriting of the direction ("passes over the stage"), there is little agreement about the placement of the directions. Several of the entrances could be classed as announced entrances, accompanied by some form of "Who comes here," which Honigmann has shown have been treated with little consistency by editors. Such stage directions

> may be meant to suggest a . . . distance between the speaker and those he fails to recognize immediately: either the full width of the stage lies between them, or the speaker sees others before they appear on the stage. In some instances there might well be a gap of several lines between the question and entry, or the entry may have to come second even though it is normally placed first.[54]

	ANTENOR	HELENUS	TROILUS	SOLDIERS
Seltzer	Capell	QF	QF	Capell
Alexander,	Capell	Capell	QF	F
Walker, Muir,				
Bevington	Capell	Capell	QF	Capell
Evans	QF	QF	QF	Capell

The treatment of the warriors' entrances offers an excellent example of how announced entrances are inconsistently placed even within a few lines of the same edition. Cressida asks "Who's that?" for the entrances of Antenor and Helenus (1.2.185, 214), "What sneaking fellow comes yonder?" (1.2.223) for Troilus's entrance, and "Here comes more" (237) for the "common soldiers." QF place all these entrances after Cressida questions the identity of each warrior ("*Cressida:* Who's that? / *Enter Antenor*"), but editors since Capell have somewhat haphazardly rearranged the stage directions. Many editors (including Foakes, Harbage, Palmer, and Taylor) follow Capell by consistently moving the stage directions so that Cressida's questions follow the entrance ("*Enter Antenor / Cressida:* Who's that?"), but many other editions show little logic in their arrangements.[55] A chart showing the placement by a selection of editors that do not follow Capell for all of these four entrances indicates that almost every possible combination is realized in variously placing the entrances both after (as QF) and before (as Capell) Cressida's questions (and, for the soldiers, her comment "Here comes more").

Hodgdon argues that Capell's rearrangement of the stage directions diminishes the "potential power" and privilege of Cressida's gaze.

> Although it is Pandarus who notices Aeneas, the first to enter, Cressida's language calls up the rest of the spectacle—a detail obvious in both Quarto and Folio but masked by edited texts which, in repositioning the stage directions so that it is Pandarus' words that "bring on" most of the Trojans, are complicit with subsuming her gaze in his. But although Pandarus certainly attempts to direct her gaze, and although his running commentary seems more knowing than her questions, the playtext also suggests that she may not be "looking his way" for she is not only the first to see but clearly owns her own gaze.[56]

Just as Cressida asks "Who were those went by?" to open the scene, the question of whether the observed characters are onstage relates to the depiction of her curiosity. If the audience is presented with a character before that character is identified, Cressida can voice the audience's question ("Who's that?"). If, however, she brings the characters onstage with her question, she in some sense orchestrates the spectacle and dialogue. While Hodgdon remarks that Pandarus's commentary "seems more knowing than her questions," Cressida's question about the "sneaking fellow" certainly seems more informed than Pandarus, who mistakes Troilus for Deiphobus.[57]

Describing and showing Troilus to Cressida is Pandarus's often stated purpose in watching the parade (with the added hope of being given the nod by Troilus), creating the crucial moment of bringing the title characters onstage together for the first time. They are only together for five scenes (1.2, 3.2, 4.2, 4.4, 5.2), but significantly in the first and last of these scenes, one of the lovers watches the other.[58] As Pandarus uninterestedly answers Cressida's questions about Helenus, he begins to wonder whether Troilus "went not forth today" (1.2.215). Pandarus's initial confidence that he could show to Cressida Troilus marching home from battle undermines the entire first scene, where Troilus had told Pandarus that he would unarm because he was too lovesick to fight,[59] and Pandarus exited declaring he would "meddle nor make no more i'th' matter" (1.1.83). The duplicity of characters is set up very early, with Troilus declaring that he is too heartsick to fight, though Pandarus knows he will, and Pandarus vowing he would not woo Cressida for Troilus but immediately doing so. In this early scene, the play can be understood to depict a society where Cressida's legendary faithlessness is just another instance of an epidemic of falsity.

In his exaggeration of Troilus's virtues, Pandarus supplies Troilus with a hero's welcome home: "Hark! Do you not hear the people cry 'Troilus'?" (1.2.221). The Oxford editors (Muir followed by Taylor, neither providing an explanatory note) are convinced that Pandarus's "Hark" and "hear" have a literal cause, and precede it with a stage direction for "Shouts off."[60] Muir's stage direction offers at least two possibilities. If the shouts are incoherent, Pandarus is interpreting chaotic noises for his purposes, perhaps obviously (as in Miller's production). But almost immediately after Pandarus says he hears "the people cry 'Troilus,'" Troilus does appear, creating the possibility (perhaps the dramatically weaker possibility) that the shouts could be as Pandarus reports them.

Chaucer has Criseyde sitting alone listening as the "men cride in the strete, 'Se, Troilus'" (2.612) and "the peple cryde, 'Here cometh oure joye'" (2.643) as she watches Troilus ride past. Rather than following Chaucer and reproducing a sentimental and heroic moment, the play offers a comic opportunity for Pandarus.[61] Davies' and Mendes' productions provide examples of how the exclusion of offstage shouts effectively foreground Pandarus's attempts to praise Troilus beyond reality. Davies had Pandarus make an excited plea, "Do you not hear the people cry 'Troilus?,'" only to be greeted by a deadpan denial by Cressida with a shake of her head, not only implying that she heard no such shouts but also that Pandarus was vastly overplaying his role. Mendes did provide shouts, but they were Pandarus's own, perhaps attempting ventriloquy when he yelled through his cupped hands, "Troilus, Troilus," but never in danger of fooling Cressida into hearing it as the people's cry. Having Pandarus himself shout showed a desire to provide a cause for the line, but allowed that cause to be purely Pandarus's creation. Mendes did experiment in rehearsal with offstage noises and shouts to accompany the entire procession, but these were soon abandoned because they were considered to be a distraction from the dialogue.[62] Many directors have included offstage noises throughout the procession, but the only evidence I have found for a specific use of shouts offstage for Pandarus's line is Miller's production, which, as noted above, had indistinguishable cries obviously misinterpreted by Pandarus.

While it is Pandarus who says he hears Troilus being greeted, it seems Cressida sees him first. The audience has of course been introduced to Troilus before and would presumably recognize him if he were onstage, posing the question again about what view the audience shares with the characters. Walker, Muir, and Bevington are among those editors who follow Capell in moving the warriors' entrances before Cressida's questions, but all revert to the QF placement of Troilus's entrance before Cressida asks, "What sneaking fellow comes yonder" (1.2.223). Muir's note that "Cressida is teasing her uncle" requires Cressida to recognize Troilus, but by following the QF placement of the stage direction, Muir wants Cressida, but not the audience, to see him. Is Cressida's irony accompanied by the audience's recognition of Troilus, and does Pandarus's misidentification precede the audience's recognition of Troilus?

The problem with identifying Troilus could be discussed on several levels. Theatrically, the issue is related to the staging (with Troilus "yonder" perhaps signifying that he is offstage, in the yard, or onstage at a distance), or a costume that masks his identity. Pandarus notices that "his helm [is] more hacked than Hector's" (1.2.230), and his unarming at the beginning of the first scene and end of the second strongly suggest he has, if not wears, a helmet. Thematically, the issue of "knowing a man if you see him" (1.2.61–62) relates to the play's central problem of establishing and communicating personal identity and self-worth. The inability of characters to recognize one another, because of helmets, darkness, lack of acquaintance, or changes in circumstances, recurs throughout the play to create episodes where characters must assert their individuality in the face of obscurity. The same situation seems to exist for the characters, the actors, and the audience when they all need to assign the famous names of the epic to living flesh and bones and voices.

When Troilus first appears to Cressida, the text poses the open questions of where, how, and when he is seen, and how he behaves in relation to Pandarus's and Cressida's descriptions of him. Does he look and go sneakingly, similar to the way Helen notices that he "hangs the lip" (3.1.136) and Agamemnon observes he "looks so heavy" (4.6.97)? Perhaps while finding the heart to go into battle, Troilus is still visibly upset from his apparent lack of success in wooing Pandarus to woo Cressida. Cressida's calling him a "sneaking fellow" could of course be merely a comic deflation of Pandarus's praises of him, but her devaluing him certainly has the deeper significance, as she explains in her soliloquy at the end of the scene, of increasing her desirability by not allowing herself to seem too easily won.

3

"Enter Cassandra"

CASSANDRA'S ENTRANCE INTO THE TROJAN COUNCIL SCENE (AFTER 2.2.96) is given different descriptive stage directions in Q and F. Attempting to discover the possible reasons for the variants is almost as difficult as determining the range of different implications in the directions. Compared with F's visual stage instruction, Q could be considered a more authorial description of the entrance, but the differences may have originated in the printing house rather than the theater or at the author's desk. One explanation for the variants may be the availability of space on the printed page. Q's shorter direction comes toward the end of a page that has two short speeches on one line, while in F the direction is given extra space, especially above it, and is centered and printed on two lines when it could have fit on one. If compositors for QF both worked from a copy that had the same stage direction, the different wording may be a printing house elaboration or reduction. If F was set from a marked up copy of Q, however, the description of Cassandra "with her hair about her ears" might have been a manuscript addition or alteration for theatrical purposes.

The possibility of compositorial influence can be investigated with reference to similar stage directions set by the same F compositor (B).[1] In *Hamlet*, Ophelia enters "distracted" in F, "playing on a Lute, and her haire downe singing" in Q1, and without any description in the Q2 stage direction (4.5.21).[2] Without venturing too deeply into the complex discussion of the *Hamlet* texts, F's Compositor B seems to have set "distracted" without knowledge of Q1's longer direction, perhaps using an annotated copy of Q2. F's Compositor B also set the passage in *Richard III*, again without any prompting from his printed copy (Q3), where Queen Elizabeth enters "with her hair about her ears" after learning of Edward IV's death. If current theories that the F copy texts of *Richard III, Hamlet,* and *Troilus and Cressida* made use of promptbooks to supplement quartos are at least possibly true, it is worth speculating that the changes Compositor B made to the quarto versions of these directions may imply that the wording of the F di-

That in their country did them that difgrace,
We feare to warrant in our natiue place.
      Enter Caſſandra rauing.
Caſſ. Cry Troyans cry:
Priam. What noiſe? what ſhrike is this?
Troy. Tis our madde ſiſter I do know her voice,
Caſſ. Cry Troyans.   *Hect.* It is Crſſandra
Caſſ. Cry Troyans cry, lend me ten thouſand eyes,
And I will fill them with prophetick teares.
Hect. Peace ſiſter peace,
                                Caſſ.

Q

That in their Country did them that difgrace,
We feare to warrant in our Natiue place.
      Enter Caſſandra with her haire about
              her eares.
Caſ. Cry *Troyans,* cry.
Priam. What noyſe? what ſhreeke is this?
Troy. Tis our mad ſiſter, I do know her voyce.
Caſ. Cry *Troyans.*
   Hect. It is *Caſſandra.*
   Caſ. Cry Troyans cry; lend me ten thouſand eyes,
And I will fill them with Propheticke teares.
   Hect. Peace ſiſter, peace.

F

8. **Enter Cassandra Q, F. Reproduced by permission of The Huntington Library, San Marino, California.**

rections derives from manuscript sources rather than with B or other printing house editors.[3]

This tangled web of textual transmission can at least lead to some theatrical possibilities. The convention of actors representing women "with their hair down" can have other meanings than madness. Alan Dessen provides examples of disheveled hair being used to portray a "female figure distraught with madness, shame, extreme grief, or the effects of recent violence."[4] Surely Ophelia, as described in Q1, represents one character who has lost her wits, but the *Richard III* direction describes a woman completely sane, only temporarily in an extreme state of grief through loss. Seen in this light, it is certainly Ophelia's mourning that is a major cause of her distraction, and her madness manifests itself with the actions of mourning. Cassandra's appearance can also be interpreted as the grief and mourning from a prophetic sense of loss as much as madness. Troilus's interpretation of her as "mad" seems not to be accepted by Hector, and editors and directors must make choices about presenting Cassandra in a way that could allow readers and audiences to question Troilus's remarks.

If the QF compositors had access to different information, the description in F may seem to have a theatrical connection, describing one aspect of the boy actor's appearance, but Dessen rightly warns against such easy interpretations of a stage direction's provenance. Just as a playwright might have written in his manuscript the theatrical convention of a stage direction, a theater document may have given only a key word to indicate a standard costume, wig, or demeanor.[5] The "plot" to *The Dead Man's Fortune* has directions for two characters to enter "mad," showing that even in what is considered a purely theatrical document there was no need for a more elaborate description of the mad character's looks or costume. Similarly, the "plot" for the untitled Trojan War play has Cassandra enter three times without any indication of the state of her hair or mind, even for her first entrance into what seems to be a Trojan council scene.

Cassandra also appears in the Trojan council scene in the first part of Heywood's *The Iron Age* with the same wording as the F direction ("Enter Cassandra with her haire about her eares" 1.1.134).[6] Priam calls her "madde," but she in turn accuses him and all of Troy of being mad (*Iron Age*, 1.1.143–44). Hector is clearly sympathetic to Cassandra's cries, calling her a "Vestall Profetesse . . . oft inspired" and begging the Trojans to "lend her gracious audience" (*Iron Age*, 1.1.157, 159). The contradictory interpretations of Cassandra's appearance and speech are also an important issue in Shakespeare's play. The character must present both visually and verbally some level of what Shakespeare's Troilus calls "brainsick raptures" (121), but at the same time convey that they are, as Hector calls them and the audience may know them to be, "high strains / Of divination" (112). Within the concerns of this study, the question to be asked is whether the different QF directions provide any significant clues as to how these contradictions can be played.

An audience's response to Cassandra's entrance could be conditioned by a prior knowledge of the character from myth, literature, and the previous references to her in the play. Pandarus twice mentions Cassandra before her entrance and both times paints a different picture than the "mad sister" (2.2.97) Troilus describes. In the first scene, Pandarus praises Cressida's beauty by comparing her to Helen, but he is interrupted just after evoking Cassandra as a paragon of wit for the similar purpose of commending Cressida (1.1.41–47). In the second scene, Pandarus describes how Cassandra laughed at the witty exchange between Helen and Troilus, seeming to imply that as an improbable candidate for laughter, Cassandra's reaction confirms the humor of the repartee. Cressida is quick to reply that "there was a more temperate fire under the pot of her eyes" (1.2.142), stressing the point that Cassandra, in Kenneth Palmer's words, "was unlikely to join with any enthusiasm in this facetious game."[7] Coming before Cassandra's first appearance, these early references may be expecting the audience to be aware of the mythic character, rather than just preparing for her later entrance.

The information readers and audiences might have about Cassandra from outside the play may be capitalized on by both the author and director.[8] Some modern productions have included in their program some sort of "Who's Who according to Legend,"[9] providing audiences with what sometimes seems essential and sometimes highly irrelevant and misleading information about characters' mythological biography. How much of this knowledge would have been assumed by Shakespeare is questionable, but knowing before Cassandra enters that she was given the gift of prophecy by Apollo, only to be subsequently prevented from having any powers of persuasion, can increase the complexity of the character and situation Shakespeare recreates.

Considering the difference between the QF directions raises questions about how mad Cassandra appears both to an audience and to other characters. The divided perception that Cassandra is both mad and sane is a distinction brought out by Chaucer and Caxton in material Shakespeare probably drew from, and audiences and readers may know. In *Troilus and Criseyde*, Troilus asks Cassandra to interpret his dream, but when she tells him:

> Wep if thow wolt, or lef, for out of doute,
> This Diomede is inne, and thow art oute.
>
> (5.1518)

Troilus dismisses her as a lying prophetess, "the victim of delusions":[10]

> sorceresse,
> With al thy false goost of prophecye!
> Thow wenest ben a gret devyneresse!
> Now sestow not this fool of fantasie
> Peyneth hire on ladys for to lye?

                                          (5.1520–24)

In both the poem and the play, an awareness of the truth of Cassandra's prophesy can contradict Troilus's denial of that truth. Hector's sympathetic treatment of Cassandra in *Troilus and Cressida* can combine with an audience's knowledge of the outcome of the war, and perhaps a knowledge of the Cassandra legend, as a way of qualifying Troilus' condemnation of her.

In a situation closer to Shakespeare's Trojan council scene, Caxton tells how Cassandra, when learning of Priam's decision to send Paris to Greece, disrupts the discussion with

> so grete sorowe as she had be folyssh or oute of her mynde, and began to crye an hyghe, saying, "Ha, ha, right noble cyte of Troye, what fayerye hath mevyd the to be brought to suche paryllis, for whiche thou shalt in shorte tyme be beten doun and thyne hyghe tourys ben demolisshid and destroyed unto the ground."[11]

For Caxton it is her sorrow that makes her act as if she were mad, but the clear implication is that she is not. Determining the subtle distinction between madness and the perception of madness, the playwright, editor, and director must make decisions concerning the degree to which Cassandra's alleged madness is apparent to the characters and the audience. If the madness is emphasized, the danger exists of readers and audiences dismissing Cassandra in the way Troilus does, but Troilus's view, and indeed the QF stage directions, should have some physical correlation. Do the different QF directions somehow indicate different portrayals of madness? Does Q's "raving" imply something more or less mad than F's description of Cassandra appearing with "her hair down"? Does the conventional appearance of madness convey more of a sense of real insanity than the vocal and physical gestures that would constitute "raving"? These are some of the questions to be explored in a critical history of the texts and performances.

Many recent editors conflate the QF directions to read, "Enter Cassandra raving, with her hair about her ears," destroying whatever integrity Q or F may have by combining the literary ("raving") with the theatrical ("hair down") directions.[12] Q's vague "raving" leaves much more to the readers' visual imagination, implying the appearance, behavior, and psychological state of a madwoman without detailing how this is conveyed, while F describes only her hair without interpreting what her appearance means. An editor's rationale for combining the directions could be that F's direction provides clarification of the period's theatrical convention of depicting a "raving" woman with her hair down, and modern readers might need both directions to be informed that raving on the Shakespearean stage indicates a particular conventional look of madness. This interpretation could, however, be provided in a note and need not be an imperative for conflating the texts.

Conflating the two directions can work to intensify them. If "raving" only implies the conventional look of madness, and the different directions are essentially the same, then an element of contradiction between appearance and reality may be preserved in the individual stage directions. By conflating the QF directions, "raving" becomes an additional aspect of her behavior rather than another way of indicating her appearance and performance, subverting any possible contradiction between perceived and real madness by describing a character who both looks and acts mad.

Miller's video production serves as a good example for exploring the presentation of Cassandra because of the detailed description that Susan Willis gives of the evolution of interpreting the character in rehearsal. She reports that, in speaking to the cast,

> Miller pointed out that Cassandra seconds Hector's opinion, displaying the irony of madness. He added that Cassandra does not seem raving mad in Hector's later arming scene and would not be played as such. Here they tried toning down the screaming madness of the standard stage Cassandra, all volume and little sense. Cassandra (Elayne Sharling) approached the table intently and earnestly but speaking in a normal voice; the men rejected not her but her words, and as Hector backed her up to the cell or cage built into the set she entreated him in an intense whisper all the way, keeping almost hypnotic eye contact. It was a stunning version of Cassandra because suddenly one was *listening* to her, hearing her words as Hector heard them, while everyone else at the table tuned her out in annoyance. . . .
>
> [Later in rehearsals] the Trojan council scene gained a slightly new approach to Cassandra. Mad with truth, she now played the whole scene locked in the cell; she cannot get to the table to tell them what they need to hear about their stupid course of action, so she cries out, Miller told the actress. When Hector walked back to the cell to calm her, she spoke in that effective intense whisper, crying out again as he left her; then, unheeded, she paced defiantly until she let out one great deep laugh as her brother gave in at the end. . . .
>
> In the last week Miller introduced all the women to the scene, not just Cassandra but Helen and Andromache as well. . . .

As a result of a joking suggestion by production manager Peter Sten-
ning, Cassandra's part was changed yet again. Sharling (Cassandra) was
asked to do the whole scene at a rip, all shouted, starting out of the cell
so two large goons, male nurses, could grab her and lock her in as she
raved. All the dignity and fascination that the character had earlier is lost
in such a rendition. Because it is also entirely opposite to the later Cassandra scene, it provides a schizophrenic pattern. The outburst was shock-
ing as they rehearsed it and disrupted everyone at the table; Helen paced,
Paris shifted, others stirred and turned. Miller left Cassandra with this interpretation, later adding a rocking, hair-chewing preliminary to it mod-
eled on the outbursts of a schizophrenic patient Miller knew. Her explosion suggests the near explosiveness of the discussion in the Trojan
council, although the earlier version of Cassandra had been refreshing
and clarifying to the role and the council scene.[13]

Miller's final decision that the character's continuity can be achieved
by interpreting her as a schizophrenic at least opens the debate of
whether Cassandra should appear the same in both her scenes. While
neither Q nor F have any description of Cassandra in her later entrances, is there enough of a difference in her speeches and the situation to suggest any significant change in appearance? Should she
look or act any less mad in her later scene, and if not, then how might
readers or audiences reconcile her recovery?

By using a real life schizophrenic as a model for Cassandra's movements and changes of temperament, Miller looked outside the play
and the myth of Cassandra to justify the radical change in her character between the scenes. Miller's final decision was to have Cassandra
present throughout the Trojan council scene with her hair down, appearing as the F direction describes. In her later scene (5.3), her hair
was neatly dressed in a net at the back of her head, and the rest of her
costume was equally ordered. She coolly reasoned with Hector not to
fight and then calmly predicted his death in a tone that suggested an
acceptance of the unavoidable certainty of the outcome rather than
the crazed prophesying she had displayed in her first scene.

Unfortunately, Willis's account of the progress of interpreting Cassandra does not include any indication of how she would have looked
in the council scene had she spoken in "a normal voice." Perhaps consideration of this interpretation never reached the point of deciding
about Cassandra's appearance, but speculation about the possibilities
serves to highlight some performance issues raised by the variant QF
stage directions. If Miller had Cassandra speak and appear as sanely
as she does in her later scene, the QF directions would have been entirely dismissed, but if she looked mad, as in the video, with di-

sheveled clothes and hair but spoke in a calm and sane voice, an unusual, but certainly valid interpretation of the F direction would have been achieved. The contradictions between the audience's and characters' perception of Cassandra would have found a physical basis in the discrepancy between her appearance and manner. The sanity, indeed the prophetic truth of her words, would have been in stark contrast to the madness of her appearance.

In his final decision, Miller can be seen to follow the conflated direction, "raving, with her hair down," but John Harrison's Birmingham Repertory Theatre modern dress production of 1963 provided an interesting interpretation of the F direction. J. C. Trewin wrote that "Cassandra (Lesley Nunnerley) appeared not as the customary raving prophetess, in whom 'high strains of divination' work, but as a leader of the Trojan peace party, carrying a trophy with the slogan 'Let Helen Go.'"[14] The anonymous reviewer for the *Stratford-on-Avon Herald* remarked that the actress "turns the mad Cassandra into a figure of startling sanity."[15] Harrison's promptbook calls for "Beatniks" to accompany Cassandra's entrance, and after they placed a box for her to stand on, they gathered around her to create the impression of a political rally, shouting and chanting during her speeches. Troilus's interpretation of her as mad became a military government's dismissive view of peace protesters.

Not only have editors changed the wording of Cassandra's entrance, but the placement of the direction is also altered in most modern editions. QF both have Cassandra enter and speak before Priam questions the source of the "shriek," but Priam's failure to recognize his daughter immediately, Troilus's identification of her from "her voice," and Hector's need to confirm her name all present a strong case that her first two speeches may be spoken from offstage. The entrance conforms to the convention of announced entrances, with the almost formulaic "What noise" answered by "I know her voice" and "It is Cassandra." Theobald first added the directions for Cassandra to speak her first two speeches from within, and moved her entrance to before her third speech. While the vast majority of editors have followed Theobald's emendation, directors have been less easily convinced.[16] What may seem like a practical issue of postponing Cassandra's entrance, because her family would surely have immediately recognized her, can eliminate what Dessen describes as the "richly suggestive" QF arrangement.

To delay Cassandra's entrance is to offer a smoother, less jolting experience for the reader or playgoer, but what if the placement of her appearance . . . is a calculated effect designed to ensure that the playgoer cannot miss the faulty seeing of the Trojan council that here is deciding the fate of their city?[17]

Dessen raises important thematic issues of the way characters are seen, understood, and valued in this play, and warns against an editorial desire to clarify the text in a way that may reduce possibilities and complexities. The theater history of Cassandra's entrance offers numerous ways of understanding the potential for the QF arrangement as well as other possible stagings.

Quayle's promptbook curiously has two entrances for Cassandra. After her first speech, she appeared upstage through a doorway, and then a note calls for her to enter downstage after her third "Cry Trojans cry."[18] Perhaps the promptbook does not note a short exit between her speeches that would have made some sense of the need to identify her, or maybe the second entrance is merely a direction to move into the main playing space. Shaw had Cassandra enter, as QF, upstage left for her first speech, then cross to upstage center for her second speech before moving downstage center for her third speech. Both Quayle's and Shaw's arrangements make the obvious point that by keeping Cassandra upstage, she can be seen by the audience without necessarily being seen by her family, and her first lines are then spoken with the added visual impact of what could be a powerful onstage presence.

While Quayle and Shaw were presented with Theobald's emendation in their promptbook edition but substantially followed the QF staging, Harrison did the reverse. He used for his promptbook Harbage's Pelican edition, which unusually follows the QF placement of the entrance, but Harrison opted instead for Theobald's arrangement. Harrison may have had knowledge of the editorial tradition for in his promptbook the direction "off" is penciled in before Cassandras first speech, and an offstage cry ("Let Helen Go") is added for the Beatniks. Although there is no marking of "off" for her second speech, the note that calls for Cassandra's and the Beatniks' entrance is given after her second speech. The Beatniks who accompanied Cassandra both offstage and onstage add to the sense of unrest that erupts first out of sight and then is brought into the council. The added offstage cry lends some support to the dramatic impact of Theobald's arrangement, where an offstage disturbance can chill both the audience and the Trojans, and effectively prepare for Cassandra's entrance.

While several more recent productions preferred the QF placement, they needed some rearranging to accommodate it. Barton's promptbook has Walker's directions for "within" crossed out, but Priam's line is moved to come before Cassandra's first speech. The promptbook reads: "Cass[andra] enter. Priam rises, [Cassandra] scream." By having Cassandra onstage for Priam's question, Barton's rearranged lines and invented scream would seem to preserve the QF reading more than the editorial rearrangement of the entrance. The Barton/Kyle promptbook also shows a change from the editorial tradition. Cassandra entered at the point indicated in QF, and Walker's later entrance is crossed out. After a cry from offstage, Cassandra entered to the ridicule and mimicry of her brothers. Before Priam's question, the promptbook notes that Margarelon and Troilus "scare her," probably causing the movement that prompted the change in Priam's line from "What shriek" to "What start."[19] The promptbook further notes that "all during Cass[andra]'s speech everybody except Hel[enus] and Pri[am] laugh and mock her." Cassandra's onstage presence was used to set up the brothers' disrespect for her before she spoke, showing another way that an early entrance can be effective.

Mendes' staging was a combination of the Barton and Barton/Kyle versions; a scream prefaced Cassandra's entry (as Barton/Kyle), Priam's line was moved to precede Cassandra's first speech (as Barton), and an editor's indication of a later point of entry was rejected in favor of having Cassandra onstage for her first line (as both Barton and Barton/Kyle). Mendes further rearranged the passage by having Troilus's "Tis our mad sister" immediately followed by Hector's "It is Cassandra" (Troilus's phrase "I do know her voice" was cut, and Cassandra's second "Cry Trojans" was attached to her third speech). The division between the brothers evident elsewhere in the scene was apparent in the different attitudes toward Cassandra, with Paris and Troilus not taking her seriously while Helenus and Hector showed compassion and perhaps some fear that she was correct. Hector quite clearly took offense at Troilus identifying her as "our mad sister," and he spoke his line ("It is Cassandra") directly at Troilus, as if to tell Troilus that she has a name and should not be so easily dismissed. The characters' compassion for Cassandra prompted the audience into questioning Troilus's treatment of her, a treatment made all the more callous when he referred to her as "our mad sister" in her presence.

As described above, the Barton, Barton/Kyle, and Mendes stagings all included a scream with Cassandra's entrance. Barton had an onstage scream while Barton/Kyle and Mendes had the scream from offstage. While the offstage screams may lend some support to the argument that Priam's line may imply an offstage cry, Barton's onstage scream can argue the reverse. Either onstage or offstage, the screams provided a more literal cause for Priam's line; being more of an incoherent noise than Cassandra's first line, the screams are a less intelligible version of the shriek implied in the text, Cassandra's "Cry Trojans Cry." By making the cause of Priam's line a scream, the directors decrease the need for Cassandra's first line to be a noise or shriek, but the need for alterations and cuts points to the implications in the text that Cassandra's cries are spoken with a certain volume and intensity. The impact of her entrance must be a strong one, injecting the debate, which especially in Troilus's previous speech is verging on abstract logic, with the significance of life or death.

Hall's New York production used Bevington's text, and was therefore presented with an edition that not only followed the QF placement, but also included a brief, evenhanded discussion of the alternatives and an explanation of the editorial tradition of postponing Cassandra's entrance. Hall elected to follow QF (and Bevington), and made use of his theater to help make sense of an early entrance for Cassandra and the dialogue that questions her identity. With the Trojan brothers locked in debate in the center stage sandpit, Cassandra startled characters and audience in the production's first use of a balcony that ran along the sides of the theater. She was suddenly present on the balcony and screaming her first "Cry Trojans Cry" in a way that had many in the theater, both onstage and in the audience, looking around, as if asking with Priam where the "noise" originated. After her first cries, she rushed down backstage stairs before reappearing on the main stage to confront Priam and his sons. In a staging that seems similar to Quayle's two entrances, Hall made effective use of both his theater's architecture and the QF arrangement with a staging that could have been performed on an early modern stage. Hall's staging allowed Priam, and indeed the audience, to be momentarily confused about the source of the cries without necessarily eliminating the power of her immediate presence.

Miller took advantage of the unique opportunities available to a video director in exploring the same themes as the theater directors. Troilus's mocking of Cassandra was also included in Miller's version, but because of some departures from the text, the video has different implications. As Willis mentions in her description of the scene (quoted above), Cassandra was present at the start of the Trojan Council scene along with Helen, Andromache, and numerous extras. During the discussions throughout the scene, some of these characters were used either in the background or as the focus of shots to register reactions to the speeches. The most obvious example was Helen, shown responding to the various views on whether she should be "back returned" (185), but Cassandra was also frequently shown, especially when Troilus spoke. During Troilus's long speech ("I take to-day a wife," 2.2.60–95), Cassandra remained almost constantly in the frame, slowly building up to the explosion where she burst from Andromache's care to confront her father and brothers. Troilus immediately signaled for help and two men escorted her to a barred cell where she was imprisoned for the remainder of the scene. While Cassandra was escorted away, the camera caught sight of Troilus holding back his laughter at his sister's madness, and when Troilus later tells Hector not "to deject the courage of our minds / Because Cassandra's mad" (2.2.120), Cassandra objects with a cry from her cell. The camera's ability to control somewhat the viewer's focus, especially in a group scene, was used by Miller to contrast Troilus's mad attempt to rationalize the war with Cassandra's mad reaction to the coldness of the reasoning.

Miller's liberties with the scene suggest some interesting possibilities inherent in the text. After Cassandra's first "Cry Trojans cry," the old, feeble, and nearly blind Priam asked "What noise, What shriek," but Miller made one of his few alterations to Alexander's text in cutting Troilus's and Hector's following speeches identifying "our mad sister," "Cassandra." Miller's blocking of the scene had Cassandra practically on top of Troilus and literally face to face with Hector for her first speeches, and therefore the cuts, especially to Troilus's line ("I do know her voice"), seem to support the need for Cassandra to be some distance from the main action during her first two speeches. Priam's inability to distinguish Cassandra's cries was, however, made to work with Cassandra already present because Miller depicted Priam as someone "whose grip on consciousness grew more slender at every rehearsal."[20] Willis describes the final rehearsal of the scene, where

> at the end [of the scene] Priam gave a mindless giggle (to which Miller responded, "I love it now that he's completely ga ga") and as the various courtiers passed by the cell Miller added a camera shot of Cassandra laughing.[21]

Miller eventually cut Cassandra's laughter during the final edit, leaving the giggling Priam as the final image of the scene. The idea of using Priam and Cassandra to close the scene would have provided a mirror image to Cassandra's entrance and Priam's reaction to it, and would have emphasized the role of both characters. The loss of control at the head of the family and state is compounded by the loss of confidence within the family itself. While Hector toys with the idea of giving Helen back and Troilus coolly reasons for keeping her for honor's sake, Cassandra's passionate response is perhaps the most sane reaction to what will inevitably become the tragic pursuit of honor.

Cassandra calling for the Trojans to weep prophetically for their destruction can signal the first tragic moment in the play. The dramatic power that these cries can have if delivered offstage is evident in the way that Poel had them repeated. After the speech where Hector seals his fate by resolving "to keep Helen still" (lines 162–92), Cassandra was again heard offstage shouting "Cry Trojans cry." Poel also sent his audience into the interval with the same offstage cry after Pandarus ushered Troilus and Cressida off to bed (3.2.207).[22] Finally, as will be discussed again in relation to the end of the play, Poel had Cassandra repeat her offstage cry during the final tableau. The repetition of Cassandra's cries testifies to the impact the lines were deemed to have when delivered offstage, haunting both characters and audience.

Theobald's emendation that has Cassandra speak from within is not only a valid interpretation of the dialogue, but has proved to be theatrically desirable. It has not, however, been universally accepted, and while some productions have supported his emendation, others have rejected it and followed the QF placement of the direction. The theatrical indecision should help fuel editorial indecision, and as with the wording of Cassandra's entrance, contribute to a productive exploration of an important, but ambiguous, moment.

4

"Good Thersites Come In and Rail"

Thersites' second scene is filled with entrances, exits, re-entrances, and descriptions of movements and locations. The variety of character groups makes the scene one of the most difficult in terms of determining the movements of the characters, especially with characters standing "within," "at the opening," or going into what the dialogue refers to as Achilles' tent (2.3.76, 83, 177). What few stage directions there are in QF often add to the complications and possibilities, and tracing the editorial and performance history reveals a wide variety of possible interpretations. Editors have often disagreed with the placement of directions in QF, while directors have reintroduced the reading of the early texts and invented alternative stagings, creating very different moments where characters are onstage or offstage, listening or deaf to certain lines.

After the Trojan council exits, Thersites is directed to enter "solus" (QF). The serious debate in which the Trojans engage, with no less than their lives and honors at stake, is framed by scenes in the Greek camp where the talk of hostilities is mainly between the factions among the Greeks. In Thersites' previous scene, he departs from Ajax, Achilles, and Patroclus vowing to leave the "faction of fools" (2.1.120), and he enters his second scene still "lost in the labyrinth" of his own "fury" (2.3.1–2). In his roles as both fool and commentator, Thersites derides his former and future employers, Ajax and Achilles, before beckoning to "My lord Achilles" (1.2.21). It is not Achilles but Patroclus who answers his call, triggering Thersites' second speech, in which he verbally abuses Patroclus in the guise of a religious contemplation. After a brief exchange between Patroclus and Thersites, Achilles enters, also asking "Who's there?"

Q's lack of a stage direction for Patroclus to enter is one of many necessary stage directions absent from Q, but F's placement of the entrance has been the subject of editorial debate, prophetically anticipated or partially caused by Hillebrand's note:

> *The history*
>
> *Enter* Therfites *folus.*
>
> How now *Therfites?* what loft in the Labyrinth of thy
> furie? fhall the Elephant *Aiax* carry it thus? he beates me,
> and I raile at him: O worthy fatiffaction, would it were
> otherwife: that I could beate him, whilft hee raild at mee:
> Sfoote, Ile learne to coniure and raife Diuels, but Ile fee
> fome iffue of my fpitefull execrations. Then ther's *Achilles,* a
> rare inginer. If Troy bee not taken till thefe two vnder-
> mine it, the walls will ftand till they fall of them-felues.
> O thou great thunder-darter of Olympus, forget that thou
> art *Ioue* the king of gods: and *Mercury,* loofe all the Ser-
> pentine craft of thy Caduceus, if yee take not that little
> little leffe then little witte from them that they haue:
> which fhort-armd Ignorance it felfe knowes is fo aboun-
> dant fcarce, it will not in circumuention deliuer a flie from
> a fpider, without drawing their maffie Irons, and cutting
> the web. After this the vengeance on the whole campe,
> or rather the Neopolitan bone-ache: for that me thinkes is
> the curfe depending on thofe that warre for a placket. I
> haue faid my prayers, and diuell Enuie fay *Amen.* What ho
> my Lord *Achilles?*
>
>   *Patrocl.* Whofe there? *Therfites?* good *Therfites* come
> in and raile.
>
>   *Therf.* If I could a remembred a guilt counterfeit, thou
> couldft not haue flipt out of my contemplation: but it is no
> matter, thy felfe vpon thy felfe. The common curfe of man-
> kinde, Folly and Ignorance, be thine in great reuerew: Hea-
> uen bleffe thee from a tutor, and difcipline come not neere
> thee. Let thy bloud be thy direction till thy death: then if
> fhe that layes thee out fayes thou art not a faire courfe, Ile
> be fworne and fworne vpon't, fhee neuer fhrowded any but
> lazars. *Amen.* Where's *Achilles?*
>
>   *Patro.* What art thou deuout? waft thou in prayer?
>   *Therf.* I the heauens heare me.
>   *Patro.* Amen.   *Enter* Achilles.
>   *Achil.* Who's there?
>   *Patro. Therfites,* my Lord.
>   *Achil.* Where? where? O where? art thou come why my
>   cheefe,
>   Q

9. Enter Thersites Q, F. Reproduced by permission of The Huntington Library, San
Marino, California.

The anonymous suggestion, recorded by the Cambridge Editors . . . that
Patroclus speaks "within" and does not enter until Thersites says "Wher's
Achilles?" in line 33, deserves more attention than it has had. It is certainly
not decisive that Patroclus says "come *in* and raile"; but the arrangement
proposed would get rid of a difficult wait for Patroclus while Thersites soliloquizes, and the speech, "What art thou deuout?" etc. would come

Whil'ft emulation in the armie crept :
This I prefume will wake him.   *Exeunt.*

Enter Therfites *folus.*
How now *Therfites?* what loft in the Labyrinth of thy
furie? fhall the Elephant *Aiax* carry it thus? he beates
me, and I raile at him : O worthy fatisfaction, would it
were otherwife : that I could beate him, whil'ft he rail'd
at me: Sfoote, Ile learne to coniure and raife Diuels, but
Ile fee fome iffue of my fpitefull execrations. Then ther's
Achilles, a rare Enginer. If *Troy* be not taken till thefe two
vndermine it, the wals will ftand till they fall of them-
felues. O thou great thunder-darter of Olympus, forget
that thou art *Ioue* the King of gods: and *Mercury,* loofe
all the Serpentine craft of thy Caduceus, if thou take not
that little little leffe then little wit from them that they
haue, which fhort-arm'd ignorance it felfe knowes, is fo
abundant fcarfe, it will not in circumuention deliuer a
Flye from a Spider, without drawing the maffie Irons and
cutting the web : after this, the vengeance on the whole
Camp, or rather the bone-ach, for that me thinkes is the
curfe dependant on thofe that warre for a placket. I haue
faid my prayers and diuell, enuie, fay Amen : What ho?
my Lord *Achilles?*

Enter Patroclus.
Patr. Who's there? *Therfites.* Good *Therfites* come
in and raile.
Ther. If I could haue remembred a guilt counterfeit,
thou would'ft not haue flipt out of my contemplation,
but it is no matter, thy felfe vpon thy felfe. The common
curfe of mankinde, follie and ignorance be thine in great
reuenew; heauen bleffe thee from a Tutor, and Difcipline
come not neere thee. Let thy bloud be thy direction till
thy death, then if fhe that laies thee out fayes thou art a
faire coarfe, Ile be fworne and fworne vpon't fhe neuer
fhrowded any but Lazars, Amen. Wher's *Achilles?*
Patr. What art thou deuout? waft thou in a prayer?
Ther. I, the heauens heare me.
Enter Achilles.
Achil. Who's there?
Patr. Therfites, my Lord.

F

more naturally if Patroclus entered just in time to see Thersites rise from
his knees.[1]

Walker was the first editor to keep Patroclus offstage until his second
speech, and many editors since have followed this arrangement.
While Hillebrand thought the F placement created "a difficult wait
for Patroclus while Thersites soliloquizes," Walker more specifically
objected to F by arguing that "it seems unlikely that Patroclus should

enter, listen silently to Thersites" imprecations, and then ask (at line 34) "art thou devout? Wast thou in prayer?"[2] Both editors' claims must be questioned: Does Patroclus's presence during Thersites' second speech create a difficult wait? Is Thersites' second speech a soliloquy? What are the dramatic possibilities for an earlier or later entrance by Patroclus, and what thematic implications arise for the range of possible reactions Patroclus could have to Thersites' speech?

The freedom such questions furnish for exploring different interpretations of the moment has not been nurtured by the way some editors have argued for individual interpretations. In agreeing with Hillebrand, Palmer at first suggests that "it is possible for Patroclus to enter [. . . at line 23] (as in F) and to watch Thersites without hearing him," but he concludes that "it is surely better that he should remain offstage during most of this ensuing speech. (F's entry might be a prompter's 'warning' or an entry from a distance.)"[3] Muir more confidently asserts that "obviously Patroclus enters here (32), in time to hear the 'Amen.'"[4] Foakes, however, is unusual in supporting the F placement, claiming that Patroclus should not only be onstage for Thersites' abuse, but should hear it as well, noting that "the Greek warriors enjoy his railing, and it is best to follow F here."[5] The juxtaposition of these three editors' judgments of what is "best," "surely better," or "obviously" correct demonstrates how subjective decisions can be cloaked in the language of objective certainty.

While critical opinion needs to be the basis for many editorial decisions, these editors' determination to argue for their choices as the "best," "better," or obvious option endeavors to provide a fixity for the text that simply does not exist. Rather than raise the kind of questions about the variants that encourage profitable exploration of the moment, their notes limit possible readings by ruling out variants. Palmer at least provides two suggested stagings of the F placement, with Patroclus watching without hearing Thersites or Patroclus entering "from a distance," but his dismissal of these possibilities, the latter suggestion even further marginalized as a parenthetic afterthought, encourages the reader to disregard the F point of entry. Perhaps the reader should be grateful that Palmer suggests a defense of F at all. Any reader who may search Muir's collation for the F placement and dare endow it with some credibility runs the risk of being rebuked by Muir's note informing them that they have failed to see an obvious need for editorial interference.

One subtle difference between Muir's note and Hillebrand's note is the distinction between Hillebrand's view that Patroclus's second speech "would come more naturally if Patroclus entered just in time to see Thersites rise from his knees," and Muir's slightly different view that Patroclus enters in time to hear Thersites say "Amen." While most editors since Walker have followed the placement of Patroclus's entrance after "Amen," none have felt it necessary to include a direction for Thersites to kneel. In offering an alternative staging by suggesting that Patroclus's question is caused by an aural rather than visual impression of prayer, Muir still retains the placement of Patroclus's entrance after Thersites says "Amen." The reader then needs Muir's note to indicate that the offstage Patroclus heard "Amen." Similarly, Walker, Palmer, and other editors who follow the postponed entrance but do not provide a note explaining Patroclus's questions, "What, art thou devout? Wast thou in prayer?" leave to the reader the task of devising a reason why Patroclus would enter after Thersites has finished speaking and suspect that he was praying.

Several of the issues debated by editors can be pursued in performance texts. While directors have not agreed on the point at which Thersites should kneel or rise, the notes added to the promptbooks of Payne, Shaw, Hall/Barton, Barton, and Mendes directing Thersites to kneel support the editors' argument that Thersites should be kneeling. If the editors' placement of Patroclus's entrance assumes that Patroclus sees Thersites kneel, there is further reason for adding a direction indicating where he kneels and rises. The need for an added direction is, however, based on the questionable assumption that Patroclus needs a staged cause or a visual as opposed to an aural cause for his question, leading back to the larger issue of where Patroclus should enter.[6] While many recent editors are convinced that Patroclus does not belong onstage until his third speech ("What, art thou devout?" line 34), directors have given a more mixed response. Not one of eleven major British productions from Poel to Judge followed the editors' suggestion of a later entrance by Patroclus, but this fact may be due to the editions used for those productions. While the scholarly editions of Walker, Muir, and Palmer, as well as some less annotated editions (including Evans's Riverside) delay Patroclus's entry, only the three productions that used Walker's edition (Hall/Barton, Barton, and Barton/Kyle), and Judge (who used Muir), were offered the emendation in their promptbooks. The changes many productions made to their promptbook editions, the business that has been used to surround Patroclus's entrance, or even the following of an edition, can offer significant commentary on the theatrical possibilities of Patroclus's entrance.

Dryden began his third act with a version of the passage under discussion. He followed F in bringing on Patroclus when Thersites called to Achilles and had Patroclus remain onstage for a shortened version of Thersites' second speech.[7] But Dryden marked Thersites' second speech as an aside up until the point where he says to Patroclus, "I have said my prayers; and the devil Envy say *Amen*. Where's *Achilles?*" (3.1.15–16). Dryden approved of having Patroclus onstage for the abuse but elected not to have him hear Thersites. The difficult wait for Patroclus of which Hillebrand complained is somewhat shorted by Dryden's cuts, but Dryden's decision to have the subject of Thersites' abuse present before the audience is the first of many dramatic judgments in favor of the F placement of Patroclus's entrance.

Like Dryden, modern directors have the option of eliminating or altering awkward moments by making cuts. Guthrie took the most severe course, cutting from the middle of Thersites' first speech ("O thou thunder darter") until Patroclus's "Amen" (lines 9–36), and then had Achilles enter with Patroclus. Slightly less ruthless were the cuts made in the three successive RSC productions of Hall/Barton, Barton, and Barton/Kyle, where Thersites' second speech was reduced to the single sentence "The common curse of mankind, folly and ignorance be thine in great revenue" followed by "Amen." The difficult language of Thersites' speech or merely a concern with the play's length may have been contributing reasons for the cuts, but the "difficult wait" for Patroclus was eliminated by reducing the time he spent onstage. While Guthrie's cuts were made using Ridley's edition, which follows F, the Hall/Barton, Barton, and Barton/Kyle productions used Walker's edition and rejected her emendation. The Barton and Barton/Kyle promptbooks have the directions "Enter Patroclus" and "within" crossed out, while the Hall/Barton promptbook only indicates in a note that the F point of entry was followed, without crossing out Walker's later direction. The cuts that these productions made to Thersites' second speech somewhat mitigate the support they can give to the F placement of Patroclus's entrance, but these three productions significantly staged the moment where Thersites curses Patroclus with Patroclus onstage.

Promptbooks can also be investigated for the amount and kinds of stage business accompanying Patroclus's presence, providing an interesting set of examples of how the moment can be interpreted. Perhaps even the lack of notes in a promptbook is significant. Poel and Payne, in following F, make few cuts to the text, and while stage actions are elsewhere described in some detail in their promptbooks, no notes accompany Patroclus's entrance or describe any movements during the ensuing speeches. While the lack of notes in the promptbooks are not proof that no business took place, the absence of detailed or premeditated movements may indicate that the directors felt no need to occupy Patroclus.

Alternatively, elaborate stage business and additional actors can suggest that Patroclus's presence was considered in need of some justification. Quayle had used Thersites' first speech in the scene ("How now, Thersites? . . . devil Envy say 'Amen'" 2.3.1–20) to conclude Thersites' first scene (2.1), and had Thersites' second scene (2.3) begin with his entrance shortly followed by Patroclus. Between the entrances of Thersites and Patroclus the promptbook has the note: "Achilles' bodyguard, walking up and down outside Achilles' tent . . . laughs at Thersites." Shaw began the scene with Thersites' soliloquy but introduced two Myrmidons to "bring on [a] tent" at Patroclus's entrance. The Barton/Kyle promptbook notes that Patroclus whistled to bring on five Myrmidons after asking Thersites to "come in and rail." While the promptbooks of Quayle and Shaw do not indicate any involvement by Patroclus in the action of the "extras," the Barton/Kyle note seems to imply that Patroclus may have busied himself with the arrival of the Myrmidons while Thersites continued in soliloquy. In all of these productions, the additional activity could have made Patroclus's silent presence seem less awkward.

Barton's promptbook reveals an even more active opening of the scene. Ajax entered with Thersites and seven Myrmidons at the beginning of the scene, but while Ajax exited before Thersites spoke, the Myrmidons remained onstage to "push Thersites down during [his] 'soliloquy.'" On an audiotape of a performance after the production's transfer from the Royal Shakespeare Theater to the Aldwych Theater, Ajax can be heard shouting "Thersites" at the beginning of the scene. The added moment is a kind of restaging of the opening of their first scene, but this time Thersites managed to escape Ajax's beating only to fall into the hands of the Myrmidons. The promptbook's use of quotation-marks for "soliloquy" does not clarify whether Thersites' first two speeches were given as a soliloquy while Thersites was being beaten, or whether the soliloquy status of the speech was knowingly ignored by having Patroclus and the Myrmidons listening to Thersites. In the first of many extra-textual appearances by the Myrmidons in Barton's production, they presented the image of a group beating that will, of course, be gruesomely repeated for Hector's death. The promptbook places Patroclus's entrance halfway through his first speech, after he asked "Who's there?" and then notes that he crossed to Thersites and dragged him across the stage. The sentence that remained in Thersites' second speech ("The common curse . . . revenue") could then be equated with the sort of abuse that he spewed at Ajax in his first scene, a short verbal response to physical force. In Barton's "Notes to the Company at Rehearsal" printed in the program, he remarked that "Thersites is at first frustrated, beaten, cowed; by the end of the play, his philosophy achieves a monstrous domination."[8] The beating that began Thersites' second scene reinforced Thersites' starting point, perhaps at the expense of somewhat delaying his role as commentator. The different but related aspects of Thersites' character, the beaten fool and the detached commentator, present a distinction that is a key issue to be explored in the staging of Patroclus's entrance, and in determining the different effects of Thersites' second speech as a soliloquy, or as a direct address to Patroclus.

Three productions in the 1980s (Hands and Miller in 1981, and Davies in 1985) provide strong opposition to the editorial opinion that Patroclus should not be present or hear Thersites' second speech. All these productions made their promptbook using editions that printed the F direction, and all three made dramatic sense of the F direction without cutting or adding characters. Hands's production is the most difficult of the three to interpret because the promptbook has been lost, and the stage manager's script is very lightly annotated; however an audiotape of the performance does supply some interesting evidence.[9] Twice during Thersites' second speech Patroclus can be heard reacting to Thersites, repeating a thoughtful grunt ("um") after "contemplation" (line 25) and "thyself upon thyself" (line 26). Thersites delivered the speech as if it were a prayer of well-being or blessing, his tone in no way suggesting malice, but whether Patroclus was reacting to Thersites' words or only his manner of expression is unclear. The amount of control Thersites or Patroclus has in the situation is important to the credibility of their characters and the nature of their relationship, both being in a position to make a fool of the other. Patroclus's questions may at first seem to imply that he did not hear all of Thersites' speech, but, as suggested above, he could have seen Thersites in a praying position or heard only his "Amen." The audiotape implies that only the inflections of the speech, perhaps combined with some gestures, were interpreted by Patroclus as praying, while the words of abuse were heard only by the audience. This interpretation suggests the further possibility that Patroclus's questions can work to defuse Thersites' abuses by electing to comment only on the form rather than the content of the speech.

Miller's video makes clear at least one of the possible interpretations of Hands's production. After Patroclus entered as in F, he kneeled and looked directly at Thersites during the prayer of abuse. The only reaction elicited from Patroclus was that he gave Thersites a small splash of the water in which Thersites was washing clothes, certainly more playful (and perhaps even baptismal) than malicious.

This performance interpretation supports Foakes's view that "the warriors enjoy his railing," with Patroclus not only hearing Thersites' abuse without reacting violently, but showing no signs at all of agitation. Unlike the possibility in Hands's production that Patroclus heard only the words and not the content, Miller's Patroclus most certainly hears Thersites, but by not taking offence at the curses, he reduces Thersites into the role of a performing fool. In the dialogue following Achilles' entrance, Patroclus becomes upset when Thersites calls him a fool, but Achilles reminds him that Thersites "is a privileged man" (2.3.55). Achilles' comment can inform the earlier dialogue between Thersites and Patroclus in at least two ways; as a licensed fool, Thersites' remarks would be allowed as performance, but Achilles' need to remind Patroclus of this may suggest that Patroclus would not have heard the earlier curses without becoming upset.

Davies' production presents yet a different interpretation showing the F point of entry as dramatically viable. Using the permanent set of a crumbling mansion with a staircase leading to a balcony, Patroclus appeared on the balcony for his first line and shouted to Thersites who stood below. While Thersites addressed the audience, Patroclus descended the stairs, seeming not to hear Thersites until he was face to face for his question, "What, art thou devout?"[10] Davies' use of stage space could support either Palmer's (rejected) suggestion of an entry at a distance, or conversely Hillebrand's claim that Patroclus has nothing to do during Thersites' speech, but it can also show that an imaginative director can find a dramatic solution. The use of a raised space for Patroclus's entrance can also suggest a possible staging on a Shakespearean stage, where Patroclus (and perhaps Achilles, and even the group entrance later in the scene) could have entered initially onto a balcony before descending onto the main stage. The time it took Patroclus to walk down would have provided the ideal opportunity for Thersites to be alone onstage for his second speech.

Davies capitalized on his specific set design to make the F placement of the direction work, but in following the F placement, he can also be seen to support the argument that Patroclus should not hear Thersites curse him. As an editor needing to make the text work on a conjectured Shakespearean stage, Taylor is faced with an obviously different set of problems. Although Taylor seems to support the notion that Patroclus should not hear Thersites' second speech, he proposed in a critical essay a unique solution that retains the F placement:

Patroclus need only appear briefly in a doorway, disappear again (or even turn back to face inside), and then reappear (or turn around). Not only is Patroclus' speech difficult to speak from "within," but unless he appears, and can be recognized, an audience can only guess *whom* Thersites is abusing in the following lines.[11]

Taylor's edited text directs Patroclus to enter "at the door to the tent," immediately exiting after his speech and re-entering before Thersites says "Amen" (33).

As an editor, Taylor included the following notes:

> 2.3.21.1 Recent editors have had Patroclus speak from within, despite F's direction; but it seems likelier that he simply appeared briefly in a doorway.
>
> 2.3.23 Prompt-books are casual about recording exits-and-quick-re-entries, and Patroclus seems to hear only the end of Thersites' next speech. He need do no more than turn back to face the tent.[12]

Taylor's insistence that the audience should be in no doubt whom Thersites is addressing is an important objection to the later placement of Patroclus' entrance, but Taylor's added exit and re-entry for Patroclus may be too prescriptive. Taylor admits the possibility, in both his critical work and his textual notes, that Patroclus "need do no more than turn back to face the tent," but his edited text seems to exclude such an interpretation by having Patroclus exit and re-enter. If Taylor can make sense of Patroclus's presence onstage by having him turn away from Thersites, would not such a staging, with Patroclus visible to the audience, make even more clear the subject of Thersites' abuse?

The directors who introduce other characters and busy the stage with action during the opening of the scene have threatened to smother any complex relationships between Thersites, Patroclus, and Achilles. While the scene is, at times, not only comical but also enacting comic routines, allowing the scene virtually to run riot can reduce the subtle, almost tragic subtext. Mendes believed this scene begins "Thersites journey as a loner," and took steps to prepare for it with Thersites' exit in his previous scene (2.1).[13] Thersites exited from his first scene after being chased from the stage by Achilles, Ajax, and Patroclus, vowing

> I will see you hanged like clotpolls ere I come any more to your tents. I will keep where there is wit stirring, and leave the faction of fools. (2.1.118)

After a quick exit he reappeared with a shopping bag and jester's stick, making it clear that he was leaving the service of Ajax as he crossed over the back of the stage. At the opening of his second scene,

Thersites, still with the shopping bag, was looking for new employ-ment, illustrating Ulysses' line explaining the reason that Ajax has to "bay" at Achilles: "Achilles has inveigled his fool from him" (2.3.90). Thersites' soliloquy that begins his second scene became, in Mendes' production, railing with the venom of an unemployed jester, which while sparking laughter from the audience, was not so much railing for fun as expressing disgust with Ajax, Achilles, and his own de-grading circumstances.

The unique staging in Mendes' production is best examined with some insight into the director's and actor's intentions. In a personal interview, Mendes elaborated on the "complexity and darkness" of the relationship between Thersites and Patroclus, saying that his pro-duction tried to "establish a sort of mutual distrust, but also a mutual binding together" between the two characters:

> We had a very specific line on that relationship, which was that Thersites saw in Patroclus a lot of what (and this could be a very romantic notion) we thought Thersites had been once upon a time; a passably beautiful hu-man being, if that is possible, and experienced all the things that Patro-clus is now experiencing, whether it be a homosexual relationship or a non-gay relationship. The whole crux of that relationship between Ther-sites and Patroclus was Thersites between the lines constantly saying "You fool, do you know what you're doing here, you're laying yourself on the line, you're going to die?" But that is also mixed with jealousy, because Pa-troclus has Achilles, is still beautiful, is what Thersites might like to be. Thersites is isolated, they are on the inside, he is on the out. But I think that's very important, because that gave a logic to Thersites' constant get-ting at Patroclus. When he says "Patroclus is a fool" he is not just picking on Patroclus because he wants to make a gag out of it, he is saying "you are a fool." There's a real meaning to that. Thersites feels that very strongly.

Simon Russell Beale, who played Thersites in Mendes' production, further reveals the thought that went into the characterization:

> What was worked out by Sam Mendes and me was the result of meeting the jester cliché head on. I decided to use a conventional joker's stick—with bells and all—and it came to serve as a reminder to Thersites of the role he had been asked, for whatever reason, to fulfil—a role that he hates but which pays the rent. The more conventionally jolly the stick, we thought, the more painful the reminder to someone as intelligent and cynical as Thersites of the position as an entertainer and his exclusion from the circle of protagonists.[14]

Thersites was shown to be an outsider in an ingenious piece of stag-ing surrounding Patroclus's entrance. At Thersites' mention of Achilles in his first speech ("Then there's Achilles," line 7), the light on the back gauze changed to give the audience a partial view into Achilles' tent, showing Achilles with Patroclus, eating an apple and relaxing to the strains of Charlie Parker's sultry rendition of "Lover Man." Looking with disdain at his jester's stick, Thersites shook it a few times and resentfully took the pose of a fool as he called to Achilles, as if to say "here we go again."

Without knowledge of Taylor's suggested arrangement, Mendes approximated Taylor's staging of Patroclus's entry.[15] Hearing a voice, Achilles motioned to Patroclus, who rose to ask "Who's there." Patroclus took a step out from behind the curtain to see Thersites and asked him to "come in and rail." Patroclus immediately returned behind the gauze as Thersites continued to rail, facing the curtain and apparently still railing in search of acceptance. Patroclus's brief appearance through the gauze and into Thersites' and the audience's view for the question "Who's there" fulfills Taylor's desire to provide the audience with concrete knowledge of whom Thersites abuses, as well as leaving Thersites essentially alone for his second speech. Rather than staging Taylor's edited text, however, Mendes' arrangement is actually closer to the suggestion Taylor offers but does not adopt, where Patroclus remained onstage but turned away from Thersites.

Mendes' interpretation demonstrates some of the advantages of having Thersites alone, as an outsider, but also illustrates the advantages of depicting what Thersites is excluded from. Patroclus's presence onstage, and in Mendes' staging the addition of Achilles' more shadowy presence as well, can add another dimension to Thersites' prayer by highlighting the fact that it is also a plea for acceptance from those whom he condemns as foolish and those who see in him nothing more than a fool. Mendes' staging endorses the option that Patroclus does not hear Thersites but confirms that much can be gained by having Patroclus onstage for the speech. Taking even further Taylor's point that the audience should know "*whom* Thersites is abusing in the following lines," Mendes' staging implies that the audience should not only be aware but be kept aware by Patroclus's continued presence.

My role of textual advisor for Judge's production provided an opportunity to observe (and slightly influence) rehearsals of the moment. The mood, tone, and movements involved in Thersites' speeches were the subject of considerable experimentation, as was Patroclus's presence or absence for Thersites' second speech. Without my mentioning the editorial debate, the scene was first staged with Patroclus entering after Thersites' opening speech, as F

10. Simon Russell Beale as Thersites, Swan Theatre 1990, Mendes. Reproduced by permission of photographer John Haynes.

(2.3.21.1). Thersites addressed his second speech directly to Patroclus, but the director and actors expressed some concern over whether this was the best approach. Should Patroclus enjoy the speech, be upset by it, or ignore it? Would it be best for Patroclus to remain inside the tent and call from within, as Muir's edition (used for their script) and most other editions have it? They next tried having Patroclus call from within and remain inside the tent for Thersites' second speech, with Thersites forcefully delivering his second speech in the direction of the tent. In the discussion of the advantages and disadvantages that followed, it was thought that some of the venom of the speech might be lost if delivered to a tent rather than directly to the character.

Having watched with interest as the director and actors explored many of the options that I might have suggested, I eventually mentioned that this passage has been the subject of editorial debate. I asked if they thought, as Taylor suggests, that the audience should be made aware of the subject of Thersites' speech by having Patroclus peer out of the tent, but then return into it, allowing Thersites to command the stage on his own. Both Judge and Richard McCabe (Thersites) thought this might be a good idea, but were still not convinced that Patroclus should remain inside for the speech. Judge had already decided that in the battlefield finale, Patroclus's death was to be staged, and his body would be carried offstage when Nestor says, "Go, bear Patroclus' body to Achilles" (5.5.17). It was also decided that Achilles would next enter carrying the dead Patroclus ("Where is this Hector?" 5.5.46). I wondered if these later uses of Patroclus's corpse were relevant for the earlier scene, and might add resonance to the end of Thersites' speech, "Then if she that lays thee out says thou art a fair corpse, I'll be sworn and sworn upon't she never shrouded any but lazars" (2.3.32).[16] Judge agreed, and immediately decided that Patroclus should be onstage for Thersites' speech, and that Patroclus could listen and enjoy the speech as the railing that he solicited ("Good Thersites come in and rail," 2.3.22).

The decision-making process for Patroclus's entrance offers a good example of the way in which the production explored editorial options, both with and without an awareness that an editorial debate existed. The seemingly simple question of where Patroclus should enter received extended discussion and experimentation during two rehearsal sessions, and it was important to the director and actors to find the staging that worked best for them. They considered the dialogue, the dramatic situation, the characters, the set, and the audience as elements that must all contribute to a decision of how the moment should be presented. Experimenting with different alternatives, such as when Patroclus entered and whether or not he heard Thersites, also led to a wider understanding of the passage. The actors and director were constantly asking how the moment helped to establish the relationship between Thersites and Patroclus, and how it gave insight into the individual characters. It was in moments like these, and there were many of them, that I was most convinced that textual ambiguity has a positive value in the way it provokes a wide range of questions about the play.

The alternatives arising from the placement of stage directions where characters can be either onstage or offstage while another character is denigrating or praising them will be returned to often in this study, especially because of the way in which the textual and performance possibilities relate to the recurring themes in the play of watching and judging.[17] The ambiguity over Thersites' abuse of Patroclus in his second speech in the scene, whether it is heard and tolerated by Patroclus as fooling, or spoken as a soliloquy or an aside, can create different interpretations of the characters and the moment. Simon Russell Beale confirms from an actor's point of view that "an insult directed to Achilles requires a different motive to one directed at, say Patroclus, and an insult muttered in private has a different tone to one meant to be heard by another character."[18] Perhaps an actor and director need to make clear interpretative decisions when choosing one of many possible stagings, but what of an editor? Directors, for example, have often made choices that emphasize the role of Thersites as commentator, but sometimes an editor can, and perhaps should, attempt to leave that characterization more to the reader's interpretation. Imposing on an edited text a decision about whether Patroclus should or should not hear Thersites and arguing for an interpretation in a way that dismisses other possibilities guides readers towards a specific but debatable interpretation of the characters. Precisely how editors can avoid making such decisions and whether readers would want the resulting open work, are issues that will continually reshape editions of Shakespeare. One ideal could be an edition that does not attempt to fix the text in places where it is open, but rather presents the options in a digestible format that encourages rereading and consideration of different manifestations of the text.

5
"Who Play They To?"

Helen's scene is rarely the subject of serious critical commentary, but when the scene is discussed, it is often portrayed in vivid detail. Foakes, for example, describes Helen relaxing

> in the sensual atmosphere of a high-class brothel, an atmosphere cloying in the heady sweetness of "love, love, nothing but love, still love, still more," to cite the opening line of Pandarus's song. The conversation is at once ceremonious and bawdy, overlaying with its repeated adjectives, "sweet," "honey-sweet," "fair," the hot blood, hot thoughts, and hot deeds of a luxurious palace.[1]

Interpreting a scene's dialogue in an attempt to characterize its setting and atmosphere is a task shared by critics and directors. Foakes's depiction of a "sensual atmosphere" in "a luxurious palace" would be at home in a theater review or in a director's or designer's notes, but critical essays are often judged by a different standard that requires writers' opinions to be validated, or at least supported by the text. Jan Kott has been both praised and criticized for his illustrative commentary, and his view of Helen's scene is typically visual:

> In the Greek camp we have seen red-faced fools, big fat, heavy barbarians mimicking one another. In Troy we meet smart courtiers with their small talk. Parody is still there, but its subject has changed. Paris kneels at Helen's knees as in a courtly romance. Page-boys play the lute or the viol. But Paris calls the lady from a medieval romance simply—'Nell'. Lovely Nell, Greek queen and the cause of the Trojan war, cracks jokes like a whore from a London tavern.[2]

Certainly Kott's images, like those of a production, should not be taken as strictly text based; there is no point in attempting to find, for example, the dialogue which implies that Paris must be kneeling before Helen. His description of a scene where "page boys play the lute or viol" does, however, highlight two important ambiguities in the texts concerning the use of music and extras.

108

Q's economy of space, with the Greeks' *Exeunt* sharing a line with Pandarus's entrance, may account for Q's not including the music or the servant in the direction.[3] Similarly, F's direction for music shares the line with the Greeks' *Exeunt*, but the explanation for the shared line is not as obvious as may first appear. Between the directions, F has a blank space, room enough to have permitted the indication of music to be associated more with the entrances than the exits, or at least to be equally spaced between both directions. It is difficult, therefore, to justify F's arrangement as an economy of space. The order of the directions, with the music preceding the entering characters, perhaps should not be interpreted too literally, but F's placement of the direction for music to begin the scene has been questioned since music is not mentioned until the thirteenth speech.

Rowe was the first editor to postpone the music, simply reversing F's wording so that "music within" immediately followed the entrance of Pandarus and the servant. Capell postponed the music even further until just before Pandarus mentions it in the dialogue: "What music is this?" (3.1.17) Editorial opinion has been divided between the Folio, Rowe, and Capell, with Bevington, Taylor, Foakes, Seltzer, and Alexander among those substantially following F, and Pope, Theobald, Palmer, and Muir among those substantially following Rowe. The editions of Ridley and Walker, used for no less than seven promptbooks, follow Capell.[4]

Q

F

11. Enter Pandarus Q, F. Reproduced by permission of The Huntington Library, San Marino, California.

Determining some of the scene's staging possibilities is further complicated when questions arising from the placement of the direction for music are studied alongside the ambiguities surrounding the entrance of Helen and Paris. The only difference between the QF versions of Paris and Helen's entrance is the spelling of Helen's name (Q has "Hellen" and F "Helena"), but editors often emend the direction to include extras. Theobald first rewrote the direction to read "Enter Paris and Helen, attended," a seemingly logical addition considering the words with which Pandarus greets them: "Fair be to you, my Lord, and to all this fair company" (3.1.43–46). Pandarus's absurd repetition of the word "fair" (nine times in two short speeches, 3.1.43–46, 48–49) must account for some of the speech's purpose of showing Pandarus as overly courteous, but by addressing a "fair company" not mentioned in the stage directions, the speech also raises questions crucial to the scene's staging.[5]

Virtually all editors and most directors have followed Theobald by including extras, but there has been some variation in their status. Seltzer qualified Theobald's "attended" by calling for "[courtiers]" (Seltzer's brackets), while Foakes specified that they are "attendants." Taylor is alone in commenting on the members of the "fair company," proposing an even more specific identity:

> Since the musicians are required later, and have been with Paris and Helen earlier off stage, they seem the likeliest candidates. Could F's anomalous "Helena" be related to its omission of the necessary "attendants" (the annotator starting to write the word, or "and," then breaking off, and the compositor taking "a-" as a suffix)?[6]

Taylor adds to the QF stage direction "attended [by musicians]" (Taylor's broken brackets), providing what he considers to be the necessary (i.e., not bracketed) presence of additional characters, while also offering the less certain (bracketed) emendation that musicians are exclusively the makeup of the "fair company."[7] Taylor later includes in his text a bracketed direction for Pandarus's phrase "Come, give me an instrument" (3.1.92) to be spoken "[to a musician]," and it is this moment and the ensuing song that Taylor presumably refers to as the reason "the musicians are required later." Bevington, who follows Taylor in having Paris and Helen enter "attended by Musicians," also inserts a prescriptive stage direction for the phrase "give me an instrument," but the difference between Bevington's interpretation that Pandarus "is handed a musical instrument" and Taylor's addition points to the indeterminacy of the moment: Taylor's direction that the line is spoken "[to a musician]" leaves open the question of whether Pandarus is handed an instrument or merely requests accompaniment, while Bevington's text, in prescribing the exchange of an instrument, does not specify who hands it to Pandarus. In his note to the line, Bevington writes that "Pandarus will accompany himself, perhaps on the lute or cittern, as he sings." [8] While he is unsure about the instrument Pandarus would use, Bevington seems confident that Pandarus himself, rather than the musicians added to the stage direction, played during the song.

The ambiguities in the directions for music within and the entrance of Helen and Paris create a wealth of opportunities for establishing the scene's mood and setting. The editorial disagreement about the timing of the music, the role of the musicians, and the number, status, and actions of extras provides many variations that can be explored in a theater history of the directions. The attention the scene often receives in reviews and in press photographs attests to the scene's potential for establishing the play's social setting. When Kott writes that Helen is "a whore in a London tavern," he is not only agreeing with Thersites' view of Helen, but he is also characterizing the scene. The parallels that can be drawn between Helen and Cressida's situation, as objects of contention in the war, and lovers in a patriarchal society, invest Helen's scene with an importance beyond its narrative significance. Directors have a further opportunity in Helen's scene to expand their interpretation of gender relationships in the play's world, and they also have a chance to enter the debate over the value of Helen. Whether a production depicts her as a whore, a goddess, or a less easily stereotyped character where the question of her worth cannot be simply answered, the frivolous dialogue cannot completely obscure a distillation of some of the most probing issues of both the love story and the war plot.

The play's dialogue, while often evoking Helen's name, gives only a few glimpses of her life in Troy. The Prologue's reductive vision of "The ravished Helen, Menelaus' queen, / With wanton Paris sleeps— and that's the quarrel" (9) introduces the deflated picture the play paints of the quarrel and its cause. While Helen and Hecuba going "up to the eastern tower . . . to see the battle" (1.2.2–4) is one of the least frivolous images of Helen in the play, it still can convey a sense of spectatorship that does not seem fully attuned to her tragic significance. Pandarus's description of Helen joking and teasing the Trojan hierarchy later in the scene (1.2.106–63) more closely resembles the depiction of Helen in her scene. The occasion Pandarus describes to Cressida is especially relevant to the present discussion because Helen is not simply alone with Paris but surrounded by Troilus (whose chin she tickled), the laughing trio of Cassandra, Hecuba, and Hector, the "chafed" Paris, presumably Pandarus himself, and an unnumbered group that Pandarus refers to as "all the rest" (1.2.162). The dubious interpretation Pandarus makes of the moment (that "Helen loves him [Troilus] better than Paris," 1.2.103–4), indeed the doubt as to whether the gathering took place at all, makes any assumptions about the story problematic. Certainly the presence of Priam's wife, daughter, and at least three of his sons constitutes a different scene from the one Shakespeare chose to write, but the joking nature of the occasion Pandarus describes and the image of Helen as the center of attention in a populated room give some clues to ways her scene can be played.

Kott emphasized the way in which Helen's scene can exaggerate the contrast between the "barbarians" in the Greek camp and the "courtiers" in Troy. Jane Adamson makes the similar point that

> coming after all those scenes fraught with the disputes and competitions of male egos (especially in the womanless and rancorous Greek camp), the seductive allure of this pampered world of pillows and music, teasing compliments and voluptuous idleness, provides a welcome change from so much animosity and frustration, the silly-sweet banter a lighter relief from high-flown intellections or foul-mouthed abuse. (If the trio's exchanges are played as nastier than this, of course the contrast is lost.)[9]

Adamson's final disclaimer about performance possibilities leads the way into a theater history of the scene, which shows that directors have interpreted Helen's appearance either as a departure from the world of the play or as a further illustration of the kind of society the production depicts. While many directors have chosen to play the scene, in Adamson's words, as either "lighter relief" or somehow "nastier," some have tried to combine the comic elements with a darker cynicism. However the scene is played, the use of music and extras often figures significantly in the interpretation.

Poel mirrored F by attaching his cue for music to his note describing the business that ended the previous scene. His penciled direction for the offstage "noise of Ajax falling" is immediately followed by the direction that the "string quartet begins." This connection highlights the ability of music to change the mood between scenes from the Greek's farcical praising of Ajax to the more domestic setting of the love stories within Troy. Parallels can certainly be found between the two scenes: Pandarus's pride in praising Cressida, suggesting, however mischievously, that his niece is "the mortal Venus" that Paris's servant describes (3.1.31), reveals a touch of the vanity afflicting Ajax. Pandarus's entire conversation with the servant is another example of the duplicity of language used by the Greeks in praising Ajax, while at the same time entertaining themselves and the audience with the double meanings of such phrases as Ulysses' "I will not praise thy wisdom" (2.3.243). Audiences are often left laughing at the end of the Greeks' scene, and Helen's scene does begin with the comic misunderstanding between Pandarus and the servant, but ultimately the scenes are very different, and music beginning as Pandarus and the servant enter can provide a tangible signal of the change.

Poel's promptbook has the words "Enter" and "attended" crossed out for the entrance of Paris and Helen, and a direction is added for them to be discovered with servants. The decision to have Helen and Paris discovered shows how their entrance can be executed by the opening of a curtain, and the music within could then be part of a scene that is revealed. Instead of having Helen and Paris approaching Pandarus and the servant, Pandarus could be seen to invade their world, more emphatically intruding on their entertainment. When the servant says that the music is being played "at the request of my Lord Paris, who's there in person; with him the mortal Venus" (3.1.30–32), he sets up the possibility of a "there" to which Pandarus goes. Such a movement need not be executed by the use of a discovery space; it could be performed by having Helen and Paris enter but appear as if they remained within their chamber.

Alan Dessen discusses several instances where a change of location takes place in the middle of a scene, the most relevant being

> *The Massacre at Paris* where the king announces hypocritically "I will go visit the Admiral" who has been wounded and is "sick in his bed." Rather than using an *exit* and *re-enter* to move the king to the Admiral's chambers, Marlowe instead keeps the royal group on stage and *"enter the Admiral in his bed"* (ll. 255, 250, 256 s.d.).[10]

The Prologue's image of Helen sleeping with Paris (lines 9–10) could be poignantly illustrated by their entrance, or discovery, in a bed. While the simple direction in QF for Helen and Paris to enter does not suggest such an entrance, the failure to include a "fair company" could show that the direction is otherwise incomplete. Speculation of the use of a bed or a discovery space does open some intriguing possibilities, but perhaps most important is the more general observation that Paris and Helen's entrance might in some way imply a change of place for Pandarus rather than Helen and Paris.

Payne followed his promptbook edition (Ridley's New Temple) in delaying the music until Pandarus mentions it, but the musicians remained "within," not entering with Helen and Paris. Payne's promptbook notes that Helen had a lute when she crossed between Pandarus and Paris, and later notes that Helen handed the lute to Pandarus after his line, "Come, give me an instrument.—Now, sweet Queen" (3.1.92). The business is especially appropriate to the last words of the speech, in which Helen is directly addressed. It is also appropriate to the way Helen associates herself with the music when she interrupts Pandarus in his message to Paris, demanding that Pandarus "shall not bob us out of our melody" (3.1.67). Payne's having Helen hand Pandarus an instrument is the kind of action that Taylor discourages by the direction for Pandarus's line to be spoken to a musician, but Payne's interpretation has no less authority and can present the action as a more highly charged moment. Furthermore, if Helen is not only enjoying music but playing it, she can be portrayed as being even further removed from the war that simultaneously takes place in her name.

Payne clarified his edition's direction for Paris and Helen to enter "attended" by adding a note for "two ladies, laughing" to enter with them. The ladies are given directions to applaud Pandarus's song, cheer when Paris kisses Helen after telling her that "hot deeds is love" (3.1.127), and sing and dance after Pandarus asks, "Is love a generation of vipers?" (3.1.129). The difficulty of interpreting what kind of accompaniment these "ladies" provide is somewhat clarified by their reactions, which imply that the extras can establish a social setting where Helen and her lady companions could enjoy themselves despite the siege. The ladies also presented a group of women, something the play rarely speaks of and only once shows (when Cassandra and Andromache are onstage together in 5.3). As mentioned above, Helen's scene creates another opportunity to portray gender relationships in the world of the play, and the editorial and theatrical addition of "attendants" can provide a chance for a slightly more expanded view of the Trojan women.

Production photographs of Quayle's staging clearly show that there were extras of a higher class than servants, with couples that embraced above and below the stairs. A single man held a glass in one hand while his other arm was in a sling, slightly acknowledging the wartime situation in which these revelers found themselves. Pandarus delivered his song while sitting on the same couch where Paris and Helen embraced, still framed by hugging couples. These extras surrounded Helen and Paris with luxurious sensuality, a setting in which Pandarus's song must have provided a fitting commentary. Like Payne's staging, Quayle provided several verbal reactions for his extras: they seconded Paris's request for Pandarus to sing;[11] they called out Cressida's name when Pandarus said "your disposer is sick" (3.1.86);[12] and they laughed and answered Pandarus during his song. Quayle's promptbook does not indicate how music was used at the

12. Helen's scene, SMT 1948, Quayle. Photographer Angus McBean, Shakespeare Centre Library. Copyright Royal Shakespeare Company.

13. Helen's scene, SMT 1948, Quayle. Photographer Angus McBean, Shakespeare Centre Library. Copyright Royal Shakespeare Company.

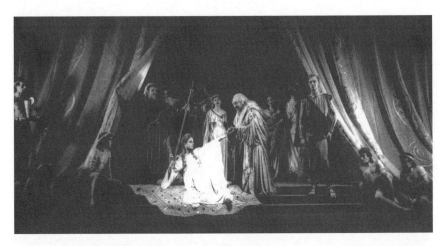

14. Helen's scene, SMT 1954, Byam Shaw. Photographer Angus McBean, Shakespeare Centre Library. Copyright Royal Shakespeare Company.

15. Helen's scene, SMT 1954, Byam Shaw. Photographer Angus McBean, Shakespeare Centre Library. Copyright Royal Shakespeare Company.

beginning of the scene, but at Pandarus's request for an instrument, a note indicates that an extra exited through a curtain and returned with a lute. The economy of movement and characters that Taylor's edition provides, with musicians as the "fair company," certainly has some persuasive logic. Its prescriptive direction, however, can inhibit a director's (or any reader's) desire to interpret a piece of dialogue with the kind of exaggerated action presented by Quayle.

Shaw's promptbook includes a note for "four royal servants" to arrange cushions as the scene began, but only one of them remained while Paris's servant entered and spoke the opening dialogue with Pandarus. Paris and Helen were accompanied by "men" and "ladies" for their entrance, and although the promptbook does not note their actions, a production photograph shows that two servants lounged on each side of the stairs, while another servant stood, holding a tray of elaborately garnished drinks. The other extras were dressed and positioned more like guests than servants, and included Alexander, whose ability to talk with Cressida of court gossip was given a belated and extra-textual foundation by his presence in Helen's scene. Alexander held a decorative spear but looked too grand to be an ordinary servant or guard, and his clothes were more like the robes of the other higher class extras than the scanty costumes of the servants. Perhaps Alexander was a master of the revels figure, both servant and courtier, and his ambiguous status extends to the five apparently upper-class extras. A production photograph shows that one of the women held a flute, while another had what appears to be a recorder, or possibly a drumstick, and part of what could be an instrument (perhaps a gong or drum) was held by one of the men. From what can be deduced from the photograph, these instruments were not, however, played while Pandarus sang and accompanied himself with a lute. The promptbook has the direction for "music within" crossed out, but there is no note describing the use of onstage instruments either for the entrance of Paris and Helen, or for Pandarus's song. The promptbook is also unhelpful in discovering how Pandarus received the lute, and if it was played by an extra as part of the music at the opening of the scene. Despite all that is unclear about the music, the relevant point is that the extras holding the instruments appear more as courtiers than servants or specialist musicians, suggesting that some of the upper-class Trojans had the leisure to indulge Helen and Paris in both music and companionship.

The program for Macowan's production describes the scene as taking place in "Helen's flat," and several reviews provide photographs with captions such as the "sophisticated cocktail party"[13] or the "sherry party."[14] James Christy describes the scene in detail:

Upstage right was a sheer drape suspended from above. In front of this, a white baby grand piano. Stage left was a furnished bar wagon with an outline of a latticed window behind it; beside these, a standing lamp with a ruffled white shade à la mode. The chairs and sofa in the room were chrome and had large leather cushions . . . It was a simple evocation of bare and expensive modernity. . . . Around the room were a number of young well-dressed people lounging around on the furniture and on the floor.[15]

A man standing at the bar may be a butler or a guest, but the other "well-dressed people" are surely guests rather than servers at the party. Exactly how Pandarus's line requesting an instrument was executed remains unclear, but the presence of the piano suggests the possibility that the phrase "Come, give me an instrument" could be delivered as Pandarus approaches or takes up an already present instrument.[16]

One of the few times Paris and Helen entered unaccompanied was in Guthrie's production. Like Macowan's version, Guthrie shocked critics with a twentieth-century setting, and Guthrie also followed Macowan in using a piano as Pandarus's musical instrument. The fact that Guthrie cut all of the opening dialogue between Pandarus and Paris's servant does significantly alter the scene's opening, but Guthrie's decision to create a less populated scene is still relevant and important. The promptbook does not note the cutting or alteration of Pandarus addressing the "fair company," raising questions about whether the extras are necessary for the phrase to make sense. Perhaps the exuberance of Pandarus's "fair words" was made even more ridiculous by his first addressing Paris ("Fair be to you, my Lord") and then Paris and Helen together ("and to all this fair company"), before specifically addressing Helen ("especially to you, fair Queen"). Pandarus's line is the only mention of a "fair company" in the scene, and while the editorial addition of extras is hard to argue against, perhaps Pandarus's enthusiasm provides some justification for interpreting the phrase to mean merely Paris's single servant, Paris, and Helen.

Guthrie began the scene with Pandarus entering to Helen, who was seated at the piano while Paris stood behind it. Again the scene and Helen received extensive press coverage.

We come suddenly on a scene in which Helen of Troy (none other than Wendy Hiller) is seated at a white and gold piano in an Edwardian conservatory. She wears a puce floor-length dress slashed to the knee in front, long strings of pearls, ostrich feathers in her hair, and brilliants all over the show. She smokes from a long cigarette-holder and plays for Paris (tall, lithe, and broad-shouldered like an Hungarian prince—but in real-

16. Helen's scene, Westminster Theatre 1938, Macowan.

ity Ronald Allen) a tune which sounded remarkably like "On Wings of Song."[17]

Helen was variously described as a "Gaiety Girl who—quite justifiably—almost stops the show,"[18] "the sort of Edwardian actress who sips champagne from her dancing shoe,"[19] "a tarnished flibbertigibbet from any shady night club,"[20] "a giddy creature from one of Chaplin's early, frenzied satires upon high society,"[21] and wearing a "shocking-pink hobbled evening dress which cannot make her piano playing an easier task."[22] The intimacy of the conservatory scene evidently made the presence of extras undesirable, or at least unpractical, and the press photographs depict a very different atmosphere without additional actors, where the loneliness and isolation of "the ravished Helen" and "wanton Paris" was visually implied. *The Saturday Review* described how "a drunken Paris debauches with her out of sheer necessity to keep up appearances,"[23] and combined with some of the reviews quoted above describing a "tarnished flibbertigibbet" or the comparison with Chaplin's satires, the lack of followers or servants might have made even more pathetic the idea of an aging Helen who still attempts to live a life of elegant high society, but can no longer command the attention she once demanded. Guthrie's staging seems to imply that by having Helen and Paris attended, a production invests them with an

17. Helen's scene, Old Vic Theatre 1956, Guthrie.

importance by virtue of their ability to attract a large social following, or a large number of servants. Such an interpretation can be misleading and too simplistic, as the age, dress, and actions of the followers could also create a scene where a group of characters are clinging to a past that has become an anomaly.

Guthrie's use of the piano is significant to the present discussion of the direction for music, but the promptbook is not very helpful in adding to the details in the reviews and photographs. Helen is seated at the piano for the opening of the scene, but the promptbook does not indicate when she plays the tune mentioned in *The Scotsman* review or the point at which Pandarus takes over the piano stool. What the promptbook does note is an arpeggio when Pandarus says, "Come, give me an instrument," and by the end of Pandarus's song, Helen is on top of the piano. Helen's relinquishing the piano stool to Pandarus, like Payne's Helen handing Pandarus a flute, reaffirms the dramatic potential of the exchange of musical instruments taking place between principal characters, rather than between Pandarus and a musician or extra.

The piano in Guthrie's and Macowan's productions highlights both the issues surrounding the possible instruments and music used at the opening of the scene and the connection that the earlier music may have with Pandarus's song. Opting for a recognizable style of music, both Macowan and Guthrie capitalized on music familiar to their audiences to help create the scene's ambience. Max Adrian, Macowan's Pandarus,

> composed the music himself in a deliberate imitation of one, Douglas Bing, who was at the time famous for singing dirty "pointed numbers" at the piano. The scene was a witty sketch of a vain and silly social set, not unfamiliar to audiences who enjoyed the plays of Noel Coward.[24]

Guthrie's music was similarly recognized by *The Scotsman* reviewer quoted above ("remarkably like 'On Wings of Song'") and *The Evening Standard* reviewer who described the scene as "champagne-drinking characters making love over a piano with overtones of early Noel Coward."[25] The style of Pandarus's bawdy song, indeed even the actor playing the role, may have elicited similar references in Shakespeare's theater to contemporary styles of song. F. W. Sternfeld carries such thinking even further, writing that "it is tempting to speculate that about this time Shakespeare promoted Armin to a more challenging and rewarding part and that Armin did, in fact, play Pandarus."[26]

The two successive RSC productions of Barton and Barton/Kyle that used Walker's edition rejected her delayed direction for "music within" and instead followed F's placement of the direction. Rather than have music played within (as F) and more closely associated with the offstage presence of Paris and Helen, Barton had musicians enter at the beginning of the scene as part of an elaborate preface to the dialogue. Five women and four men set a bed and bowed to Paris's servant before exiting, while servants with large fans and the musicians settled around the stage. The bowing shows the director's interest in establishing the status of the extras, raising Paris's servant above the others not only by virtue of his having dialogue, but also by their deference to him.

The way Barton prefaced the scene, while departing from the F text, offers several possible readings of F. If extras are required by Pandarus addressing a "fair company," do they necessarily enter with Paris and Helen, as in most editions? The fact that Pandarus only speaks to the "fair company" after Paris and Helen arrive suggests that extras would accompany their entrance, but the greeting of Paris and Helen could merely provide the opportunity for Pandarus to acknowledge the presence of extras that were onstage from the opening of the scene. Rather than being in the copy from which F was set, F's inclusion of the servant entering with Pandarus, where Q has only Pandarus enter, could merely be a compositor or collator noticing their copy's failure to bring on a speaking character. The need for extras, however, requires reading the dialogue more closely. F's direction for "music sounds within," and the servant's comment that the musicians play "at the request of Paris my lord, who's there in person; with him, the mortal Venus" (3.1.30–32) gives the impression that Paris and Helen are accompanied offstage, at least by musicians. But the fact that Pandarus is speaking with a servant does make it possible that the servant is only one of a number of servants or attendants who are also onstage from the beginning of the scene. Such extras could serve a similar function of setting the scene as Barton's extras who placed cushions and populated the stage, establishing a lavish atmosphere that Helen and Paris enter into, rather than bring with them onstage.

The Barton/Kyle production again dismissed Walker's delayed direction for music, but this time the F arrangement of music from within began the scene. Audiotapes of the Barton and Barton/Kyle productions reveal an interesting decision about the music, both productions having it come to an abrupt halt at the point when Pandarus commended it ("here is good"), prompting him to finish "broken music" (3.1.49). The meaning of "broken music" has been debated at length, but most commentators agree that it is a technical musical term.[27] More relevant to the present discussion is the editorial question implied by the staging. When editors include a direction for music to start, should they attempt to indicate, either in a note or a stage direction, possible points where the dialogue might imply that the music should stop? Whatever the meaning and implied action in Pandarus's phrase "good broken music," Paris's response uses Pandarus's image of "broken music" to accuse Pandarus of disrupting the entertainment: "You have broke it, cousin, and by my life you shall make it whole again" (3.1.50–51). Paris's words could merely refer to Pandarus interrupting their enjoyment of the music, and while his interruption need not signal that the music must stop at that point, the directors offer a possible interpretation that deserves consideration.

Discussing Pandarus "interrupting the musical entertainment of Paris and Helen," T. McAlindon makes the point that

> it is only in the love scenes involving Troilus and Cressida that the full import of Pandarus's "broken music" is perceived. Whatever slight chance the dialogue of the lovers might have had of developing into lyrical duets is completely eliminated by him. He is always present at some point, interrupting and commenting, turning poetry into prose and passion into lust.[28]

The decision by Barton and Barton/Kyle to stop the music highlights Pandarus's ability to debase love by presenting a concrete example of his altering the mood. The possible difference in the style of music at the opening of the scene and the song which Pandarus performs could also show how Pandarus interrupts a romantic moment, and when asked to mend it sings a bawdy song. Interpreting stage action from dialogue is often problematic, and while there are advantages to the interpretation of "you have broke it" as meaning that the music has stopped, perhaps a stage direction would be too prescriptive and too limiting an invasion of the text. The Barton and Barton/Kyle rejection of Walker's delaying the music at the beginning of the scene shows one form of profitable dialogue between the theater and the editor; the directors' decision to stop the music at a point when Paris would seem to observe its disruption represents another way that theater history can provide suggestions and commentary on editorial questions.

The stage direction for Helen and Paris to enter is preceded in Barton's promptbook by a note for the entrance of soldiers, presenting extras who make clear the cost of Helen and Paris being together. The only other promptbook note for the soldiers is their exit (accompanied by the servants with fans and the musicians), after Paris says "let us to Priam's hall / To greet the warriors" (3.1.145–46).[29] While the "us" in Paris's speech might apply only to himself and Helen, the group exit shows that Barton could have had the words directed at the extras. In addition to the obvious purpose of having soldiers onstage as a reminder of the war, a military presence could also suggest the inability of the lovers to have any semblance of a private relationship. The lovers being surrounded by a large group of silent extras with little or no stage business could heighten their loneliness in a society where they receive attention, but not companionship.

The group exit that left them alone for the scene's final speeches could also have created an intimacy and seriousness that was in stark contrast to what went before.

The use of extras in the Barton and Barton/Kyle productions is especially interesting because both productions cut the reference to the "fair company."[30] Perhaps it was judged to be inappropriate in Barton's 1968 version to address the soldiers, servants, and musicians as "fair company," again implying that the lines may suggest a higher social class of extras, or even a more active group. Although the sentence was similarly altered in the Barton/Kyle production, the scene was in many ways staged differently. Instead of populating the scene with musicians, soldiers, and servants, only the servant that spoke with Pandarus at the opening of the scene was present when Pandarus greeted Helen and Paris. The whole project of trying to determine the number and class of extras implied by Pandarus's phrase ("fair company") becomes questionable in light of the seemingly contradictory interpretations: Guthrie allowed Pandarus to speak of a "fair company" when only Paris and Helen were onstage with Pandarus, but Barton and Barton/Kyle cut the phrase when there was a servant or a group of extras onstage. By far the most common staging follows the editorial direction for attendants of some kind, but the different ways productions have used extras raises questions concerning the thematic implications of the various theatrical interpretations. There is, however, a danger in assuming a necessary link between the number of extras and the tone of the scene, as is evident in the differences between the Barton and Barton/Kyle productions.

In the "director's notes to the company at rehearsal" printed in the 1968 program, Barton describes how

> all the characters in the play are made up of inconsistencies, opposites and extremes. Each of these jarring elements should be played for what it is, and not smoothed out: The Trojans turn HELEN into an ideal—"a theme of honor and renown." The Greek DIOMED sees her as a whore. She herself, in her brief appearance, is neither. Shakespeare doesn't label her, but gives us a glimpse of a human woman.[31]

Irving Wardle's review confirms that the scene was played subtly, more sympathetic and less ironic than most productions, and without too much business.

> The Helen-Pandarus scene is usually played satirically, but here Sheila Allen gives it an erotic charge that makes other matters seem unimportant compared with a shimmering golden robe and a hand exploring a cheek.[32]

The conflict the play repeatedly shows between the public and private lives of individuals, especially the internal conflict between lover and warrior, can certainly become a performance consideration in Helen's scene.[33] Are Paris and Helen oblivious to the war, or portrayed as somehow insulated from it? How much should the war intrude on Pandarus's visit to Helen and Paris? Should Paris's mention of his "Nell's" desire for him not to fight be spoken in a scene where soldiers or other images of the war are present, or should Paris's remark and the trumpets signaling that the soldiers have "come from field" (3.1.145) be in stark contrast to what Foakes calls Helen's "high class brothel?" Can Helen live, in Barton's phrase, simply as "a human woman"?

The play's theater history can suggest some possible answers to these questions, but it also becomes evident that the use of extras can help characterize Helen and her lifestyle in many different ways. Barton's desire to present "a human woman" would seem to resist the tendency to overproduce the scene, but many critics disagree with Barton's view that "Shakespeare doesn't label her." A common critical observation is that Helen's scene shows that Hector is right in arguing that "she is not worth what she does cost / The holding" (2.2.50, Q reads "the keeping"): Muir believes that "the one glimpse we have of her only confirms" the opinion of Hector, Priam, Diomedes, and Thersites that "Helen is an unsatisfactory war aim"; A. P. Rossiter judges her as "silly and empty"; Arnold Stein similarly thinks that her scene shows "the absolute gap between the emptiness of Helen the person and the attributes she has demonstrably acquired as a symbol. . . . Even our laughter, as our dramatic interest, is directed at the utter disproportion, at the gap, at the disjunction between what she is and what she means"; and T. McAlindon writes that "the glorious Helen described by the servant a few moments earlier has turned out to be jolly 'Nell.'"[34] The play constantly deflates the Trojan and Greek legends, and it would be hard to argue that Helen is sympathetically portrayed, but Barton's comment suggests the ambiguity that does exit. The more Helen is degraded, the easier it is to dismiss her as "not worth what she does cost," but a more complex interpretation might deflect the focus on her character to the more general issue of whether any woman can be a satisfactory cause of war. In suggesting an alternative vision of Helen, Barton at least points the way to some of the different possibilities in setting the scene and using extras.

When Barton next directed the play with Barry Kyle, Helen's scene was very different. John Nettles, who played Thersites in that production, recalls that

Barton had this lovely idea—about seven years into the war, Helen must have been a bit over the top. And there you have the reason for the war had actually gone wrong. And the blast of mortality had actually shaken her beauty a little. And it was even more pointless; their youth was dying.[35]

Barton's earlier description of a "human woman" that "Shakespeare doesn't label" becomes more defined, and more readily judged. Richard David praised the staging, but he also found fault with the way the Barton/Kyle production went too far in presenting the erotic entertainment the lovers enjoyed.

The scene at court in which Pandarus tries to coax Paris, as he dallies with Helen, into covering up Troilus' absence on the evening of his assignation with Cressida, a scene that frothily exposes the worthlessness of what Greeks and Trojans are fighting for, was a delightful piece of team-playing, and Barbara Leigh-Hunt, without overweighting it, made of Helen not the mere affected feather-head of most productions but a genuinely vicious woman, *blasée*, and uncomfortably aware of her own degradation. The scene is consummated in Pandarus' song, "Love, love, nothing but love." I am not joining Harold Hobson in complaining that the Stratford directors are always introducing obscenities into Shakespeare's chaste plays. The song is grossly obscene. Shakespeare meant it so; but to have Pandarus mime its lubricities with a giant bolster is (somewhat to misapply the metaphor) gilding the lily.[36]

Compared with the earlier Barton production, Barton/Kyle provided a more unequivocally lascivious scene, and a clearer subtext for Helen ("over the top" and "uncomfortably aware of her own degradation"). It is perhaps surprising that when Barton described Helen as a "human woman," there were extras setting her bed at the start of the scene, servants fanning her, and musicians playing for her, but in the production criticized for its indulgent staging of the scene, only the speaking characters appeared.

For an example of the creation of the scene in a production that "was accused, with some justice, of interpretative excess"[37] and too liberal employment of extras and stage business, the notes that the stage manager made during the rehearsals of Hands' production makes interesting reading:

30 April
flowers for Cupid . . . to throw
Golden apple in Paris' hand for Helen to bite into
Helen on a trolley that the boys pull to centre
Rubens—Triumph of Silence

18. Helen's scene, RST 1976, Barton/Kyle. Thos F. and Mig Holte Collection, Shakespeare Centre Library. Copyright Shakespeare Birthplace Trust.

12 May
Rolf Saxon as a Goddess (there will be another Eunuch type thing in this scene as well I think)
Swanee whistle for a Cupid
The fig leaf that Paris puts on Pandarus has actually been "plucked" from [a] Goddess!

28 May
Cupids will collect the gold cloth from somewhere up C vicinity & *They* will hook it up:
all as part of the setting up of the brothel scene.
Perfumed aromiser fan for Juno & some head gear too
Blindfold for Sion—constant deluge of flowers
feather bed—Helen

At the top of the scene—under the Cupid/Pand dialogue, the 3 new boys are picking up the "Ajax" mess [broken orange crates] from the previous scene before the gold cloth comes in.

These notes register the time spent on devising the actions, identity, and costumes for the "fair company," revealing a concern, however indirect, with several of the editorial issues. The attention paid to the transition between scenes ("picking up the 'Ajax' mess"), decorating the "brothel scene," and having Helen rolled in, all relate quite specifically to the ways music and extras can signal the change of scenes, and help Helen's entrance to become impressive and resonant.

If Hands's desired aim was to disturb, he was successful, as nearly all reviewers spent some time deriding his interpretation of the scene. It is worth quoting a selection of these reviews to show the range of visual images Hands evoked: "Helen (Barbara Kinghorn) becomes a raddled doxy who likes being pleasured by half-a-dozen men at once. The servants are pretty boys in curly wigs."[38] "The Helen scene is a bit of a mess (something like Zsa Zsa Gabor playing Dietrich in a camp floor show conceived by Giraudoux)."[39] "Mr Hands has also gone over the top, or perhaps groped for the bottom, in an orgy scene between Paris and Helen of Troy that owes more to Raymond's Revuebar than to the Bard."[40] "Both the narrative point that Pandarus wants Paris to cover for Troilus's absence and the satire of the Helen-Paris relationship were buried beneath an atmosphere of contrived decadence in which Helen and Paris had to be groped ritually by be-rouged Cupids to achieve orgasm."[41]

One of the few critics who found a justification for Hands's interpretation was Michael Billington, who wrote that "sex between Paris and Helen has dwindled into a spectator sport with nightly orgies on gilt carpets. In such a bankrupt, frenzied world, Cressida's infidelity seems the merest peccadillo."[42] In what the stage manager's script titles the "brothel scene," and what Michael Shulman called "an orgy scene," there can be little chance for showing Helen as simply a "human woman," or involved in anything approaching an intimate love relationship. The options certainly exist for a director to achieve a balance between the view of Helen as a goddess and Diomedes and Thersites calling her a whore, but the opportunity also exists for proving either opinion correct. Dressing the servants as Cupids, one talking with Pandarus at the opening of the scene and the others rolling Helen in on a cart, used the trapping of the goddess myth to present the whore. In contrast to Barton's production that had servants, soldiers, and musicians create a somber atmosphere, Hands's production employed what seemed like a serving class to create a "contrived decadence." Billington's observation that love had in this society become, like the war, a "spectator sport" provides an explicit example of the way Helen's scene comments directly on how the society at war would invade and destroy the relationship of the lovers that Pandarus brings together in the following scene.

The crowds, servants, lewd gestures, and other trappings of previous productions were combined in Hands's version of the scene, and practically all were stripped away in Miller's video. Stanley Wells wrote that "Paris and Helen's lovemaking during Pandarus' song was modest in Miller's version, especially by comparison with the Aldwych orgy" in Hands's production.[43] Miller followed his edition's (Peter Alexander's) direction for "music within" at the opening of the scene, and the Elizabethan music continued in the background until Paris and Helen entered, when the music merely drifted away as Pandarus addressed the lovers. Miller did not, however, follow Alexander's direction for Paris and Helen to enter attended. They appeared alone, and the scene was played with only the speakers present. At the beginning of Pandarus's song, a brief shot of Paris's servant showed that he had not "exited," and Pandarus spoke the line "give me an instrument" while looking past Helen and Paris and pointing to an unseen character or group of characters. Perhaps he was speaking to Paris's servant, but no instrument was handed. Instead, he was accompanied by the same unseen ensemble that opened the scene. Again the point is made that the appearance of attendants, onstage musicians, or even a musical instrument was considered unnecessary for the scene. Pandarus addressed his line "fair be to you, my lord, and to all this fair company" directly at Paris, with no sign or sound of any other character until Helen arrived alone. The relative quiet of the scene, especially compared with the more populated and inventive versions in other productions, created a very different atmosphere that in Miller's production became, despite all the joking, a melancholic and serious occasion. Nowhere is this more evident than when Pandarus leaves Paris and Helen alone, and their intimate, seductive exchange turned quite sad.

Davies' promptbook titles the scene "Paris and Helen's Party," and Paris's man was one of seven attending the party that opened the scene into which Pandarus entered. The extras were playing a form of musical chairs (as an inventive and ingenious interpretation of "music in parts" and "broken music") that continued while Pandarus tried to converse with Paris's man over the loud music. Interestingly, the music faded out at precisely the point where editors have placed the direction for the start of "music within." Pandarus's remark ("what music is this") quite intelligibly referred to the music that just ended rather than just begun.

Davies' staging questions both the editors' delayed music and the arrival of attendants with Paris and Helen. In creating a scene initially populated with Paris and Helen's followers, Pandarus was confronted by more than the one servant to humiliate him. The group ridiculed Pandarus's suggestion that Cressida fit the servant's description of Helen as the "mortal Venus," and as they carried Pandarus up to the balcony, he vainly tried to impress them with his mission: "I come to

19. Helen's scene, RST 1985, Davies. Joe Cocks Studio Collection, Shakespeare Centre Library. Copyright Shakespeare Birthplace Trust.

speak with Paris from the Prince Troilus" (3.1.38–39). The extras then hung Pandarus from the balcony by his ankles, and handed him down so that he landed at the feet of the entering Paris and Helen with his trousers having fallen to the floor (see illustration, where Helen is pulling up Pandarus's trousers as Paris pours a drink). The group that confronted Pandarus from the opening of the scene helped establish the party atmosphere but also emphasized visually the dismissive treatment Pandarus receives from Paris' servant.

Vivian Thomas had high praise for the portrayal of Helen in Davies' production, calling it "one of the most fascinating scenes of this enormously rich and resonant production."

> The scene reeked of decadence. As disaster drew ever closer the audience was afforded a view of night life in the recesses of Troy: high-spirited debauchery constituted the essence of a scene which possessed two moments of poignancy: coarse gaiety was fractured for a second when Helen rested her forehead on Pandarus' chest and gave expression to a terrible anguish with the line "this love will undo us all. / O Cupid, Cupid, Cupid!" (III.i.105–6) As the scene closed Paris was luxuriating in the garish Helen's beauty while she conveyed a sense of impotent desolation as she gazed beyond him to the audience and the world outside.[44]

Davies' production bridges the gap between a populated and bare scene, a sensuous and sensitive atmosphere, where attendants humiliated Pandarus while being subservient to Paris. Thomas's description of the way the "gaiety was fractured" also suggests some advantages of setting up quiet moments as a contrast to the hectic party atmosphere of the rest of the scene. Ralph Berry, not commenting specifically on Davies' production, similarly notes the linguistic as well as the physical change that takes place in the scene: "After Pandarus's departure, Paris and Helen are left alone, and the dialogue he initiates is in verse. It is a complete change of tone and mood, signifying (after the company-gaiety of the encounter à trois) a reversion to seriousness."[45]

Mendes' production raises some questions about the different possibilities for staging F's direction of "*Musicke sounds within.*" The musicians at the Swan Theater were positioned throughout the production high above the stage at the back of the upper balcony, virtually, but not entirely out of the audience's sight.[46] Mendes followed his promptbook edition by having the music start at the beginning of the scene, and it continued through Pandarus's line "here is good broken music" (3.1.49). Before Paris responded to this, however, he raised his arm above his head and snapped his fingers, and the music abruptly halted for his line "You have broke it." The gesture served not only to stop the music (and interpret the line as Barton and Barton/Kyle had done), but also increased Pandarus's unease by the dramatic way Paris let it be known that Pandarus had disrupted the mood. Mendes' musicians were not literally "within," but neither were they onstage or in any way miming acknowledgment of Paris's signal to stop playing. Similarly, Pandarus's line "Come, give me an instrument" (3.1.92) was not directly addressed at the musicians, but they accompanied his song. Their ambiguous presence hints at some of the possibilities for the musicians to occupy a space somewhere on the periphery of the stage in any theater, and be incorporated or excluded from the onstage action.

R. V. Holdsworth noted Mendes' departure from the more common interpretation of the scene.

> Normally presented as bit of frivolous dalliance, it here becomes a bleak and chilling erotic ritual reminiscent of De Sade, in which Helen, shrouded in gold, is carried in on a platter and unwrapped like a giant sweet.[47]

By acknowledging the scene's theater history, Holdsworth highlights the way Mendes' staging of Helen's entrance, taking over a minute of wordless action, provides a clear statement of another director's decision to create a unique and memorable moment. Four servants entered carrying on their shoulders a small platform with an unidentifiable figure completely wrapped in gold. As they placed the platform in the center of the stage, Paris, with a glass of champagne in one hand, watched and waited upstage before coming downstage to slowly remove the cloth. He revealed Helen, seated on the velvet covered platform, in a "bright scarlet dress wearing high-heeled shoes, covered in heavy gold jewelry (necklace, earrings, bangles), lips painted with matching rouge and eyes heavily made up."[48] When Paris finished unwrapping Helen, he moved to kiss her, but as their lips were about to touch, Pandarus interrupted by addressing the couple with his "fair words." The music that was played at the beginning of the scene, a lone flute, continued as Helen was brought in and unwrapped, significantly contributing to the sultry mood that Pandarus broke.

The servants remained present but essentially motionless after bringing Helen in, except when silently instructed by Paris to remove Pandarus's jacket and hat while Helen teased and tickled him. The servants helped humiliate Pandarus, and as in Davies' production they heightened his discomfort in the presence of Paris and Helen. Mendes and Norman Rodway (Pandarus) both confirmed their desire to show that Pandarus was not normally part of this royal society, and that his attempts to marry his niece to a prince were seen through by everyone from the servants to the royals themselves.[49] Even the servants' silent presence at the side of the stage, looking with disdain on Pandarus's attempt to infiltrate high society, worked to diminish Pandarus's status.

Perhaps such subtextual interpretation can distort the dialogue, but the strong ambience created in the scene was given considerable praise in reviews. Michael Billington commented that

> as an example of Mendes's mastery of mood, I would cite the scene with Trojan Helen who is played by Sally Dexter as a sensationally voluptuous Hollywood queen who regards all men as easy prey and whose passion for the stodgy Paris has clearly passed its sell-by date. The whole scene reeks of exhausted, melancholic lust.[50]

The darkness of the presentation, what Billington called "melancholic lust" and Holdsworth characterized as "a bleak and chilling erotic ritual," can be in part due to the use of extras who were menacingly silent onlookers, presenting a very different onstage audience to the boisterous extras used in other productions.

20. Helen's scene, Swan Theatre 1990, Mendes. Reproduced by permission of photographer John Haynes.

Mendes' production provides one of the strongest testimonies of the dramatic opportunities that Helen's entrance affords. His elaborate dumb show created a spectacle in which the audience could share in the revelation of Helen but also be implicated in Pandarus's voyeurism. While such possibilities for staging push the limits of what is specifically validated by the text, perhaps a director's freedom helps to explore the possibilities that do exist in the texts, especially where QF have sparse and ambiguous directions. The editorial rewriting of the music and extras in the scene is never accompanied by notes that directly address the importance of the directions in creating a crucial setting, but the directors' and reviewers' attention to the scene confirms the potential for different arrangements not only to set the tone and mood, but also to provide a social setting that has reverberations throughout the play.

6
"I'll Bring You To Your Father"

CRESSIDA'S BEING "KISSED IN GENERAL" (4.6.22) BY THE GREEKS OFFERS a significant test point in charting the interpretative stance of critics and directors. The vast number of critics that have closely studied Cressida have almost universally commented on this moment and its critical tradition. Ulysses' judgment of Cressida as one of the "daughters of the game" (4.6.64) was once commonly endorsed by critics, but since about 1980, both productions and feminist critics have reassessed the Greeks' reception of Cressida.[1]

The rich theatrical and critical history of the scene where Cressida meets the Greek hierarchy is mostly outside the scope of this study, since there is not sufficient theatrical comment on editorial issues. Cressida's exit from the scene does, however, have textual problems which can be related to theatrical decisions. As in the earlier chapters discussing the entrances of Cassandra (2.2) and Patroclus (2.3), where the different dynamics of having a character onstage or offstage for certain lines were explored, Cressida's exit raises similar questions about the editorial and theatrical interpretations of placing a stage direction. Cassandra's and Patroclus's entrances, or their lines spoken from within, trigger an assessment of their character by those onstage. The possibilities for staging Cassandra being called "mad" or Patroclus as the subject of Thersites' contemplation encourage a study of the alternatives in developing the relationships between characters. The play's relentless concern with value and identity has become something of a critical commonplace, but the matrix of textual and performance options for positioning the valuer and the assessed on a theoretical or practical stage can have significant repercussions in establishing credibility and sympathy. There are few moments where this is more clearly presented than the staging of Ulysses' damning commentary on Cressida after she has been kissed by the Greeks.

The relevant issues for this study are the interpretations of Diomedes' line "Lady a word. I'll bring you to your father" (4.6.54),

Vliſ. Neuers my day, and then a kiſſe of you.
Diom. Lady a word,ile bring you to your father.
Neſt. A woman of quick ſence.
Vliſſ. Fie,fie vpon her,
Ther's language in her eye, her cheeke her lip,
Nay her foote ſpeakes,her wanton ſpirits looke out
At euery ioynt and motiue of her body,
Oh theſe encounterers ſo glib of tongue,
That giue a coaſting welcome ere it comes,
And wide vnclaſpe the tables of their thoughts,
To euery tickliſh reader, ſet them downe,
For ſluttiſh ſpoiles of opportunity:
And daughters of the game.   *Flowriſh enter all of Troy.*
                                                              All.

of Troylus and Creſſeida.

All. The Troyans trumpet.
Agam. Yonder comes the troup.
Æne. Haile all the ſtate of Greece : what ſhalbe done,

Q

Troylus an

Vliſ. Neuer's my day, and then a kiſſe of you,
Diom. Lady a word, Ile bring you to your Father.
Neſt. A woman of quicke ſence.
Vliſ. Fie, fie, vpon her :
Ther's a language in her eye, her cheeke, her lip,
Nay, her foote ſpeakes, her wanton ſpirites looke out
At euery ioynt, and motiue of her body :
Oh theſe encounterers ſo glib of tongue,
That giue a coaſting welcome ere it comes,
And wide vnclaſpe the tables of their thoughts,
To euery tickling reader ſet them downe,
For ſluttiſh ſpoyles of opportunitie;
And daughters of the game.   *Exeunt.*
    Enter all of Troy, Hector, Paris, Æneas, Helenus
          and Attendants. Floriſh.
    All. The Troians Trumpet.
    Aga. Yonder comes the troope.
    Æne. Haile all you ſtate of Greece : what ſhalbe done

F

21. "There's language," Q, F. Reproduced by permission of The Huntington Library, San Marino, California.

and F's "Exeunt" after Ulysses' speech (64.1).[2] Rowe first omitted the
F "Exeunt" and has been followed by virtually all editors. Since Pope's
second edition, nearly all editors have had Diomedes and Cressida
exit after Diomedes says "I'll bring you to your father."[3] While the in-
ference that Diomedes and Cressida should exit together has not
been questioned, Taylor has argued that the F placement should be
followed. Taylor emended his text first by adding a bracketed, and
thus self-doubting direction for Diomedes and Cressida to "talk
apart" after Diomedes says "I'll bring you to your father." He then
merely clarified the F "Exeunt" after Ulysses' speech to read "Exeunt
Diomedes and Cressida," but again enclosed even that direction in
brackets.

Taylor's textual note condemns the editorial placement of the direction because it "leaves the Folio *Exeunt . . .* inexplicable," and asserts that his own "arrangement . . . makes equally good dramatic
sense."[4] In his critical essay "*Troilus and Cressida:* Bibliography, Performance and Interpretation," Taylor makes the most explicit use of
his title when discussing this moment, using theater history to support his critical and bibliographical assessment:

> There is no reason why Cressida could not remain upstage (as she did in
> the 1948 Anthony Quayle production at Stratford-upon-Avon), having "a
> word" with Diomed, while Nestor and Ulysses are talking about her down-
> stage; there is, on the contrary, an obvious dramatic point in the juxta-
> position. And again, nothing in the context could have misled even a cur-
> sory reader into supposing the "need" for an "exeunt" here.[5]

Taylor attacks the editorial tradition and seeks to justify his interpretation of F by examining the moment through the eyes of the compositor, critic, and modern director. This juxtaposition of viewpoints
is also the method that is employed in this study, making Taylor's remarks a useful starting point in exploring the moment in more detail.

Taylor would seem to be correct in asserting that "nothing in the
context could have misled even a cursory reader into supposing the
'need' for an 'exeunt'" where F places it, but there may have been
some misleading annotations in the copy used for F that could have
caused the direction to be misplaced. Q prints "Flowrish enter all of
Troy" on the right margin at the end of a page (I1^v). If F was set from
a copy of Q with manuscript annotations, as is commonly supposed,[6]
the names F supplies ("Hector, Paris, Aeneas, Helenus and Attendants") may have been added to Q in a note that crept up the side of
the margin, causing some confusion over the placement of the "Exeunt." The manuscript "Exeunt," if written in the margin immediately
before the addition F makes to Q's "Enter all of Troy," may have ap-

peared to be part of the same direction. The annotator's desire to insert an exeunt for Diomedes and Cressida alongside Diomedes' speech could then have been misinterpreted as the beginning of the additions to Q's "Enter all of Troy," causing the compositor to set "Exeunt" and "Enter all of Troy" as successive directions. Whether this highly conjectural scenario or any other theory may provide a reason for a misplaced direction, the F arrangement still deserves to be considered for the possible stagings it suggests.

Diomedes' line, "Lady, a word. I'll bring you to your father" has not only been presumed to indicate an exit that neither Q nor F provide at that point, but it is also used to justify the exclusion of Calchas from the stage direction that opens the scene. Theobald first argued for the removal of Calchas, in terms that now sound absurdly confident.

> If Diomede leads Cressid off, as the Poet certainly means he should, in order to deliver her up to her father, 'tis plain, as the Sun at Noon-day, that Calchas cannot be supposed upon the Stage: His Name must be expung'd from among the Names of Those that are said to enter.[7]

Kittredge, Ridley, Seltzer, and Foakes are some editors who do not see the sun, and include Calchas in their editions. Unfortunately, none of these editors provides a defense of Calchas's presence, and they all curiously follow Pope in having Diomedes and Cressida exit after Diomedes says, "I'll bring you to your father."

The editorial interpretation of Diomedes' line and the emendations needed to support that interpretation, raise the obvious question of whether there is a staging that will allow the QF texts to be followed. If QF are believed and Calchas is onstage, then Diomedes need not take Cressida offstage to meet her father, and F's "Exeunt" after Ulysses' speech would then seem to imply that after a silent reunion, Cressida and Calchas move offstage. Diomedes may not even be among those exiting, and the editorial addition of a re-entrance for him before Agamemnon says "Here is Sir Diomedes," common to all editions since Pope, would be unnecessary. Agamemnon's line could merely signal Diomedes' return to center stage from a more peripheral position. A similar movement may occur after the duel when Hector says, "Aeneas, call my brother Troilus to me" (4.7.38). As will be discussed in more detail below, most editors (Taylor is an exception) believe Hector's line implies that an onstage Troilus is being requested to move to a more central position.

Calchas's presence onstage poses several interesting dramatic possibilities, depending on whether he sees Cressida being kissed or whether he is oblivious to the action. Taylor's direction for Diomedes and Cressida to "talk apart" certainly has the potential of presenting a visual commentary for Ulysses' assessment of Cressida, with his description of her "wanton spirits" being accompanied by her speaking privately with Diomedes. But Cressida speaking with her father, or being taken to a group that includes her father can provide a different visual commentary that may suggest to the audience a more sympathetic interpretation than Ulysses describing her as one of these "daughters of the game."

Paul Gaudet has argued that Calchas could be present as the QF direction states, but he does not believe Calchas should still be onstage when Diomedes says "I'll bring you to your father."

> A range of options would be open for staging an ineffectual Calchas, marginalized, even humiliated by the intervening Greek generals who appropriate his paternal authority. This would be all the more probable if one were to retain the Q and F punctuation of Agamemnon's first response to Calchas's petition in 3.3: "What would'st thou of vs Troian? make demand?" (TLN 1865–66). By preserving the second interrogative rather than adopting the modified imperative, "Make demand," employed by Rowe and subsequent editors, one could suggest that Calchas's position with the Greeks is tenuous, merely tolerated, a suggestion that playing the Q and F versions of 4.5 could extend and embody. With Calchas on stage as a visual reminder of what this scene was supposed to be, the kissing sequence could be viewed more immediately as an ironic distortion and rivalrous subordination.[8]

Gaudet does not want to dictate "performance variables," and so does not speculate on "the timing and nature of [Calchas's] exit"; however he is clearly reluctant

> to supply a deferred reunion that the "text" neither mandates nor precludes. Whatever its details and shape in performance, a staged reunion could probably not avoid the destabilization of its context. The Greek failure or refusal to acknowledge Calchas directly, his ritualized subordination, the concomitant vulnerability of a "fatherless" Cressida, the associative implication of Calchas in the devaluation of Cressida, all of these impressions would combine to make this family reunion much different and much less than its narrative promise.[9]

Gaudet's belief that Calchas should be included in the Greeks' entrance but excluded from F's "Exeunt" after Ulysses' denunciation of Cressida creates a presence that could add to an audience's thwarted expectations of a staged reunion. Calchas's shadowy presence and mysterious disappearance might create a more politically orchestrated moment that denies any opportunity for paternal sentimentality.

While Gaudet does not want to speculate on Calchas's actions if he were included, it is very much within the mandate of this study to begin to offer some staging alternatives. Both Cressida's exit and Calchas's presence constitute similar difficulties for this study, since editors (especially of editions used for promptbooks) do not argue for or offer the QF alternatives, and nearly all productions follow their editions. Two productions do, however, stage Cressida's exit in a manner that comments on the QF placement, and these stagings lead to ways of discussing the possibilities of Calchas's presence.

Taylor's brief reference to Cressida's exit in Quayle's production needs to be expanded upon for the present discussion. The opening of the scene is simplistically diagrammed in the promptbook, showing the main characters in a group at the center of the stage on a raised platform that is being roped off for the lists, while peripheral groups of characters and extras are dotted around the stage. There is an arrow showing the movement of Ajax from the central group to a smaller group stage right that includes the trumpeter, a movement that presumably took place when Ajax offered his purse (4.6.6). When Diomedes says "I'll bring you to your father," the promptbook notes that Diomedes and Cressida crossed the stage to "stop and talk to Ajax," and after Ulysses' speech Cressida and Diomedes exited at the point of the F direction. The rationale of having the exiting couple speak with Ajax is something of a mystery, but perhaps its irrationality emphasizes Quayle's desire to have Cressida present for Ulysses' speech. Although their stopping to speak with Calchas would have a more obvious dramatic point that specifically relates to the dialogue, their talking apart in some less conspicuous way makes Cressida's presence available, without being overwhelming.

The bare description of the movements in Quayle's promptbook at least shows that the F placement was followed, despite using an edition that printed an earlier direction, but it is difficult to make any further conclusions about how the moment was played. The inadequacy of promptbooks is further seen in Davies' production, where the scene's feminist interpretation, complained of and praised in reviews and critical articles, is not evident from the simple notes for movements.[10] Most relevant to the present discussion, the promptbook does not indicate a departure from the promptbook edition's placement of Diomedes and Cressida's exit, but the archive video shows the exit was staged in a way that clearly lends support to F's placement and Taylor's argument.

Diomedes did begin to escort Cressida offstage to Calchas after saying "I'll bring you to your father," but the route they took up the long staircase and along the balcony at the back of the stage allowed most of Ulysses' remarks to be spoken with Diomedes and Cressida still in full view. Cressida kept looking back at the Greeks as she walked up the stairs, and as Ulysses said "O these encounterers so glib of tongue" (4.6.59), she paused on the balcony and looked down over the Greeks, finally exiting with Diomedes as Ulysses spoke the words "ticklish reader" (62). By repeatedly looking down at the Greeks and pausing before she exited, Cressida constantly called attention to herself, making her long walk up the stairs and across the balcony much more noticeable than a simple exit. Juliet Stevenson's Cressida seemed much more interested in what was being said below than in being with Diomedes or in rushing off to see her father. Whether she was meant to hear Ulysses is debatable and could have been left intentionally ambiguous, but her slow departure allowed the audience a further chance to consider whether they agreed with Ulysses that "Her wanton spirits look out / At every joint and motive of her body" (58).

Since editors until Taylor have neither presented (except in collations) nor argued for the possibility of Cressida remaining onstage for Ulysses' assessment of her, it not surprising that Quayle and Davies are the only directors I have found that leave evidence of something resembling the QF placement of the exeunt. Similarly, the editorial exclusion of Calchas from the scene corresponds with his absence in productions before Judge. While the way Judge followed F, with both Calchas's presence and the placement of Cressida and Diomedes' exit, will be discussed below, Quayle's staging of Cressida's exit does, however, suggest some ways of exploring the possibilities of Calchas's presence in the scene.

Quayle's decision to have Cressida and Diomedes speak with Ajax before departing points forward to the issues of stage grouping that will be explored in the following chapter, which studies the editing and staging of the duel between Ajax and Hector. Where is Ajax when Cressida is kissed, and why is he not involved? Quayle offers the possibility, seconded by other productions (as will be seen in the discussion of the duel), that Ajax is preparing for his fight on a different part of the stage. It is this possibility that suggests a place for Calchas, apart from the Greeks who are kissing Cressida but still onstage, perhaps in a group of spectators anticipating the duel. If Calchas is present, his placement within a group, his reaction or lack of awareness to what goes on, and the possibilities for his movements could have a significant impact on the scene. Without a stage history that explores these possibilities, the Trojan legend can be read to offer some critical and theatrical insight into Calchas's reunion with Cressida.

Davies and his designer (Ralph Koltai) set their production in the Crimean War and asked the company to research attitudes and situations that parallel *Troilus and Cressida*.[11] Superimposing an apparently unconnected historical period onto the play invites a set of connections clearly from outside the text. The Crimean War becomes relevant to an early seventeenth-century drama about the Trojan War when their juxtaposition offers insights and new ways of understanding the characters, relationships, and dramatic situations in the play. The freedom of a director and designer to inspire their creative interpretation of a play can similarly be claimed for a critical mining of versions of the Trojan War story, not merely to recreate the process of authorship with speculation about sources, but simply to offer ways of interrogating the play and generating images for potential stagings.

Of course there is no dialogue in *Troilus and Cressida* which implies an onstage reunion between Cressida and Calchas, but very different and very meaningful possibilities arise from his inclusion in the QF stage direction: Calchas could be mute, Calchas could be absent, Calchas's inclusion may have been considered and then rejected. While it is possible that Calchas was mistakenly included as a printing error, if that error records a rejected idea, then a crucial compositional decision is preserved. The difference between a scene with or without a mute Calchas could be significant, but there would seem to be an enormous difference between the tone of a scene originally conceived that included dialogue for Calchas and a scene totally excluding him.

Tracing the different versions of the reunion between Calchas and Cressida in the legend not only suggests the kind of silent reunion that might take place in *Troilus and Cressida* but can also help in understanding the absence of a reunion. For example, Boccaccio has Calchas greet Criseida "joyfully,"[12] and Chaucer adds that "twenty tyme he kiste his doughter sweete" (5.191). The joy of Boccaccio's Calchas is an easily staged action if Calchas is present, or at least provides a useful contrast to a more aggressive greeting by the Greeks in *Troilus and Cressida*. Similarly, the paternal kisses Chaucer describes offer performance options and signal the differences between the poem and play within the literary context of the legend.

QF's inclusion of Calchas for Cressida's greeting by the Greeks at least makes explicit the absence of a speaking reunion that has been not only anticipated in the play but also would be expected by anyone who knew the legend. In studying Chaucer's use of Benoit's *Roman de Troie*, Barry Windeatt remarks that

> when Briseida arrives at the Greek camp she rebukes Calchas roundly for his treachery to Troy, and suggests that his powers of divination have led him astray (*Troie*, 13721 ff.). Chaucer echoes this passage but quite alters

the context, shifting the material earlier into Criseyde's long speech to Troilus on their last night together, where she describes how she will deal with her father. By this stroke the English Criseyde's remonstrations with her father remain confined to her intentions, or, at least, Chaucer prefers not to narrate them.[13]

Troilus and Cressida parallels Chaucer's poem when Cressida speaks against her father after she hears of the exchange ("I have forgot my father," 4.3.22; "O Calkas, fader, thyn be al this synne!" 4.761), but unlike Shakespeare, Chaucer makes explicit the nature of their actual reunion. Chaucer's Diomede leads Criseyde "unto the Greek oost" (5.16), and after his initial wooings, leaves her with Calchas.

> Hire fader hath hire in hise armes nome,
> And twenty tyme he kiste his doughter sweete,
> And seyde, "O deere doughter myn, welcome."
> She seyde ek she was fayn with hym to mete,
> And stood forth muwet, milde, and mansuete.
> But here I leve hire with hire fader dwelle,
> And forth I wol of Troilus yow telle.
>
> [5.190]

Ann Thompson notes Criseyde's "stunned silence," commenting that "she is too preoccupied with the grief of being separated from Troilus to be more than polite to" Calchas.[14] In place of Chaucer's "muwet" Criseyde, QF *Troilus and Cressida* offers a mute Calchas.

Caxton refers his reader to Chaucer for a fuller description of the lovers' story but expands on Breseyda's arrival in the Greek camp: "Breseyda was ledde unto the Grekes whom they receyved honourably."[15] Already this seems a more public reception, but two private conversations follow, first with Diomedes and then with Calcas. Diomedes "accompanyed her unto the tente of her fader," where "Calcas resceyvyd her wyth grete joye."[16] Breseyda directly confronts her father with being a traitor,[17] accusations that are seen as ironic coming from a woman renowned for her falsity: "she blamed her fader of the vyce of trayson which she her self excersised in forgetying her contre and her trewe frende Troyllus."[18] A sympathetic explanation of Breseyda's "forgetying" is offered in the passage following her conversation with Calcas: "the comyng of Breseyda plesid moche to alle the Grekes," and they "fested her" and "promysyd her to kepe her and holde her as dere as her doughter. And eche man went in to hys owne tente and ther was none of hem but that gaf to her a jewell." The warmth of this welcome convinces Breseyda to "forgate annone the noble cyte of Troye and the love of noble Troyllus."[19]

Chaucer and Caxton couple Diomedes' early wooing with the initial reunion between Criseyda/Breseyda and Calchas. While neither of these events is staged with dialogue in *Troilus and Cressida*, both could be either staged as silent actions or simply assumed to have occurred without the audience seeing them. Nonetheless, the moods and explanations that Chaucer and Caxton evoke suggest many different ways of reading and performing *Troilus and Cressida*. The rebellious and independent-minded accusations with which Breseyda greets her father can be compared to Cressida's retorts to the requests by Menelaus and Ulysses for a kiss. The kisses that the Greeks give Cressida do not, however, seem designed to persuade her that she has found a new home in the company of fatherly Greeks. The development of a paternal relationship has been sacrificed in favor of a confrontation with the cuckold Menelaus and the political mastermind Ulysses, where a battle of wits and ambiguous kisses replace a disputatious or sentimental reunion. As will be discussed in relation to the Ajax and Hector duel, Caxton's weaving the plots of Breseyda's exchange and Hector's challenge to single combat makes the point that Cressida's arrival is not in the familial comfort of her father's tent, but at a tournament presumably with some military preparations taking place.

The Iron Age offers another interesting twist on the relationship between Calchas and Cressida. Chaucer, Caxton, Lydgate, and Shakespeare all include a version of Calchas requesting the Greeks to make an exchange that will reunite him with his daughter,[20] but Heywood stages Calchas persuading Cressida to instigate her own defection and "flye to safety" (*The Iron Age*, 3.1.70). After the duel between Ajax and Hector, Priam (via a herald) invites the Greeks (and Calchas) to a feast within the Trojan walls (2.5.69). Thersites provides a commentary as "Euery Troian Prince intertaines a Greeke, and so march two and two, discoursing, as being conducted by them into the Citty" (3.1.9.2). The banquet begins after Thersites deliberates over hiding his "hutch-backe" and playing "a spruce Courtier" in a soliloquy (3.1.10) at times very close to Richard III's soliloquy after wooing Anne (*Richard III*, 1.2.215).

> Lowd Musicke. A long table, and a banquet in state, they are seatted, a Troian and Greeke, Hecuba, Polixena, Cresida, and other Ladies waite, Calchas is present whispering with his daughter Cresida. (*The Iron Age*, 3.1.28.1)

Thirty-nine lines of bittersweet banter between the warring sides occur before Calchas speaks "*to* Cressida" (3.1.67). Calchas has only recently defected to the Greeks after receiving the oracle telling of the imminent destruction of Troy, and it is the fate of Troy that he is explaining to Cressida. Dramatically, he makes her choose whether she will "take Diomed and Liue, / or Troilus and thy death" (72), to which she immediately responds "Then Troilus and my ruine" (74). After only a few lines of insistence, Cressida chooses to live: "Diomed and you I'le follow, Troilus shun" (82). The dialogue immediately shifts to another part of the table where Troilus aggressively protests against Diomedes' claim of having "with his Launce dismounted Troilus" (114).

If QF *Troilus and Cressida* is correct in having Calchas onstage, then Diomedes' manner of ushering Cressida from the Greeks to her father and the action that might take place between Cressida, Calchas, and Diomedes during Ulysses' speech ("There's language in her eye") could be establishing many different ways of reading Cressida. Chaucer's emotional but essentially mute reunion could serve as a contrast to Ulysses' wanton reading of Cressida, highlighting the image of a heartbroken woman finding some comfort with her father. Caxton's version suggests that if Cressida met Calchas at the site of the duel in *Troilus and Cressida,* she could disappoint Calchas by not being particularly pleased to see him, and the strength that Cressida showed in rebuking Menelaus and Ulysses might continue with a mimed coldness to her father. *The Iron Age* also raises the possibility that some action might imply that Calchas is persuading Cressida to be receptive to Diomedes. Calchas assumes the role of pander when he hands his daughter over to Diomedes in the scene watched by Troilus, Ulysses, and Thersites (*Troilus and Cressida*, 5.2), but this can be prefaced by Calchas miming his consent, or even his encouragement, to the relationship as Cressida departs from the kissing Greeks. Again, the action would be a backdrop to Ulysses' speech and would deflect some of the blame for Cressida's betrayal of Troilus.

Calchas is included in the QF stage direction that brings on the Greek hierarchy in their vain attempt to visit Achilles (2.3.67.1). Because Calchas says nothing and is not referred to, he is often excluded in editions and productions from what would be his first appearance. Calchas's last scene includes only two short speeches, answering Diomedes' call and telling Diomedes that "she comes to you" (5.2.5). QF print "Enter Diomedes" (5.2.0), and most editors follow Hanmer in having Calchas speak his lines from within, further contributing to the editorial diminution of Calchas. Editors that cut Calchas from the two stage directions where he is included but mute (2.3.67.1, 4.6.0) and then have him speak to Diomedes from within (5.2), limit his visual appearance to his single speaking scene (3.3).

The lack of a direction for a speaking role is a relatively common oversight in QF, but the possibility of Calchas's final lines being spoken from within does seem dramatically viable, and most directors follow their editions in having him speak within.[21]

Increasing Calchas's appearances embodies another pull on Cressida, while cutting his stage presence can add responsibility to the characters of Cressida and Pandarus, both of which are desirable alternatives. *Truth Found Too Late* provides another opportunity to explore the effects of increasing Calchas's role. While it has been persuasively argued that Dryden altered Calchas's role in order to critique the English clergy of the 1670s,[22] the additions still offer insight into the character in *Troilus and Cressida*. Dryden rearranged the passage surrounding the duel between Ajax and Hector quite radically, and Calchas's reunion with Cressida presents the first obvious move toward an ending closer at times to *Romeo and Juliet* or *Antony and Cleopatra* than *Troilus and Cressida*. The Greeks' kissing Cressida is not staged but is reported by Pandarus to Troilus ("Never was a woman in Phrygia better kiss'd," *Truth Found Too Late*, 4.2.361), serving as the final humiliation that causes Troilus to reject Pandarus ("Hence from my sight," 4.2.85). This rewriting will be discussed again in relation to the duel and the final dialogue between Troilus and Pandarus, but Calchas's altered role is relevant here. Because *Truth Found Too Late* does not stage Cressida greeting the Greeks, her first scene after leaving Troilus is when she meets with Diomedes in the Greek camp, with Troilus, Ulysses, and Thersites watching. Dryden added dialogue for Calchas and Cressida before Diomedes arrives to court Cressida. Calchas instructs Cressida to "dissemble love to Diomede still" (4.2.254) as part of his ill-fated plot to return to Troy, and near the end of the play, as Diomedes and Troilus are about to fight, Calchas again reminds Cressida that Diomedes is their "Protector here" (5.2.189).

As in *The Iron Age* and Caxton's *Historyes of Troy*, Calchas's involvement in *Truth Found Too Late* lessens Cressida's responsibility for her actions, while also diminishing her independence and resourcefulness. Where Dryden's Calchas needs to remind Cressida twice that Diomedes' affection for her can be used to their advantage, in *Troilus and Cressida* she can be seen to arrive at (dare I say embrace) similar conclusions on her own. When Cressida calls Diomedes "my sweet guardian" (*Troilus and Cressida*, 5.2.8) she may be recognizing the similar need that Dryden's Calchas had expressed for a "Protector."

All of Cressida's scenes can be viewed as battles, and her introduction to the Greeks is an especially fierce one. The kisses and defiance in Chaucer and Caxton can suggest options for a mute Calchas and

Cressida reunion in *Troilus and Cressida*, but kissing and reproaches could also be seen to take place without Calchas. The present study endeavors to consider what has often been dismissed, but it does not necessarily seek to reverse the status of rejected and accepted options. The traditional editorial decisions to exclude Calchas from the scene and have Cressida and Diomedes exit before Ulysses' speech still have a strong case for editorial preference and stage viability. Perhaps it is best to conclude by questioning how such choices might be received in the rehearsal room: how many actresses playing Cressida would want Calchas onstage to share their scene with, and how many actors playing Ulysses would prefer Cressida to remain onstage during their "daughters of the game" speech? From the characters' point of view, how would these changes contribute to their vying for attention, sympathy, or even playing space? There seems to be at least room for exploring some of the options created by the indeterminacy of the text.

When I first met with Ian Judge to talk about my working as a textual advisor for the production, we spoke about some of the editorial debates. He was especially interested in the opportunity for Calchas to be onstage for Cressida's entrance into the Greek camp, and for Cressida to be present for Ulysses' speech later in the scene. The possibility of Calchas's presence for the scene led Judge to thinking about how Calchas's inclusion might contribute to Cressida's entrance, but he was also eager to make more use of the excellent actor Raymond Bowers who was playing Calchas. During the first blocking rehearsal of the scene, Judge decided to have Calchas approach Cressida as she entered through the gates of the Trojan Wall. Calchas moved from among the Greeks with outstretched arms to welcome his daughter, but she immediately walked away from him, reaffirming the attitude with which she heard the news of her exchange, "I have forgot my father" (4.3.22). Her scorn left Calchas somewhat stunned, and he remained onstage as a powerless and disappointed onlooker, but did not call attention to himself for the remainder of the scene as the Greeks kissed Cressida.

Although Cressida scorned her father's embrace, she was much more curious and accepting of the welcome she received from the Greeks. After a kindly, fatherly kiss by Agamemnon, and a somewhat too eager grandfatherly kiss by Nestor, which she squirmed away from, Cressida seemed to enjoy Achilles' lustful kiss, and Patroclus's two ravenous kisses. These kisses gave Cressida a kind of confidence and power, which fuelled her exchanges with Menelaus and Ulysses. Cressida was in the down stage left corner when Ulysses told her, "Never's my day, and then a kiss of you" (4.6.53), and Ulysses was

22. Ulysses and Cressida, with the Greeks and Calchas, back right, looking on, RST 1996, Judge. Photographer Malcolm Davies, Shakespeare Centre Library. Copyright Shakespeare Birthplace Trust.

standing center stage, with all the Greeks (and Calchas) behind him. Diomedes began to approach Cressida for his line "Lady, a word. I'll bring you to your father" (54), but neither Diomedes nor Cressida moved to exit as Nestor commented "A lady of quick sense" (55), and Ulysses responded with his damning description of her ("Fie, fie upon her!" 55). Ulysses stood with the large group at his back, and although he interpreted Cressida for their benefit, he delivered the speech directly at Cressida in a harsh and disgusted tone. Judge and Victoria Hamilton (Cressida) thought this to be a key moment and wanted the audience not only to see Cressida during the speech, but also to see her react to the speech. They believed that Ulysses' speech provided Cressida with a painful revelation about herself, and she registered a shocked understanding that her enjoyment of the kisses and her witty repartee branded her one of these "daughters of the game" (64). Her sexuality may be empowering, as in playing hard to get with Troilus, or enjoyable, as when kissing Troilus or even the hero Achilles, but she was unprepared for how men would read her sexuality. Ulysses' speech offered another opportunity to show Cressida's struggle to know herself, to know what she wanted, and to know how her actions would be interpreted by others.

After Ulysses' speech, Diomedes approached Cressida, and escorted her offstage. Because Calchas was onstage, Diomedes' earlier line, "Lady a word. I'll bring you to your father" was changed to "Lady a word. I'll bring you to your father's." In early rehearsals Calchas remained onstage for the duel between Ajax and Hector, but a few days before the first preview it was decided to have Calchas immediately follow Diomedes and Cressida offstage. I suggested that it might be desirable to have Calchas exit sooner, either sometime before Diomedes and Cressida, perhaps with Cressida, or with Diomedes and Cressida, as discussed above. These ideas were rejected because of the potential distraction that might be caused if Calchas drifted offstage earlier in the scene, and it was thought that Calchas would be intruding on the important image of Cressida and Diomedes exiting together.

While I presented the company with options either buried in the collation or not found in their editions, they used these options to create moments that I had not previously considered. A reunion (or a rejected reunion) between Calchas and Cressida before she was kissed, and Ulysses' speech being delivered directly to Cressida, are two examples of stagings I had not seriously considered, but which are certainly valid responses to the usually emended Folio directions. My idea that Cressida and Diomedes could talk with Calchas during Ulysses' speech about Cressida was never a serious possibility because of the way Judge staged the scene. There were no separate groups of characters preparing for the duel, and with all onstage paying close attention to Cressida, it would have been very awkward for Calchas to be present without watching her. Similarly, the claustrophobic blocking of the scene would have made it difficult for Cressida to be onstage without hearing Ulysses. Without ruling out the possibility of different character groupings, Judge's staging made use of the characters in a way that had a profound impact on the scene. Rather than sideline the characters whose presence has been questioned by editors, Judge made Calchas and Cressida pivotal in moments when nearly all productions have them offstage.

7

"They Call Him Troilus"

THE WAY THAT LEGENDARY AND HISTORICAL CHARACTERS IN *TROILUS and Cressida* extend off the page and stage and into the individual and collective significance of their names and stories challenges the critical taboo on wondering what happens at points in the story that are not dramatized. Throughout the different versions of the Trojan legend, authors comment on previous poets and historians who have told the story and expect (or demand) from their audience a certain awareness of the legend. Chaucer tantalizingly refers to the relatively unknown Lollius as his chief source, although Boccaccio's *Il Filostrato* appears to be the primary extant source of *Troilus and Criseyde*.[1] Lydgate and Caxton constantly extol and denigrate previous authors and translators, and Heywood cites past writers as part of the pleasure of reading his play:

> I presume the reading there of shall not prooue distastfull vnto any: First in regard of the Antiquity and Noblenesse of the History: Next because it includeth the most things of especiall remarke, which haue beene ingeniously Commented, and labouriously Recorded, by the Muses Darlings, the *Poets:* And *Times* learned remembrancers; the *Historiographers.* (*The Iron Age,* "To the Reader")

The connection and division between poetry and history is blurred throughout the legend, with commentary about the process of interpretation, translation, invention, and disputation at times taking precedence over the narrative.

Troilus and Cressida most obviously recognizes its own legendary tradition when the lovers and Pandarus pledge by their renowned and infamous traits (at the end of 3.2), but Ulysses' speeches about Cressida (4.6.55) and Troilus (4.6.98) offer a different kind of insight into the digesting of the historic and literary versions of the Trojan War.[2] Ulysses reduces Cressida into an open book for every "ticklish" (Q) / "tickling" (F, 4.5.62) reader, but how are we to read Ulysses and his motives? Ulysses' interpretation of Cressida can lead to questions about how the stories of Cressida have been read by poets and historians, and how the play confirms or revises these readings. When Ulysses describes Troilus to Agamemnon, he ends with a kind of reference note attributing the description to Aeneas. After observing the language of Cressida's physical presence, a very different character analysis is given of Troilus, not least because Ulysses fails to respond to Agamemnon's remark about Troilus's heavy looks. Ulysses somewhat disqualifies himself as a reader of Troilus, emphasizing that he is offering a reported account rather than his own insight of the character who presumably stands before him. It is especially appropriate that Ulysses' version of Aeneas's translation of Troilus refers to Troilus as "a second hope as fairly built as Hector" (4.6.112), since a long list of translators (Benoit, Guido, Chaucer, Lydgate, and Caxton) refer to Troilus as either a second Hector or second to Hector as a warrior.[3] Ulysses' comment about reading Cressida and his reporting Aeneas's translation of Troilus implies the kind of reading, reporting, and translating that occur throughout the transmission of the legend.

The occasion and content of Ulysses' speeches on Cressida and Troilus deserve some comparison at least because of their proximity, with only thirty-three lines between two relatively long descriptions of the title characters in their first scenes after they have been separated. Muir offers the readers of his edition a note that links the speeches perhaps too closely:

> Ulysses is given a character-sketch of Troilus to balance his previous description of Cressida; we must accept both, or neither; both prepare the way for the development of the two characters before the end of the play as slut and Trojan leader.[4]

What seems at first a connection gone too far becomes a condemnation and glorification that is at least contentious. As mentioned in the preceding discussion of Cressida's speech, the critical tradition of seeing Ulysses as an authorized judge has been overturned by more recent critics who emphasize that Ulysses has just been asked to beg a kiss (or two kisses in Johnson's emendation).[5] Whatever the relative objectivity or subjectivity of Ulysses' assessment of Cressida, it seems much more attributable to his personal view than the second-hand description he gives of Troilus.

Ann Thompson also links Ulysses' speeches about Cressida and Troilus, but adds Ulysses' brief description of Diomedes in claiming a possible connection with Chaucer:

> It is interesting that Chaucer interrupts his narrative at exactly this point to give us some formal and almost entirely external portraits of Diomede,

Criseyde, and Troilus in that order. If we include the sketch of Diomede given by Ulysses at the beginning of this scene

> 'Tis [Diomede], I ken the manner of his gait:
> He rises on the toe. That spirit of his
> In aspiration lifts him from the earth
>
> (14–16)

Shakespeare is like Chaucer in following this slightly ambiguous description with a fuller, detached, and (relatively speaking in Chaucer's case) condemnatory view of the heroine, and then finishing with a favourable passage about Troilus (Chaucer, 5.799, 806, 827).... The fact that Ulysses, the most practical of the Greeks, voices opinions which are authorial in the source may justify our seeing him as Shakespeare's spokesman, but I do not feel this can be felt consistently throughout the play, and even here the position is dubious.[6]

Not only does Ulysses echo Chaucer's narrator, but his assessments also have parallels with authorial moralizing throughout the legend. The condemnation of Cressida and the explicit or implicit generalization of her conduct as a comment on all women can be seen to be debated in many different versions of the story. Windeatt observes that Chaucer's abrupt two-line transition from Cressida's reunion with her father to Troilus's sorrow comes at the expense of cutting Boccaccio's "account of Criseida's wretched life, and forecast of her rapid change of heart."[7] While Lydgate quite harshly judges Cressida, he balks at condemning all women, and reproaches Guido, who "hath delyt to speke cursidly / Alwey of wommen through-out al his bok."[8] Lydgate not only takes offense at Guido's antifeminist remarks within the fiction, but supports the virtue of women with citations from legend and personal experience: "I dar wel affermen by the rode, / Ageyn oon badde ben an hundrid gode."[9] Even if Ulysses is taking up a narrator's position and expressing views found in the sources, such moral judgments are more likely to be one of a number of opinions, and rarely simple statements of agreed truth.

The contentiousness that characterizes the assessment of Cressida throughout the different versions of the legend contrasts with the more historical approach to Troilus. Just as elements of Ulysses' version of Aeneas's translation of Troilus can be traced through the sources to Dares, the duel between Ajax and Hector, which provides the opportunity for Agamemnon to question the identity of the heavy Trojan, is a complex mingling and rewriting of events in the legend. Each version of the Troilus and Cressida story differently alternates between the love and war plots in ways that emphasize and diminish characters and events. Chaucer, Lydgate, and Caxton have passages describing Cressida's entrance into the Greek camp, and Chapman, Lydgate, and Caxton have relevant passages about fights between Ajax and Hector.[10] Caxton and Lydgate defer to Chaucer for a more thorough and poetic version of the love story, but in their redactions of Guido (or in Caxton's case, his translation of Le Fevre's redaction of Guido), Lydgate and Caxton present the love story as one of many events in the war. While Chaucer gives some account of Antenor's capture and the truce that occasioned the exchange that reunited Calchas and Criseyde, no mention is made of Hector's actions during the truce (except when he protests against the exchange: "We vsen here no wommen forto selle" 4.182). Lydgate and Caxton both expand, at times considerably, on Guido's version of the events surrounding Cressida's exchange, but Guido, Le Fevre, Lydgate, and Caxton all follow the narrative structure first found in Benoit: Calchas's request for Cressida is followed by reports of Hector challenging Achilles to single battle, and then the story returns to the lovers' separation and Cressida being reunited with Calchas. Although it is Hector alone that goes to the Greek camp to challenge Achilles, the way the challenge is interspersed with Cressida being requested and delivered to the Greeks may have provided Shakespeare with the inspiration of having the heavy looking Troilus enter with Hector as Cressida exits before the duel between Ajax and Hector.[11] As Presson observes, Chaucer's "Troilus gets no closer to the Greek camp than the wall of Troy where, watching the road below, he expects Criseyde to appear (5.1191)."[12] Combining the duel with Cressida's exchange creates the opportunity for Troilus to visit the Grecian tents and be guided by Ulysses to see Cressida's betrayal.

The editorial problems surrounding Cressida's exit from the kissing Greeks are somewhat mirrored by the ambiguity of Troilus's entrance and position during Ulysses' speech about him ("They call him Troilus" 4.6.100). As discussed above, F has Ulysses' speech damning Cressida immediately followed by the directions "Exeunt / Enter all of Troy," and editors have questioned the placement of both the exeunt and entrance. A. P. Rossiter hears an aural pun in the cry recognizing "The Trojans' Trumpet," both announcing the entering Trojans and denouncing Cressida as "the Trojan strumpet."[13] Whether or not the pun was intentional, it emphasizes the stage action, especially if F indicates that Cressida exits as the trumpets sound and the Trojans enter. A simultaneous or consecutive exit and entrance has the newly separated lovers narrowly missing each other, but precisely how this is staged is questionable. While F has no dialogue between the exeunt and the entrance, another effect of the editorial tradition that has Cressida and Diomedes exit before Ulysses' speech is that Cressida's exit and Troilus's entrance are separated. Besides advancing Cressida's exit to before Ulysses' ten-line speech, most editors since Hanmer (1744) postpone the Trojans' entrance another two lines until immediately before Aeneas speaks, even further separating Cressida from the Trojans' entrance.

Taylor believes that F regains its manuscript authority at the point of the F exeunt after Ulysses' speech about Cressida (4.6.64.1),[14] but in the subsequent direction, F's expansion of Q's direction for "all of Troy" to enter has been considered incomplete by editors since Capell. Troilus is not named in the entrance, but he is noticed by Agamemnon (97), and is the subject of the important speech by Ulysses (99). While it is reasonable to assume that Troilus would be onstage for Agamemnon's question and Ulysses' response, he must at least enter before the combat, as he encourages Hector to "awake" (118) during the fight, and afterwards speaks with Ulysses (4.7.161). Perhaps Agamemnon's line asking "What Trojan is that same that looks so heavy?" (4.6.96) is the point at which Troilus could first enter, provoking Agamemnon's question. However, despite F's not naming Troilus, there seems little justification for mistrusting QF's direction that "all of Troy" enter together merely because Troilus is not named.

Taylor interprets F as including Troilus by considering Troilus one of the attendants (his edition reads: "Enter all of Troy: Hector [armed], Paris, Aeneas, Helenus, and attendants, among them Troilus" 4.6.65.1), but it seems strange that Troilus is considered an attendant while the mute Paris and Helenus are named in the F direction. Perhaps the named Trojans indicate a group, and Troilus's absence from the direction signals his being outside the group. Separating Troilus from the other Trojans could also help dramatize why Agamemnon questions his identity and notices his heavy looks. While a debate over the value of Troilus's presence for Ulysses' speech may not have the same significance as the staging possibilities surrounding Ulysses' speech about Cressida, there is at least a similar concern with how the lovers' presence can contribute to the lines which evaluate them. The failure to include Troilus is, if not terribly significant, at least ironic when comparing Ulysses' description of Troilus with his earlier assessment of Cressida: while F seems to have Cressida onstage for Ulysses' speech about her and Troilus offstage for Ulysses' speech about him, nearly all editors and most productions have the reverse.

The dialogue surrounding the duel between Hector and Ajax has many clues that suggest distances between characters and possible groupings of characters, but these clues are often ambiguous, and have been the subject of considerable debate and emendation. Immediately before Ulysses' F only line, "They are opposed already" (4.6.96), Capell added a detailed stage direction: "Ajax and Hector enter the lists, Aeneas and Diomed marshaling: Greeks range themselves on one Side, and Trojans upon the other, without." Malone shortened the direction to "Ajax and Hector enter the lists," and nearly all subsequent editors have included a similar direction. Dividing the armies on opposite sides of the stage certainly seems reasonable, but within such a staging there are important questions to ask about the position and movement of the characters.

Ulysses' F only line ("They are opposed already") comes in response to Agamemnon's observation that "The combatants being kin / Half stint their strife before their strokes begin" (4.6.95). The rhyming couplet allows Ulysses to change the focus and observe some action. Palmer defines "opposed" as "set face to face in the lists" (249). While Palmer's gloss seems probably the best interpretation, perhaps there are other ways of understanding the "opposed." The word appears nineteen lines earlier, where Ajax is referred to as the "knight opposed" (4.6.77) to Hector, meaning Ajax is the knight that Hector will fight. Rather than changing the subject to what he sees, Ulysses could be answering Agamemnon's comment about the kinship between Hector and Ajax. "They are opposed already" could mean that there is no remedying the situation of a "maiden battle" (89) since the cousins are "opposed already," or selected as opponents.

Some distance between spectators and the combatants seems implied by Agamemnon's instruction to Diomedes to "Go, gentle knight, / Stand by our Ajax" (90), and Ulysses' F only line referring to Ajax and Hector as "opposed already" (96). When Agamemnon asks about the Trojan "that looks so heavy" (4.6.97), he also suggests a distance between himself and Troilus, presumably the space that separates Greek from Trojan spectators. For the fight itself, QF have the direction for "Alarum" (4.6.115) preceding Agamemnon's remarks that "They are in action" (116). QF also agree that the trumpets cease after three cries of encouragement to the fighters, and before Diomedes' line "You must no more" (4.7.1). Most editors follow Rowe in rewriting QF's "Alarum" (4.6.115) as "Hector and Ajax fight," and also follow Capell's direction for the characters to enter the lists when Ulysses says "they are opposed already" (96). Nearly all editions, therefore, have Ulysses' description of Troilus (98–115) occur after the combatants are in the lists, with the fight beginning as the speech concludes. After the fight, Hector tells Aeneas to "call my brother Troilus to me" (4.7.38), again suggesting that Troilus and other spectators are some distance from the area of single combat.

Achil. A maiden battell then, Oh I perceiue you.
  Aga. Here is fir *Diomed*? go gentle knight,
Stand by our *Aiax*. As you and Lord *Eneas*
Confent vpon the order of their fight,
So be it, either to the yttermoft,
Or els a breath, the combatants being kin,
Halfe ftints their ftrife, before their ftrokes begin.
Vlisses: what Troyan is that fame that lookes fo heauy?
  Vlf. The yongeft fonne of *Priam*, a true knight,
Not yet mature, yet match'effe firme of word,
Speaking deeds, and deedleffe in his tongue,
Not foone prouok't nor beeing prouok't foone calm'd,
His heart and hand both open and both free.

                    I 2   For

The hiftory

For what he has he giues, what thinkes he fhewes,
Yet giues hee not till iudgement guide his bounty,
Nor dignifies an impare thought with breath;
Manly as *Hector*, but more dangerous,
For *Hector* in his blaze of wrath fubfcribes
To tender obiects, but he in heate of action,
Is more vindicatiue then iealous loue.
They call him *Troylus*, and on him erect,
A fecond hope as fairely built as *Hector*:
Thus faies *Æneas* one that knowes the youth,
Euen to his ynches: and with priuate foule
Did in great Illion thus tranflate him to me.   *Alarum,*
  Aga. They are in action.
  Neft. Now *Aiax* hould thine owne.
  Troy. *Hector* thou fleep'ft awake thee.
  Aga. His blowes are well difpo'd, there *Aiax*.   *trumpets*
  Diom. You muft no more.   *ceafe.*
  Æne. Princes enough fo pleafe you.

                                                        Q

23. "The youngest sonne," Q, F. Reproduced by permission of The Huntington
Library, San Marino, California.

Achil. A maiden battaile then ? O I perceiue you.
   Aga. Here is fir, *Diomed* : goe gentle Knight,
Stand by our *Aiax* : as you and Lord *Æneas*
Confent ▼pon the order of their fight,
So be it: either to the vttermoft,
Or elfe a breach: the Combatants being kin,
Halfe ftints their ftrife, before their ftrokes begin.
   Vlif. They are oppos'd already.
   Aga. What Troian is that fame that lookes fo heauy?
   Vlif. The yongeft Sonne of *Priam* ;
A true Knight ; they call him *Troylus* ;
Not yet mature; yet matchleffe, firme of word,
Speaking in deedes; and deedeleffe in his tongue ;
Not foone prouok't, nor being prouok't, foone calm'd ;
His heart and hand both open, and both free :
For what he has, he giues ; what thinkes, he fhewes ;
Yet giues he not till iudgement guide his bounty,
Nor dignifies an impaire thought with breath :
Manly as *Hector*, but more dangerous ;
For *Hector* in his blaze of wrath fubfcribes
To tender obiects ; but he, in heate of action,
Is more vindecatiue then iealous loue.
They call him *Troylus* ; and on him erect,
A fecond hope, as fairely built as *Hector.*
Thus faies *Æneas*, one that knowes the youth,
Euen to his inches : and with priuate foule,

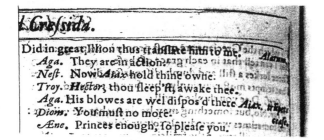

Crefsida.

Did in great *Ilion* thus tranflate him to me.
   Aga. They are in action.
   Neft. Now *Aiax* hold thine owne.
   Troy. *Hector*, thou fleep'ft, awake thee.
   Aga. His blowes are wel difpos'd there *Aiax.*
   Diom. You muft no more.
   Æne. Princes enough, fo pleafe you.

F

The most contentious direction in the passage comes before Ajax
announces that "Great Agamemnon comes to meet us here" (4.7.43),
where F reads, "Enter Agamemnon and the rest" (42.1, there is no direction in Q), although there has been no direction or clear indication that they had left the stage. Rowe's rewriting of the F's only direction to "Agamemnon and the rest come forward" merely alters the
vagaries of the F text while only partially determining the stage action. Interpreting the stage direction to signal a movement of onstage

characters rather than their entrance eliminates the need to add an exit for "Agamemnon and the rest," but several questions remain. If they are to come forward, when did they move back? Do they come forward from the position where they kissed Cressida, where they commented upon Troilus, where they watched the duel, or where they moved once the duel had finished? Crucial to a visualization of the movement is an attempt to define who "all the rest" includes. Is it merely the Greek hierarchy coming from their position as spectators to greet Hector, is it a movement of both Trojans and Greeks toward each other, or is it a mixed group of Trojans and Greeks moving into a central position that had stood for the lists?

Several editors have attempted to clarify the staging of QF's direction and Rowe's emendation, beginning with White's note in his 1865 edition.

> In Shakespeare's time . . . ["Agamemnon and the rest"] probably remained in the inner or second apartment of the stage, which was sometimes shut off by a curtain. The front of the stage was probably used to set out the lists; and at this speech by Ajax, Agamemnon and the other Greeks came forward into the arena of the fight.[15]

Since White suggests that the Greeks *remain* on the inner stage, he would apparently have the beginning of the scene played there, providing a more crowded, and perhaps more claustrophobic space for kissing Cressida. White's conjecture at least points to the possibility that the Greeks occupy an upstage position from the time they enter until Ajax says "Great Agamemnon comes to meet us here" (4.7.43). This staging also suggests one way to separate the Greeks throughout the scene from the Trojans, who presumably in White's staging occupy a position downstage from the Greeks.

White's conjecture can be extended to suggest an interesting staging for the early part of the scene. The audience and the Greeks could see Cressida and Diomedes as they cross the stage. QF have no entrance for Cressida and Diomedes, and while Capell first added a direction before Agamemnon asks "Is not yond Diomed with Calchas' daughter?" (4.6.14), nearly all editors follow Theobald in delaying their entrance several lines until immediately before Agamemnon asks "Is this the Lady Cressid?" (18). A later entrance is certainly viable as an announced entrance where Cressida and Diomedes are seen by the characters before they appear onstage, but White suggests another option. The use of the stage in a way that creates a distance allows an earlier entrance to have the different resonance available if the audience and the Greeks are watching Cressida being escorted some way to the enclave of the Greeks.

Just as White's notion of an inner stage is questionable, so too are conjectures about tents or other uses of the stage that postulate structures to emphasize a stage grouping or the arrangement of characters. When dialogue refers to physical structures or specific locations, such as tents, lists, battlefields, or walls, it may be that the structures are simply being described for the audience without anything on-stage representing tents, battlefields, lists, or walls. Nevertheless, exploring staging possibilities must still remain an important study.[16] When Aeneas reads Hector's challenge in the Greek council scene, the site of the duel is designated as "Midway between your tents and walls of Troy" (1.3.275), but the use of a tent or a partially enclosed space for the Greeks should not be too quickly dismissed.[17] Agamemnon ends the duel scene (or scenes, according to Taylor's argument discussed below) by instructing the peers of Greece to "go to my tent" (4.7.155). He presumably means a tent not in sight, and some distance from the field of combat where the duel takes place, but he could also refer to a door dressed as a tent.

Kenneth Palmer also offers a staging of the duel that emphasizes the separation of the armies in an attempt to justify F's direction "Enter Agamemnon and the rest":

> Whereabouts on his own stage Shakespeare supposed the list and the spectators to be, it is uncertain, unless we assume (as producers nowadays for *Richard II*) that the spectators are on an upper stage and the lists on the platform. In that case, the Greeks would go off, and re-enter on the main stage. F would have been right in retaining *Enter*, but wrong in failing to give an *Exeunt* (or indeed, any indication of *Above*). However, all this assumes that we know where (and how) the play as we have it was played; and we do not.[18]

Palmer's proposal for the use of the upper stage comes with a significant warning, implying that we cannot trust Qa's title page assertion that the play was performed "at the Globe." The notion that Shakespeare was writing specifically for a space different from the Globe may be a possibility, but how a performance at the Globe would be envisioned or enacted differently than one at another venue remains unclear. While the size of the stage, the access to the stage, or the lack of an above or a discovery space could limit staging possibilities, it still seems worthwhile to offer such conjectures as Palmer's and White's based on what little we know or can assume about the Globe.

Palmer's note remains an interesting theory, but he takes no further editorial action in adding stage directions for the use of an above. The conjecture has its merits though, separating the groups of characters and placing the spectators in an ideal position for viewing the fight. Without expecting too much realism and without wanting to ban Greeks from ever using spaces above, it is still worth noting two objections to Palmer's staging: A balcony is somewhat at odds with the earlier description of the duel's location as "between our tents and walls of Troy," and observers on the balcony could also suggest the Trojan Walls, certainly not the place for the Greeks to observe the fight. The advantages of separating the observers by using a balcony was, however, employed by Heywood in *The Iron Age*, which has the direction for some of the Trojans to enter "aboue vpon the wals" (*The Iron Age*, 2.5.0) to see "the warlicke combate 'twixt" (2.5.3) Hector and Aiax Telemon. Heywood's play is much more specific about the fight, with a stage direction that makes clear that the lists are onstage: "Heralds on both side: the two Champions Hector and Aiax appeare betwixt the two Armies" (2.5.21.1). Agamemnon urges "None presse too neere the Champions" (22), and Troilus gives instructions for the "Heralds on both sides, keep the souldiers back" (23). With this scene in place, there are still 29 lines (24–53) before the fight commences: Hector gives a speech very close to the one in *Troilus and Cressida* where he wished he could divide Ajax so that he could spill only the Grecian blood (*The Iron Age*, 2.5.26–35, *Troilus and Cressida*, 4.7.4–22). Heywood's Hector would rather Achilles were his opponent, but Ajax claims he will prove "equal both in strength and minde" (*The Iron Age*, 2.5.52) to Achilles, boasting of his shield, sword, and javelin. The fight that follows is described in an elaborate stage direction:

> Alarum, in this combate both hauing lost their swords and Shields, Hector takes up a grat peace of a Rocke, and casts at Aiax; who teares a young Tree vp by the rootes, and assailes Hector, at which they are parted by both armies. (2.5.53)

The "Alarum" with which the direction begins recalls the "Alarum" in QF *Troilus and Cressida* at the point where the fight would presumably begin, and the *Troilus and Cressida* direction may be a shorthand indication of what would be elaborated on in rehearsal and performance. While there is no evidence that the fight in *Troilus and Cressida* was nearly as dramatic as in *The Iron Age*, or used such props as a "grate peace of Rock" or a "young Tree," other versions of the duel suggest interesting staging possibilities.

Troilus and Cressida and *The Iron Age* differently evoke the rich tradition of characters, themes, and incidents available in the different versions of the encounters between Hector and Ajax. Chapman, Lydgate, and Caxton all include fights between Ajax and Hector, either in an arranged duel, in the field, or both.[19] In the second scene of *Troilus and Cressida,* Alexander tells Cressida that Ajax "coped Hector in the battle and struck him down" (1.2.103). This field meeting causes Hector to become angry, fast and wake, chide Andromache, strike his armourer, and rage into battle. No reference is made to this earlier encounter at the duel, but the blood relationship between Hector and Ajax is an issue at both meetings.

Alexander's report provides a picture of Hector's domestic reaction to the battlefield encounter, but in Caxton and Lydgate there are crucial military consequences. Ajax dissuades Hector from pursuing an advantage that could have won the war for Troy. Caxton's field battle between Ajax and Hector is particularly relevant to the duel in *Troilus and Cressida* because Caxton sets up the moment as an example and a rationalization of Hector's tragic failing: "the Trojans had vittorye of alle the Grekes," with Hector "at the above of his enemyes and myght have slayn hem all," but as he was fighting with Ajax "they spak to geder and therby Hector knewe that he was his cosyn germaine."[20] In *Troilus and Cressida,* Hector's description of Ajax as "cousin-german to great Priam's seed" (4.7.5) makes it likely that Shakespeare knew the passage in Caxton where Ajax persuades Hector to "cesse the bataill for that day and that the Trojans shold leve the Grekes in pees."[21] Caxton concludes the episode by emphasizing that

> this was the cause wherfore the Trojans lost to have the victorye . . . And therfore Virgile sayth, Non est misericordia in bello, that is to saye, There is no mercy in bataill. A man ought not to take misericorde but take the victorye who may gete hit.[22]

Heywood stages this meeting in battle between Ajax and Hector as the scene following Patroclus's death. Hector enters accompanied by Paris, Troilus, and Aeneas "with burning staues and fire-bals" (*The Iron Age,* 3.4.0), and "Al the Troians" crying "strike, stab, wound, kill, tosse firebrands, and make way" (3.4.1), but Ajax enters and immediately pleads with Hector "this day leave thine advantage" (3.4.14). The scene and act end with Ajax remaining onstage after the Trojans' exit, making clear that "Greece was this day / At her last cast, had they pursude aduantage" (3.4.26).

While *Troilus and Cressida* does not dramatize the field battle nor emphasize its significance as in *The Iron Age,* some of its importance is infused into the arranged duel and into Hector's character throughout the play. Ulysses' speech describing Troilus is significant not only for what is said about Troilus, but also as an important comment about Hector. In his comparison of Troilus to Hector, Ulysses makes the crucial point that "Hector in his blaze of wrath subscribes / To tender objects" (4.6.108). Combined with Ajax's response to Hector stopping the duel ("Thou art too gentle and too free a man," 4.7.23), the duel provides an occasion for twice voicing the same characteristic in Hector that Caxton observed. When Troilus chastises Hector as they prepare for the play's battlefield finale, Hector's "vice of mercy" (5.3.37) becomes a reiteration of what the audience has learned of Hector immediately before and after the duel.[23] Troilus complains to Hector that

> When many times the captive Grecian falls
> Even in the fan and wind of your fair sword,
> You bid them rise and live.
>
> (5.3.40)

Hector's answer, "O 'tis fair play" (5.3.43), significantly prefaces his actions during the battlefield scenes, where he pauses in his first fight with Achilles (5.6.14), perhaps abandons fair play in his pursuit of the sumptuous armour (5.6.27), and finally appeals vainly to Achilles, "I am unarmed. Forgo this vantage Greek" (5.9.9). From his first speech to his last, the great warrior Hector can be seen attempting to avoid fighting, or at least to be arranging fights that can be halted for chivalric reasons. After first arguing that Helen should be returned (2.2.16), Hector changes his mind and announces he has issued the challenge to single combat (2.2.207). But when the combat actually occurs, only "half Hector" comes to fight his cousin. Within the context of this study, it is important to ask how the textual ambiguity surrounding the single combat between Hector and Ajax can generate possible stage images that can confirm, contradict, and expand our understanding of the characters and the situation. How does the scene change if there is more ceremony than ferocity, if political maneuvering overwhelms the military spectacle? While such questions about staging choices may seem most appropriate in a rehearsal room, they can also be pursued in a study of the possibilities arising from the text's failure to offer an authoritative stage picture.

In contrast to the alarum and the dialogue that give only vague clues to the staging of the duel in *Troilus and Cressida*, *The Iron Age* not only has the stage directions quoted above, but also has a woodcut on the title page that depicts the duel between Ajax and Hector. The woodcut agrees with the stage direction that the combatants "appeare betwixt the two Armies" (*The Iron Age*, 2.4.22), and the woodcut depicts these armies as soldiers with spears watching from behind and around the walls of Troy and through the Grecian tents. The lack

The Iron Age:

Containyning the Rape of *Hellen* : The siege of *Troy*: The Combate betwixt *Hector* and *Aiax* : *Hector* and *Troilus* slayne by *Achilles* : *Achilles* slaine by *Paris* : *Aiax* and *Vlisses* contend for the Armour of *Achilles* : The Death of *Aiax*, &c.

Written by THOMAS HEYVVOOD.

Aut prodesse solent audi Delectare.

Printed at *London* by *Nicholas Okes*. 1632.

24. Title page of Heywood's *Iron Age*, 1632. Reproduced by permission of The Huntington Library, San Marino, California.

of any indication of a stage distances the woodcut from firm conclusions about how the scene looked in the theater, but the division of
the armies, the depiction of walls and tents, and the foregrounding
of the combatants and selected other principals at least offer a few
staging possibilities. Foakes interprets Heywood's comment in the
epistle that *The Iron Age* was "Acted by two Companies, upon one
Stage at once" to imply that there were resources for making "possible a decent shot at showing the two armies . . . watching Hector and
Ajax fight."[24] Agamemnon's and Troilus's comments, quoted above,
requesting the soldiers not to "presse too near" (*The Iron Age*, 2.5.22)
and to "keep the soldiers back" (23) add the impression of a stage
crowded with anxious soldiers. In either *The Iron Age* or *Troilus and
Cressida* the duel could have been an opportunity to use extras to create different settings from savage chaos to absurd chivalry.

Editors and critics have referred to similar scenes in Shakespeare's
other plays to help visualize the way the duel could be staged. Palmer
and Taylor draw very different parallels between the staging of the
single combats in *Richard II* (1.3) and *Troilus and Cressida*. Palmer (in
a parenthetical remark, quoted above) makes the seemingly insup-
portable assertion that modern directors of *Richard II* have "the spectators on an upper stage and the lists on the platform."[25] Taylor, however, alludes to the scene in *Richard II* to strengthen his theory,
detailed below, that the dialogue in both *Richard II* and *Troilus and
Cressida* "clearly suggests that [the lists] are offstage."[26] The alternatives for placing the lists, the combatants, and the spectators in ways
that differently emphasize or diminish the importance of the groups
are also apparent in Andrew Gurr's comment about the stage history
of *Richard II:* "the scene which receives the most variable handling is
1.3, the combat scene."[27] The same may be said for the duel scene in
Troilus and Cressida. The theatrical variations are not merely a result
of embellishments or departures from the texts, but the textual ambiguity invites seemingly contradictory conclusions about staging the
fights.

C. Walter Hodges's drawing of "a possible Elizabethan staging" of
the *Richard II* duel scene (1.3) shows all the spectators on the same
level, and the placement of the marshal signifies that the fight will
take place between the pillars.[28] Eliminating Richard's "chair of
state," the drawing still suggests that the decorated pillars and the
grouping of the actors behind their knight would provide a sufficient
separation and identification of the armies, and the juxtaposition of
groups of fighters, marshals, and spectators could all be similarly
staged in *Troilus and Cressida*.[29] The use of the doors as the gathering
points for the armies could be utilized to extend the stage to accom-

modate more soldiers if the doors were open. The doors and pillars might also be decorated to suggest either Grecian tents or Trojan walls, separating the onstage spectators from the combatants either before, during, or after the fight, and F's direction "Enter Agamemnon and the rest" may signal a movement from within a tent, a doorway, or some other peripheral space.

Chapman, Caxton, Lydgate, and Heywood all give vivid descriptions of the armor and weapons used in the fights between Ajax and Hector.[30] The variety of horses, spears, swords, shields, stones, and trees referred to in the legend would have been known to Shakespeare and his actors, but QF's entrance for Ajax "armed" (4.6.0) is the only hint of costume, and the alarums and the dialogue that signal the fight do little to clarify what kind of action takes place. Lydgate and Caxton (but not Chapman) relate how the kinship of Ajax and Hector, either consciously or instinctively, prevents mortal combat between the cousins, but especially in Lydgate the fighting is allowed to become quite fierce ("lyke Tygres or lyownes"[31]) before breaking off.

In *Troilus and Cressida*, Aeneas informs the Greeks before the fight that because "Ajax is half made of Hector's blood . . . half Hector stays at home" (4.6.85). Achilles and Agamemnon then expect "a maiden battle" (89) where both combatants "Half stint their strife before their strokes begin" (95). While Achilles may be somewhat relieved that Ajax will not receive too much glory from the fight, Agamemnon could be expressing true disappointment that the duel might not, and because of Hecuba's letter (5.1.36) ultimately does not, have the anticipated effect of inciting Achilles into battle. Despite all the dialogue anticipating and describing Hector's reservations about the single combat, a fight does occur. The play and the scene alternate between the heroic and the ironic in a way that allows, and even encourages consideration about how the duel can either be a short nonevent, or an extended stage action with some competitive combat.

Troilus's encouraging Hector to a fiercer combat with his shout "Hector, thou sleep'st! Awake thee!" (4.6.118) provides an almost immediate example of the difference between the brothers highlighted in Ulysses' previous speech describing Troilus ("Manly as Hector, but more dangerous," 107). Troilus's call for Hector to "awake" is also crucial for determining the action of the combat, confirming that Hector is not fully committed to the fight. While Hector was not able to sustain his objection to the war in the Trojan council scene (2.2), the eventual outcome of the duel with which he intends to rouse the Greeks ends with "embracement" (4.7.32). For all Ulysses' plotting in selecting Ajax to oppose Hector, it is Hector who seems in control of the duel, ultimately providing an occasion to display not his military prowess, but his chivalry, gentleness (as Ajax calls it, 4.7.24), or, as Caxton's citation of Virgil terms it, "misericorde."

Barry Nass has charted a critical history of the duel, noting that "Reuben A. Brower speaks for the majority [of critics] when he observes, with disappointment, that 'the effect of the scene is lamely anti-climactic.'"[32] Nass also cites Seltzer's similar view, influential if only because it appears in the introductions to his Signet edition and the Signet Complete Works, that the staging of the fight is

> a red herring for the director, because this combat, when it finally happens, is dramatically uninteresting compared to other portions of the scene—Ulysses' enthusiastic praise of Troilus, for example. . . . If the director plans the moves of his actors to emphasize the apparent climax of the episode, he will find that the real interest of the scene has shifted elsewhere, that the point of the action is not what he thought it was, and that whatever this scene should be, it is not a scene of pageantry.[33]

Nass goes some way toward countering these arguments from a critical perspective, seeing the duel, and especially the "blended" Ajax as offering another of the play's instances of dividing the self, as Cressida partitions herself ("One eye yet looks on thee / But with my heart the other eye doth see," 5.2.109) and Troilus divides her in her final scene ("This is and is not Cressid," 5.2.149). Susan Snyder presents a middle ground, interpreting the duel as important precisely because it is another example of thwarted expectation in the play:

> if Hector's challenge and the abortive joust with Ajax lead to nothing in terms of consequent events, they lead *into* the ways of this play very directly. The rhythm of buildup followed by collapse into anticlimax is in a sense what *Troilus and Cressida* is all about.[34]

The duel provides an opportunity for Hector's personal sense of honor and the Trojan pageantry to confront directly Greek manipulation (Ulysses), military lunacy (Ajax), and inflated pride (Achilles). Shakespeare's invention of the rigged lottery has Ulysses setting up the duel as a political charade, and the duel itself becomes an opportunity, like much of the play, for a parody of ceremony. Thersites' reported image of Ajax going "up and down the field asking for himself" (3.3.237)[35] anticipates a burlesque duel. The opening lines of the duel scene, where the unanswered trumpet deflates the vaulted language with which Ajax requests a parley to Hector (4.5.7–11) is not too far from Thersites' performance of "the pageant of Ajax" (3.3.262). Ralph Berry comments that the chivalric pretensions are now too openly discredited to be anything but an invitation to stage business,[36] and the by-play with *trumpet* provides some sour notes. Ajax's command to his trumpeter has to be read twice to be disbelieved:

> Now Crack thy lungs, and split thy brazen pipe.
> Blow, villain, till thy spheréd bias cheek
> Outswell the colic of puff'd Aquilon.
> Come, stretch thy chest, and let thy eyes spout blood;
> Thou blowest for Hector.
>
> (4.5.7)

"No trumpet answers" is the stage direction, voiced by Ulysses, and silence is the best comment on Ajax's rhetoric. Then follows Cressida's entrance. Again, for all the lumpish gestures of gallantry made by the Greeks, this is a cartoon of chivalry, Hanoverians viewed by Gillray. . . . Chivalry appears in better shape for the combat, with its preliminaries and aftermath. Greek and Trojans rise to a self-conscious level of chivalric emulation: the word knight (used six times in the scene) helps define the event.[37]

The extent to which the "chivalric pretensions" in the dialogue are transformed into stage business will go some way in determining the tone of the scene. Aeneas's F only speech (4.5.145), which ends the scene immediately before the duel, leaves the word "chivalry" hanging in the air as the Greeks enter for the combat. Ritson, Malone, and Tannenbaum believe that Aeneas's speech is part of a theatrical interpolation.[38] If the lines were added by Shakespeare or the actors, or indeed if they were cut, the alterations could signal different staging choices that coincide with the added or cut dialogue. While the F only dialogue is just five lines, it may have been helpful to cover some preparations for the duel scene, such as readying and arranging extras or stage decorations. Even without such speculation about stage business, the dialogue itself alludes to making "ready" (4.5.144) and "chivalry" (145), and adds to the expectations, however fulfilled or thwarted, that the single combat would be an event replete with pageantry and ceremony.

Charles Edelman has reassessed the possibility of "the combat, even though sporting, as being spectacular and exciting to witness."[39] With reference to accounts of fifteenth- and sixteenth-century tournaments for examples of single combats, he argues that the fight between Ajax and Hector was "a 'foot combat,' possibly 'at barriers,' and fought either with swords or axes."[40] Edelman agrees with Palmer that when Aeneas asks if the fight is to be "to the edge of all extremity" (4.6.70), he is enquiring if they will fight *à l'outrance*, "the accepted medieval term for a combat with sharpened rather than bated

weapons."[41] Similarly, when Agamemnon instructs Diomedes to confer with Aeneas whether the fight will be "either to the uttermost /
Or else a breath" (4.6.93), Edelman argues that "the term 'uttermost'
. . . in this context clearly means not 'to the death,' but 'until one of
the combatants is unable to continue.'"[42] Regardless of these quali-
fications, Edelman believes that "far from being a lacklustre affair this
tournament foot combat between Hector and Ajax might be a breath-
taking display."[43]

An antidote to the wealth of images associated with the fights between Ajax and Hector in the sources and analogues is Taylor's view
that the stage directions and dialogue in *Troilus and Cressida* indicate
that the fight takes place offstage. Like Palmer and White, Taylor
wants to interpret literally F's entrance for "Agamemnon and the
rest," and not rewrite it as an onstage movement. He therefore adds
an exit for Ajax, Diomedes, Hector, and Aeneas in the middle of
Agamemnon's line "Or else a breath. The combatants being kin"
(4.6.94), arguing that

> Capell's arrangement, followed by all editors (usually reduced to "Ajax
> and Hector enter the lists"), puts the lists on stage; the remainder of the
> scene (see following notes) clearly suggests they are off stage, as in *Richard
> II* (1.3). It also seems preferable to mark the direction here, with the re-
> maining line and a half addressed to Ulysses: this allows an interval which
> makes "They are oppos'd already" more credible.[44]

What Taylor finds problematic about Ulysses' F only line, "They are
opposed already," is why Ulysses would "say this if the opponents were
clearly visible both to Agamemnon and the audience."[45] He concludes that Ulysses' line is "wholly superfluous unless the action in
question takes place offstage."[46] Furthermore, he questions why
Agamemnon should "notice 'that [Trojan] that looks so heavy' if
preparations for the crucial combat were in progress onstage. Could
an audience be expected to attend properly to Ulysses' long description of Troilus if such preparations were going on behind him?"[47]
These important questions will be explored in some depth in relation to the different versions of the speech in Q and F, and in the theater history of the passage that follows, but first it is important to see
how Taylor edits other moments in the scene.

After Ulysses' description of Troilus, Taylor retains the QF
"Alarum" (4.6.115) as an indication of the fight beginning offstage.
Before the QF direction for "Trumpets Cease" Taylor clears the stage,
and begins a new scene with the entrance of "Hector and Ajax, fight-
ing, and Aeneas and Diomedes interposing" (4.7.0.1) before the
"Trumpets cease" and Diomedes says "You must no more" (4.7.1).

Taylor's justification for the scene break again relates to the F only entrance for "Agamemnon and the rest," and the need to have the group exit sometime after Agamemnon's line "His blows are well disposed. There, Ajax!" (4.6.119). Taylor offers the following textual notes for the passage:

> 4.6.119 *Exeunt*] . . . The following dialogue seems to presume their absence. (Both Q and F frequently omit exit directions.) The only motive for an exit is an excited move closer to the lists, which must therefore be presumed to be off stage (see note to 4.6.94.1 [quoted above]) The exeunt could be naturally managed in stages, a few characters at a time crowding forward and off during [the lines which follow Agamemnon's "They are in action"].

> 4.7] The exeunt and entrance apparently required at this point result in a clearing of the stage and a change of location (though little or no time has elapsed) and so represent a proper scene-break.

> 4.7.0.1–2 *Enter . . . interposing*] Hector and Ajax must enter fighting, in order to explain their movement from off to on stage (with imaginary lists).

> 4.7.0.2 *trumpets cease*] . . . It seems likeliest that the ambiguous QF marginal position indicates that the trumpets cease between Agamemnon's speech and Diomedes'; but it would be most natural for the trumpets to bridge the proposed scene-break, stopping only when Diomedes and Aeneas signal or move to stop the fighting.[48]

Whether the dialogue after the "Alarum" presumes the combatants' absence, rather than simply a distance between the spectators and the fight, must remain questionable. Taylor's arrangement would, however, allow for a certain level of heightened drama, with the audience having only the spectators' comments as a clue to how the fight was progressing. The entrance of the characters fighting followed by the spectators could also be used to show the fight being somewhat out of control, similar to the picking up the tree and stone in *The Iron Age*. Conversely, if most of the fighting takes place offstage, it could add to the thwarted expectations of the event and invite the audience to question their desire to see the fight. Perhaps the most relevant change for the present discussion is how the imaginary offstage lists would alter Ulysses' speech about Troilus, relieving the speech from the distractions of onstage preparations for the fight. While Taylor's proposals may not be altogether convincing, they at least provide an opportunity to question the differing effects of foregrounding or diminishing the preparations for, and the enactment of the duel.

Taylor's interpretation of the F only entrance for "Agamemnon and the rest" requires several more emendations, and his edited text reads:

HECTOR
 Aeneas, call my brother Troilus to me,
 And signify this loving interview
 To the expecters of our Trojan part:
 Desire them home.   *[Exit Aeneas]*
      Give me thy hand, my cousin.
 I will go eat with thee, and see your knights.
   Enter Agamemnon and the rest: Aeneas, Ulysses
   Menelaus, Nestor, Achilles, Patroclus, Troilus, and
   others
AJAX
 Great Agamemnon comes to meet us here.
HECTOR *(to Aeneas)*
 The worthiest of them, tell me name by name.

                (4.7.38)

Taylor argues that "Aeneas is sent to fetch the others who (according to our proposed reconstruction, and as the instruction itself implies) are off stage."[49] While the instruction can imply that Troilus is off-stage, there is, again, just as much reason for supposing Troilus to be onstage but at a distance from Hector. Furthermore, Aeneas was only instructed to call Troilus to Hector and to send the other Trojans home. Hector does not request that Aeneas fetch the Greeks, and the curious entrance for "Agamemnon and the rest" has been inter-preted by some editors (Rowe, Pope, Theobald, Hanmer, Warburton, Johnson, Kittredge, and more recently Evans and Muir) to refer only to the Greeks. Aeneas could be sent to one side of the stage to relay Hector's message to the Trojans while the Greeks, seeing the fight has ended, either enter or come forward, perhaps being similarly sum-moned by Diomedes. Taylor is surely right in having Hector's speech directed "to Aeneas" when he asks to be told "name by name" the ap-proaching Greeks (except Achilles), but what Aeneas does between Hector's request to call Troilus (4.7.38) and when Aeneas identifies Menelaus (in his next speech, 4.7.60) is debatable. When Hector ac-cepts Ajax's invitation to go to the "Grecian tents" (4.7.35), his speech (ending "I will go eat with thee, and see your knights," 42) could in-dicate that Hector is on the point of exiting. Ajax's answer ("Great Agamemnon comes to meet us here," 43) might interrupt him, stress-ing that it is "here" where the initial meeting will take place.

The Greeks' meeting with Hector signals another of the play's many identity parades, highlighting the ways that the play and the scene repeatedly ask questions about how individuals are known and assessed. Ulysses' speeches about Cressida and Troilus not only provide comments about the title characters, but as the consummate politician and tactician, Ulysses' views must always be questioned in light of his possible motives. The tenuous nature of evaluating others is emphasized by Ulysses' having been scorned by Cressida, and by his attributing the translation of Troilus to Aeneas. The instability of the stage directions surrounding the speeches adds to the multiplicity of staging alternatives and character grouping that contribute to the sympathy and credibility of the valuer and the valued. The textual problems with Troilus's speech are particularly appropriate, as there are not only staging questions, but variants in the dialogue that offer alternatives of how Troilus is named by Ulysses.

Pope was the first editor to omit the F only "they call him Troilus," and Knight (ed. 1841) offered the explanation that the words should be omitted because they are repeated later in the speech. Although most editors have agreed that F's repetition of the phrase "they call him Troilus" is a mistake, there have been different theories offered to explain the F reading. Chambers proposed the influential hypothesis that the words "they call him Troilus" were originally written at the beginning of the speech, as printed in F, but Shakespeare "then reserved them for a point later in the speech, replacing them by 'a true knight,' and made a mark of deletion which the printer failed to observe."[50] Greg mostly agreed, confidently stating that F includes "an unquestionable false start," and concluded that because "Q duly omits the cancelled words proves that it was printed from a properly edited manuscript."[51] These strong words have become the linchpin for the argument that prefers Q as copy text, but several voices have been raised in opposition.

James Nosworthy, while agreeing that Q is "obviously correct," was unconvinced that F preserves a false start. Instead, he offered the theory that F's extra "'they call him Troilus' was added to the foul papers by Shakespeare to indicate an intended cut" of the lines between the repeated phrase. He argued that the central lines of the speech are

> expendable in the sense that they relate to an aspect of Troilus, his military prowess, which is not fully developed in the play as it stands. Ulysses' lines, admitting the cut . . . would clearly be quite adequate to the presumed needs of the revision.[52]

Honigmann turns this argument on its head, suggesting that the lines between the repeated phrase "were a later insertion, added to point forward to the sequel, where Troilus would naturally figure more as a warrior than as a lover."[53] Honigmann questions why "so elaborate a character-sketch, conventional enough when a character appears for the first time, should be given near the end of the play."[54] Both Nosworthy and Honigmann have elaborate theories of the occasion for revision that will become relevant again in the chapter on Pandarus's final speech, but their proposals offer important views about the purpose and expendability of the speech that will be explored in the stage history which follows.

While rejecting the first shot theory, Nosworthy still believes that F mistakenly prints "they call him Troilus" twice, but Honigmann is ambiguous about whether or not the addition of the lines purposefully include the repeated phrase. Taylor, however, argues

> that the speech could reasonably be left as the Folio gives it, with "They call him Troilus" repeated—just as Troilus (in 5.11) repeats "Hector is dead," or as Pandarus, in the course of identifying for Cressida's benefit another Trojan warrior, repeats "That's Helenus" [1.2.215, 216]. There is also a simple theatrical motive for adding the Folio's half line at the beginning of Ulysses' speech: without it, some or even many spectators may not know who Ulysses is talking about for the first twelve lines of the speech. The stage is full of Greeks and Trojans; Agamemnon identifies the object of his inquiry only as "that same that lookes so heavy"; unless Troilus is hamming dreadfully, the identification need not be self evident to every spectator—the more so if, as I will argue below, Troilus and the others are all looking offstage at this moment.[55]

Honigmann objects, arguing that Troilus would be immediately recognized as the subject of Ulysses' speech "since (i) Troilus is the one Trojan with a reason to 'look so heavy,' and (ii) his extreme youth has been stressed throughout [1.2.78, 108, 111, 231, etc.]."[56] Certainly there are many ways to stage the moment where the object of Agamemnon's inquiry could be made perfectly clear, and even the simplest pointing during Agamemnon's question or Ulysses' response, or a blocking that isolated Troilus, could resolve any confusion.

Taylor's appeal to the other repeated phrases may be comparing very different instances of repetition, but he does make the significant point that in a speech identifying Troilus, the repeated phrase draws attention to their watching and naming him, and underscores the reported nature of the identification. In attempting to understand how the phrase "they call him Troilus" is being used, it is helpful to look at a similar phrase earlier in the play, as well as the possible sources for Ulysses' speech. Alexander identifies Ajax for Cressida in a speech that closely parallels Ulysses' first use of the phrase in F:

> The noise goes this: there is among the Greeks
> A lord of Trojan blood, nephew to Hector;
> They call him Ajax.
>
> (1.2.12)

The pattern of giving lineage, chivalric title (lord or knight) and name is similarly repeated in the F reading of the beginning of Ulysses' speech: "The yongest Sonne of Priam; / A true Knight; they call him Troilus."[57] The second instance of the phrase ("They call him Troilus") in F (and the only instance in Q) is part of the comparison between Troilus and Hector: "They call him Troilus, and on him erect / A second hope as fairly built as Hector." When Cressida earlier tells Pandarus that "there's no comparison" (1.2.60) between the brothers, Palmer provides what must surely be a somewhat ironic note contradicting Cressida by giving examples of the brothers being compared in Chaucer, Caxton, and Lydgate.[58] As noted above, the comparison of Troilus to Hector, and especially his being second to Hector, can be traced from Dares through the medieval translations, histories, and poems of the legend, but in Lydgate's version the comparison includes a close parallel to the phrase repeated in F: "a knyght, / The seconde Ector for his worthyness, / He called was."[59]

Alexander's naming Ajax and Lydgate's description of Troilus may offer support for the first shot theory, with Shakespeare beginning Ulysses' speech with a structure similar to Alexander's description of Ajax, before finding the phrase "they call him Troilus" useful in rewriting Lydgate. Bevington rightly warns that while theories, especially Chamber's, about the repetition may be used in trying to determine the relationship of Q to F, the repeated phrase is not "a strong instance upon which to generalize about the prior composition of F throughout."[60] More profitable than such theorizing is the guidance these parallels offer to the ways Ulysses' speech can work. F's first "they call him Troilus" is more purely an identification, and part of the first lines of the speech which name Troilus. In F's second "They call him Troilus," the comparison with Hector stresses that the Trojans "erect on him a second hope as fair as Hector." The phrase distances Ulysses and Agamemnon from the Trojan view, amplifying the perspective of the speech, where Ulysses merely reports Aeneas's views of Troilus.

Moments before Agamemnon questions Troilus's identity, Aeneas and Achilles enact one of the play's many naming rituals ("If not

Achilles, sir, / What is your name," 4.6.77). In a play so concerned with identity and reputation, F's repeated "they call him Troilus" should be a welcome underscoring to the action of pointing at and translating Troilus. Q's single instance of "they call him Troilus" can, however, still retain some of the significance of F's repetition. Q and all editions, excepting F and Taylor, have the phrase appear only late in the speech as part of its climax, and along with the fact that the audience would know who Troilus is, the naming of a familiar character invites the audience to take particular notice of the act of identification and estimation.

Nosworthy's and Honigmann's arguments that the speech was either lengthened or cut pose questions about how the speech reads without the lines between F's repeated phrase. Taylor thinks it "possible" and Foakes believes it "probable"[61] that the repetition indicates a cut, but only Palmer offers a more elaborate argument citing the reasons why a cut would be desirable:

> Certainly, as it stands, the full set-piece "character" is not highly dramatic, and serves to distract an audience's attention while the combat is prepared. Hence, the length of the implied cut in F is simply a clue to stage conditions in some early production.[62]

While the Trojans' view of Troilus as "a second hope" would be retained, and even given greater prominence by the cut, the contrast between the brothers would be lost. It may be argued that Troilus's potential ruthlessness and Hector's "misericorde" are represented sufficiently elsewhere in the play, as they are only moments later when Troilus shouts for Hector to "awake" during the fight with Ajax. Perhaps it is best to allow for debatable alternatives: either the central part of Ulysses' speech is providing another important iteration of the brothers' difference, or it is an expendable repetition of a familiar theme.

Palmer's view that the possible cut may reflect a performance judgment that the speech may "distract an audience's attention while the combat is prepared" comes close to Taylor's questioning whether "an audience [could] be expected to attend properly to Ulysses' long description of Troilus if such preparations [for the duel] were going on behind him?"[63] The fencing match between Hamlet and Laertes offers a parallel situation, where the preparations for the duel occur during a speech. After Hamlet and Laertes choose their foils, Claudius has a thirteen-line speech calling for the wine to be put on a table, and detailing the cannons, trumpets, drums, and drinking that will ensue if Hamlet "give the first or second hit" (5.2.215). Be-

fore Claudius's speech, F has the direction "Prepare to play," and after the speech there is the direction "They play."[64] Perhaps Claudius's
speech has not received the same criticism as Ulysses' because
Claudius is speaking specifically about the fight, but similar questions
could be asked about the attention that would be paid to either
speech during the preparations. In *Hamlet,* with the combatants already having chosen their weapons, all that seems left to prepare is
the area where the fight will take place and the table for the drinks,
and part of the purpose of Claudius's speech could be to provide the
time for these arrangements. Similarly, Ulysses' speech, rather than
being upstaged by the activity surrounding the duel, as Taylor and
Palmer suggest, could instead be useful in allowing the preparations
to take place.

While Taylor and Palmer believe that Ulysses' speech would be
overwhelmed by the activity of the duel, Seltzer, as quoted above, offers the contrasting view that the duel is "dramatically uninteresting
compared to other portions of the scene—Ulysses' enthusiastic
praise of Troilus, for example."[65] The perceived battle for the audience's attention between the preparations for the duel and Ulysses'
speech points to some important questions in interpreting and staging the moment. How is Troilus's assessment framed by action before and after Ulysses' speech, and how does the scene change if the
comments and reactions of the onstage spectators are emphasized
or marginalized? If the conversation between Ulysses and Agamemnon is competing with the duel's preparations for the attention of
the theater audience, it should also be questioned why Agamemnon's attention has drifted from the main event to an inquiry about
Troilus.

The duel between Ajax and Hector was always an opportunity for
political and psychological maneuvering rather than a real concern
with the fight and its outcome. Within the narrative progression of
the play, the duel also seems more important for the situations which
it sets up, where Hector and Achilles meet, and Ulysses escorts Troilus
to watch Cressida's betrayal. To help understand the importance of
the scene, the legend provides some appropriate parallels in the versions of the abandoned duel between Hector and Achilles that occurred during the truce in which Breseyda was exchanged. Caxton
introduces Hector's visit to the Greek camp to challenge Achilles to
single combat with a passage telling how "Achilles beheld hym gladly
for as moche as he had never seen hym unarme. And at the requeste
of Achylles Hector wente in to hys tente."[66] Hector and Achilles agree
to a single combat that will decide the war, but both Greeks and Trojans reject the idea. Juxtaposed with the story of Breseyda's exchange,

the passage serves to emphasize the way individual desire can be negated by the community.

After Shakespeare's Ulysses confronts Achilles with the idea that "against your privacy / The reasons are more potent and heroical" (3.3.185), Achilles voices his

> woman's longing,
> An appetite that I am sick withal,
> To see great Hector in his weeds of peace,
> To talk with him and to behold his visage
> Even to my full of view.
>
> (3.3.230)

Rather than a return to the sanctioned chivalric male desire for combat, Achilles expresses a personal yearning to see Hector not as a warrior, but as a civilian. Achilles' withdrawal from battle provides the conflict between an individual and a community that is a major theme in Trojan War stories, and a particularly apt theme for analyzing the occasion of Ulysses' speech about Troilus. Agamemnon's comment directing attention away from the combatants to the heavy-looking Trojan moves the focus from a public spectacle to a lover's personal struggle.

Troilus is poised at a point between the worlds of love and war that are never clearly exclusive in a war fought over the possession of a woman. From his first speech he articulates the contradictions inherent in being a lover and a warrior. As a statesman, Troilus illustrates his political and moral philosophy with examples from domestic life ("I take today a wife," 2.2.60), and as a lover he woos with the images of war ("O virtuous fight" 3.2.66), but at the duel these opposites are observed in him. Within the context of a military event, Agamemnon sees him looking heavy, and in the description of his military prowess he is described as "more vindicative than jealous love" (4.6.110). Troilus's vindictiveness not only contrasts with Hector's tenderness, but, as Kenneth Muir notes, Ulysses' simile (or his quotation of Aeneas's simile) for Troilus's vindictiveness "ironically foreshadows Troilus' jealousy."[67]

While Ulysses does not comment on Troilus's heaviness, his description of Troilus as "more vindicative than jealous love" is not only an accurate prediction of how the lover and warrior will merge, but is also a part of the description which Ulysses himself does not seem to appreciate fully. If "The providence that's in a watchful state / Knows almost every grain of Pluto's gold" (3.3.189), then Ulysses should know of Troilus's love for Cressida, but perhaps Ulysses is only kept abreast of the loves of his own countrymen. When Ulysses asks

Troilus if Cressida has a lover in Troy (4.7.172), and in failing to identify why Troilus becomes so upset at watching Cressida and Diomedes
("You shake, my lord, at something," 5.2.50) Ulysses displays, at least
to Troilus, ignorance of a relationship between Troilus and Cressida.
Ulysses plays the pander to Troilus's jealousy by escorting him to see
the betrayal, which will eventually spur Troilus to the vindictive rage
which Ulysses himself describes during the battle:

> [Troilus] hath done today
> Mad and fantastic execution,
> Engaging and redeeming of himself
> With such a careless force and forceless care
> As if that luck, in very spite of cunning,
> Bade him win all.
>
> (5.5.37)

Troilus's cry for Hector to "awake" during the duel gives some hint
of the vicious fighter that will emerge, but before the duel Agamemnon notices a very different Troilus, whose heaviness singles him out
for scrutiny. In response to Taylor's view that F's first "they call him
Troilus" is useful because "unless Troilus is hamming dreadfully, the
identification [by Ulysses] need not be self evident to every spectator," it is worth questioning whether Troilus can look heavy enough
to be noticed without, as Hamlet says, "tear[ing] a passion to tatters"
(*Hamlet*, 3.2.11). Gertrude speaks of Hamlet's "vailèd lids" (1.2.70),
and may provide a clue to how her son's sorrow is evident from his
demeanor, and not simply from his "inky cloak" (1.2.77). There are
several relevant instances in Shakespeare where onstage characters
are said to look heavy. In *Titus Andronicus,* Young Lucius asks Titus to
"leave these bitter deep laments," to which Marcus replies, "Alas, the
tender boy in passion moved / Doth weep to see his grandsire's heaviness" (3.2.49–52). The circumstances of the moment (coming in the
scene which follows Titus, Marcus, and Lavinia carrying off the severed heads and hand), along with Titus's previous speech, would require little physical confirmation of the character's heaviness. In
Richard III, Clarence's scene in the Tower begins with him being
asked "Why looks your grace so heavily today?" (1.4.1),[68] but again the
circumstances (Clarence was last seen going to the Tower, 1.1.118)
and dialogue (he immediately describes his "miserable night . . . of
fearful dreams," 1.4.2) make clear Clarence's disposition without
much need for corresponding gestures. Perhaps most visual are two
examples in *Richard Duke of York* (*3 Henry VI*): F has the direction "Enter one blowing" before Richard asks the messenger "But what art
thou whose heavy looks foretell / Some dreadful story hanging on

thy tongue?" (2.1.42.1–43). In a later scene, Queen Margaret also explicitly highlights the visual nature of her state when she explains that

> Our people and our peers are both misled,
> Our treasure seized, our soldiers put to flight,
> And, as thou seest, ourselves in heavy plight.
>
> (3.3.35)

What is different about Troilus's heavy looks is that the audience, and not the characters discussing him, is aware of the reason for his despair. While the other occurrences of characters' noticing heavy looks form part of an exploration into the cause and importance of the heaviness, Ulysses makes no response to Agamemnon's perception of Troilus' emotional state.

When Chaucer's narrator shifts from Cressida's reunion with her father to focus on Troilus (5.195–96), seventy stanzas tell of Troilus's sorrow in being separated from Cressida (5.197–686). For members of the audience that have read Chaucer, these stanzas can be seen to be concentrated into Troilus's heavy looks which prompt Agamemnon's question. The audience watches the way in which Troilus deals with his separation from Cressida while he is also required to uphold his place as one of the principal spectators at the duel. Although Ulysses does not comment upon his demeanor, the speech that characterizes him as a warrior is spoken with Troilus looking like a dejected lover. The following stage history of the passage will explore the importance of the physical presence of the characters, and some of the ways their gestures, movements, and groupings can confirm, contradict, expand upon, and illustrate the editorial problems.

~

Dryden serves as a useful bridge into the theater history of the passage, providing another version of the Trojan legend, with alterations and reactions to *Troilus and Cressida* that comment directly on the editorial and performance issues surrounding the duel. In *Truth Found Too Late* the Greeks strangely pass by Achilles on their way to the single combat between Ajax and Hector, and after Achilles and Patroclus consider Achilles' fallen status (using the *Troilus and Cressida* dialogue from 3.3), the Greeks reenter for the duel. The speeches by Agamemnon and Ajax requesting a "loud note to Troy" (*Truth Found Too Late*, 4.2.54) that will crack the lungs of the trumpeter are followed by the direction "Trumpet sounds, and is answer'd from within," and immediately "Hector, Aeneas, and other Trojans" enter (4.2.59.1). The overzealous calls by Agamemnon and Ajax for a trumpet blast are not answered by the undercutting silence of "no trumpet answers," as in *Troilus and Cressida* (4.6.12). Instead, Dryden uses similar dialogue for what seems the very different effect of heightening and glorifying the epic and chivalric pretensions.[69]

Dryden cut the dramatization of Cressida being kissed by the Greeks, opting instead to have Pandarus report the event to Troilus after Troilus has seen Diomedes and Cressida together (4.2.354–61, as part of a sequence of events that will be discussed in relation to Troilus's rejection of Pandarus). The other relevant cut Dryden made to the passage is the dialogue between Ulysses and Agamemnon concerning Troilus. These cuts streamline the action of the duel, postponing the mingling of the love story with the war plot until after the duel is completed. Instead of following Ulysses' F only line ("They are opposed already") with Agamemnon's question about Troilus ("What Trojan is that"), Dryden uses Ulysses' line as a link between the preparations for the duel and the start of the fight:

> *The Trumpets sound on both sides, while* Aeneas *and* Diomede *take their places, as Judges of the Field: The* Trojans *and* Grecians *rank themselves on either side.*

ULYSS. They are oppos'd already.

> *Fight equal at first, then* Ajax *has* Hector *at disadvantage: at last* Hector *closes,* Ajax *falls on one knee,* Hector *stands over him but strikes not, and* Ajax *rises.*

> (4.2.81.1)

Some of what Dryden achieves in his fight can be linked directly to the dialogue he cut. Instead of having Ulysses say that "Hector in his blaze of wrath subscribes / To tender objects" (*Troilus and Cressida,* 4.6.108), Dryden shows Hector pausing over the fallen Ajax. Dryden may also be interpreting the lines he cut from *Troilus and Cressida* in prescribing the way the fight progresses. Troilus's shout for Hector to "awake" (*Troilus and Cressida,* 4.6.118) coincides with "Ajax has Hector at disadvantage," but it is uncertain whether Agamemnon's following comment ("His blows are well dispos'd. There, Ajax," *Troilus and Cressida,* 4.6.119) refers to Ajax's or Hector's blows. Either Agamemnon is confirming the implication from Troilus's remark that Ajax has an advantage, or, as in Dryden's version, Hector recovers and has an advantage. Agamemnon's line in *Troilus and Cressida* could then be referring to Hector's "well dispos'd" "blows," before offering some needed encouragement to Ajax.

Dryden's stage management of the scene comments on several of the editorial issues of the passage. In anticipating Capell's direction

for the Trojans and Greeks to "rank themselves on either side," Dryden merely describes what seems the logical assumption that the
armies would be on separate sides of the stage. He does not, however,
indicate in any detail how the spectators were separated from the
combatants and the "Judges of the Field." This separation becomes
most important in the interpretation of the F only entrance for
"Agamemnon and the rest." Dryden has "Agamemnon, and the chief
of both sides approach" (4.2.112.1), while Rowe and some editors, as
mentioned above, only have the Greeks approach. Dryden's group
obviously includes Troilus, because not only had Hector requested
that Aeneas call Troilus (as in *Troilus and Cressida*), but Dryden also
adds the direction for Agamemnon's greeting, "My well fam'd lord
of Troy, no less to you," to be spoken "To Troilus" (4.2.115). Rowe
added the direction ("To Troilus") in his second edition, and nearly
all editors of *Troilus and Cressida* include the emendation. But if
Troilus is to be called by Aeneas and then spoken to by Agamemnon,
when (in Rowe, and the many editors following Rowe) does Troilus
approach? What is the point of rewriting the F direction as an onstage
movement that only covers the Greeks' movement when a Trojan
movement is also required? Perhaps the dialogue that indicates
Troilus's approach eliminates the need for a stage direction, or perhaps Rowe's interpretation points toward a more substantial movement for the Greeks from an alternative space, such as above (as
Palmer suggests) or within.

   While editors have continued to debate the possibilities of rewriting F's entrance for "Agamemnon and the rest," directors have been
more likely to explore the problems Dryden first saw with Ulysses' F
only line "They are opposed already." By cutting Ulysses' assessment
of Troilus, Dryden lends support to the critics who think the speech
either undramatic or a poorly judged accompaniment to the preparations for the duel. The rewriting also shows how Ulysses' F only line
can suggest an immediate start to the duel. In contrast to my suggestion that Ulysses' speech about Troilus could be used to cover the
preparations for the duel, Dryden and some directors have found the
speech (4.6.98–115) an unwelcome delay to the impending fight.

   Nearly all editions used for promptbooks follow Malone in having
the direction for Ajax and Hector to "enter the lists" before Ulysses
says "They are opposed already," but this has been variously interpreted by directors. While Malone's direction is crossed out in the
promptbooks of Poel and Payne, both directors seemed to follow it
to some extent. Payne has a note for extras to "make a barrier with
their spears," thus providing a marked off area for the fight, but the
promptbook does not indicate when the combatants entered the

area. Many directors will be seen to cut Ulysses' speech about Troilus in a way that offers support to Nosworthy's theory that the F repetition of "they call him Troilus" indicates an intended cut of the lines between the repeated phrase. Poel, however, offers more support than most, cutting only those lines between the repeated phrase (from "Not yet mature" to "jealous love," 4.6.100–110), and leaving the surrounding lines and speeches intact. After Ulysses remarked that Troilus is "A second hope as fairly built as Hector" (112), the promptbook has a note for "blows and drums," and after Ulysses' speech there is another direction for "blows" before Agamemnon says "They are in action" (116). The term "blows" might indicate a start to the fighting before Ulysses finishes his speech, or it might indicate trumpet blasts, but the promptbook elsewhere has directions for "trumpets." In either case, Poel had the cut version of Ulysses' assessment of Troilus delivered amidst noises of the fight, or at least the preparations for the fight.

Capell's added direction at the beginning of the scene for "Lists set out" (4.6.0) has been included in many editions, including those of Ridley and Walker that were used for so many promptbooks. Quayle's promptbook is, therefore, surprisingly unique in noting that the di-

25. **Ajax and Hector fight, SMT 1948, Quayle. Photographer Angus McBean, Shakespeare Centre Library. Copyright Royal Shakespeare Company.**

rection was followed. Two extras were "uncoiling rope" while another measured paces before Agamemnon entered (see illustration, showing the fight, with the rope faintly visible in the foreground, stretched between two spears).[70] These extras then saluted Agamemnon as he moved to the center of the lists. After Cressida exited and the Trojans entered, and just after Agamemnon and Aeneas finished discussing the conditions of the fight, Quayle's promptbook notes that the "Generals confer together on lists." The ensuing dialogue between Aeneas and Achilles took place during this conference, and can begin to show how the scene can break up into smaller groups.

Frank Marshall added a note to *The Henry Irving Shakespeare* objecting to Capell's direction for "Lists set out": "this is absurd, and introduces unnecessarily the customs of medieval chivalry in the Grecian camp" (332). While it may be easy to defend the chivalric nature of Capell's direction, the need to demarcate a fighting arena, and the placement of the direction at the beginning of the scene remain contentious. As will be demonstrated, the stage history shows that when directors have decided to do something resembling setting out lists, the action usually occurred after Cressida exited. Even Quayle's action of roping off an area for the fight at the beginning of the scene does not fully support Capell's staging. Since Quayle cut from Ulysses' F only line through the dialogue about Troilus that precedes the duel (4.6.97–115), the time these lines would have taken was not available to prepare for the fight, and may have contributed to the director's decision to set out the lists well in advance of the fight.

Guthrie's promptbook has a note for two trumpet blasts at the point of Malone's direction for Hector and Ajax to enter the lists. During the first blast Hector saluted, and for the second blast there is the note "Hector etc. in pit." Without crediting his source, Christy gives a detailed description of the fight.

> Guthrie had two sailors hold a colored rope in front of Agamemnon and his staff as they looked down to the orchestra pit into which Hector and Ajax descended as into the lists. At the height of the excitement about the imagined duel, soldiers of both sides standing in the rear broke ranks yelling with enthusiasm to peek over the shoulders of their commanders.[71]

Guthrie's staging certainly gives support to Taylor's suggestion of imaginary offstage lists, but the alterations somewhat mitigate that support. Like Quayle, Guthrie cut from Ulysses' F only speech ("They are opposed already") through all of Ulysses' description of Troilus (4.6.97–115). Agamemnon's speech instructing Diomedes to consult with Aeneas and "consent upon the order of their fight" (4.6.92) was

26. Spectators at the Ajax and Hector fight, Old Vic Theatre 1956, Guthrie.

therefore followed by the combatants' (and presumably the mar-
shalls') descent into the pit. Agamemnon then immediately continued by announcing, "They are in action."[72] One of the most important aspects of Taylor's editorial staging is that by placing the fight
offstage, the focus of attention is placed upon the observers of the
fight. Guthrie probably achieved a similar result, but without the
purpose of spotlighting Ulysses' description of Troilus. Nevertheless,
Taylor's argument that the dialogue indicates that the fight takes
place offstage, and the point at which the combatants exit, is given a
retrospective vote of confidence by Guthrie.

Two major New York productions provide some relevant comments on issues already discussed, and also offer some insights that
will become more common in later British productions. At the point
of Capell's direction for Ajax and Hector to enter the lists, the
promptbook for Henry Herbert's Players' Club production of 1932
has the direction "Greek and Trojan Soldiers take up shouts in combat; Trojan and Greek captains place Barriers." This curious note
mixes what would seem to be directions for the fight followed by
preparations for it, reflecting the confusion in the QF texts about
where the preparations end and the fight begins. Perhaps the shouts

were not for the fight itself, but in anticipation of it, and the barriers were used to hold back the enthusiastic spectators. The late placement of the barriers also argues against Capell's direction for setting up the lists at the beginning of the scene, and shows how the action, along with the shouts, could begin to raise the audience's expectation of the fight. Like Poel, Herbert cut the lines of Ulysses' speech that appear between the repeated F phrase, providing another vote for the expendability of much of Ulysses' description of Troilus.

Joseph Papp (in his production at New York's Delacourt Theater, 1965) cut the same lines from Ulysses' speech as Poel and Herbert ("Not yet mature . . . jealous love," 106–10), but Papp also cut the last three lines of the speech ("Thus says Aeneas . . . to me," 113–15). In addition, Papp moved Ulysses' F only speech ("They are opposed already") to come after his identification of Troilus, a conscious decision that was included in his production notes to the edition he co-edited. Papp seems almost apologetic for disregarding the editorial tradition of having lists, writing that "the fight itself did not employ lists and consisted of a contest with quarter staffs."[73] Papp's concerns highlight the relation between the blocking of the scene and the interpretation of the F only line. What is Ulysses describing when he says "They are opposed," and if the inclusion of the F only line is not merely due to a compositor error, then what different picture is given in the two texts?

Five years before Papp's production, Hall and Barton (1960) similarly attached Ulysses' F only line to the end of his description of Troilus. The only note in the promptbook for movement is that Troilus sits on a stool before Agamemnon asked "What Trojan is that same that looks so heavy?" This simple action could help single him out for both Agamemnon and the audience, providing a way for the audience to know immediately who was looking heavy without requiring him, in Taylor's phrase, to be "hamming incredibly." Ulysses' speech about Troilus was again cut, but not exactly as the F repetition may imply:

ULYSSES:	The youngest son of Priam, a true knight;
	His heart and hand both open and free;
	Manly as Hector, but more dangerous;
	They call him Troilus, and on him erect
	A second hope, as fairly * built as Hector: *Go orch
	They are opposed already. (on fight)
AGAMEMNON:	They are in action.[74]

The concerns of the directors seem to be in offering an action which confirms that Troilus looks heavy, but also that the description of Troilus does not go on for too long, and is not competing with a fight or any movements (such as preparations for the fight) that warranted mention in the promptbook. The orchestra and fight that did finally interrupt the description occur near the end of the speech, and in the rearranged version, were noticed by Ulysses (in the transposed F only line) and confirmed by Agamemnon.

When Barton next directed the play (1968), there were similar emendations and deletions. The promptbook does not have a direction for Troilus to do anything that would make him look heavy, but drums and trumpets were sounded, signaling some military activity, before Agamemnon asked about Troilus. Ulysses' F only line was cut, so that Agamemnon's speech continued as it does in Q (but did not, of course, include the Q only "Ulysses:"). There were again cuts made to Ulysses' description of Troilus, from the second to the eighth line of the speech, bringing together the lines "The youngest son of Priam, a true knight: / Manly as Hector, but more dangerous." The comparison of Troilus with Hector was reinforced by retaining the latter half of the lines between F's repeated phrase ("Manly as Hector . . . jealous love"), and unlike the cut version in the Hall/Barton production, Troilus's rage was anticipated by Ulysses speaking of his being "more vindicative than jealous love."

The alterations made to the end of Ulysses' speech are different in the promptbook and the audiotape. The promptbook has Ulysses' F only line ("They are in action") cut out of its place in the text and pasted alongside the line ending "as fairly built as Hector" (112). The line, however, has a partially erased pencil line though it, which may mean that it was originally cut, either in its original or altered place, but was subsequently reinstated. While this scenario could be true, it is certainly true that the line was at some time cut altogether, as it is not spoken on the 1970 audiotape. The speech on the tape finishes with "They call him Troilus," creating a half line that was completed by Agamemnon's "They are in action." Between the two speeches there were drums and trumpets, and the noise of fighting on the tape (after Agamemnon says "They are in action") implies a fight that started and stopped.

The changes Barton made to the text, and the differences between the promptbook and the audiotape, at least signal a perceived difficulty with the moment, and a concern to rearrange it in a way that would work for the production. Over twenty years after the production, John Barton reflected on some of the factors that went into staging the passage.

> It is a matter of focus and distraction. However you interpret "they are opposed already," some military action or preparation is going on and you don't listen to the Agamemnon and Ulysses on Troilus bit, which is

very, very important. That's why one changes it. However you interpret "they are opposed already," they've got to do something, and a duel is a pretty conspicuous thing.

You've got to make Troilus look different than everybody else who is looking forward to the duel. Everyone else is thrilled about it. It is a very tricky bit because the whole build-up is waiting for the duel, and everybody is assembled to see the duel. Troilus is there, and disconsolate, and you have to steady the scene and focus on him—which is difficult.[75]

Barton not only stresses that the audience's attention will be divided between the groups of characters, but the characters themselves are also differently occupied. The choices for a director involve finding ways to guide the audience between the preparations for the duel, the heavy looking Troilus, and the commentary by Agamemnon and Ulysses. While it may seem advantageous to allow each group their importance without overwhelming the others, the nature of performance must also admit the opportunity to emphasize and diminish actions and speeches as will best suit the production. In relation to the textual ambiguity of the passage, it can be questioned how the F only line ("They are opposed already") is either a welcome acknowledgement of the action, or a problematic distraction from the dialogue about Troilus which follows. Similarly, the F repetition (of "they call him Troilus") can justify cutting an awkwardly long speech, or, conversely, can stress the importance of noticing, assessing, and naming Troilus in Ulysses' speech.

Barton's next production, codirected with Barry Kyle, shared some of the textual changes made to the two previous RSC productions, but there were also some significant differences. Ulysses' F only speech ("They are opposed already") was again cut, but without an indication that it was moved. Ulysses' description of Troilus was once more trimmed, but unlike the two previous RSC versions, the second line was retained, giving a reading that is less supportive of the theory that F indicates a cut after the first line. The third through the eighth lines were cut, but again the promptbook and the audiotape are different. While the promptbook cuts from the half line after "They call him Troilus" until the end of the speech (as the 1970 audiotape of Barton's production), the 1977 audiotape of the Barton/Kyle production retains "They call him Troilus, and on him erect / A second hope as fairly built as Hector." The way the Barton/Kyle promptbook and the Barton audiotape were cut make the half line "They call him Troilus" the finale of the speech, giving further prominence to the act of singling out Troilus for recognition. The line and a half added to the 1977 audiotape ("and on him erect . . . Hector") returns the focus to Hector, ending the speech with the name Hector as the fight begins.

Davies' production used an elaborate arrangement for the combat, and Malcolm Ranson, the fight director, described in the program some of the thought that went into creating a duel suitable for the production's Crimean War setting.

> The sabre-fighting we're using for the duel is the Prussian military version of student "schlaeger" duelling . . . [where] you stand still and slug it out aiming only at the face, to produce the much-loved duelling scars. In the military version the body and arms are valid targets, and the right foot is allowed to move but the left had to stay fixed—it was a great dishonour if you moved it. So it's a sort of cross between chess and Russian roulette.[76]

Ranson's final image shows both the formality and the ferocity that were considered desirable for the duel. The "lists" were two tables that Hector and Ajax stood upon, and as these tables were being set up, Ulysses approached Agamemnon. Ulysses' F only line ("They are opposed already") was cut, and as he stood with Agamemnon downstage left, Agamemnon pointed with his cane downstage right at Troilus while he asked "What Trojan is that." Ulysses' response was again cut, creating a speech that read:

> The youngest son of Priam, a true knight,
> Not yet mature, yet matchless; firm of word
> For what he has he gives, what thinks he shows;
> Manly as Hector, but more dangerous;
> For Hector in his blaze of wrath subscribes
> To tender objects, but he in heat of action
> Is more vindicative than jealous love.
> They call him Troilus, and on him erect
> A second hope as fairly built as Hector.

The cuts eliminate five lines of the description of Troilus, and the final three lines naming Aeneas as the source, resulting in a speech predominantly about comparing the brothers. Although the speech is cut almost in half (retaining 9 of 17 lines), the nine lines still comprise a substantial speech, and one which came across clearly as the preparations for the duel were taking place upstage. Without Ulysses saying "They are opposed already," there may not be the need to have the combatants in place, allowing for more of the preparations to take place during Ulysses' speech about Troilus. Davies' staging also provided a division of the characters onstage that made dramatic sense. The combatants prepared to fight (arming themselves, limbering up, and taking practice swipes) and the spectators created some commotion as they positioned themselves upstage, while the conversation between Ulysses and Agamemnon was clearly delivered downstage. The audience's sight line to the combatants had first to take in the downstage Ulysses and Agamemnon, allowing their dialogue to guide them toward noticing Troilus.

Miller's video offers interpretative comments on many of the editorial issues in the passage. Agamemnon's speech telling Diomedes to "Go, gentle knight, / Stand by our Ajax" (4.6.90) was used to direct not only Diomedes but all Trojans and Greeks to begin moving toward the lists. After instructing Aeneas and Diomedes to determine the "order of their fight" (92), Agamemnon was left relatively isolated with Ulysses and Nestor, and he softened his voice to tell them "The combatants being kin / Half stints their strife before their strokes begin" (94). Ulysses' F only reply ("They are opposed already") may be a comment on the position of the combatants, but none of the trio looked toward the lists, and the fighters did not appear at all in the frame. Ulysses and Nestor flippantly giggled at the line, as if Ulysses' remark that "They are opposed already" came as an enigmatic but humorous reply to Agamemnon's disappointment at their being kin and not likely to fight at full strength. Miller apparently did not perceive any need for a physical confirmation that Ajax and Hector are "opposed."

As Agamemnon asked about the Trojan "that looks so heavy," Troilus appeared in the background, simply as one of the crowd and not doing anything that drew attention either to himself or his heaviness. Perhaps it was part of the decision to have his presence available but inconspicuous that prompted an important change to the published text. While the BBC edition of the play that accompanied the video notes most changes and cuts to Peter Alexander's text, no mention is made of the departure from Alexander's text in having Ulysses follow F's repetition of "They call him Troilus." This decision, unique among editors and directors until that time, does seem to support Taylor's reading of F, where the additional "They call him Troilus" is considered useful in identifying the subject of the speech. The movements of characters from the position where Cressida was greeted and where Aeneas hailed the Greeks is chaotic, with the camera moving in closer to Agamemnon, Ulysses, and Nestor while Troilus was one of a group drifting offscreen.

Taylor's interpretation that the fight takes place offstage also receives some support in Miller's version, but there are important differences. Noises of the fight can be heard throughout Ulysses' speech about Troilus, and the difficulty of a divided focus for the audience was enacted by the attempts of Agamemnon and Nestor to move away from the long-winded Ulysses, and towards the duel. Agamemnon's line, "They are in action," was given during the end of Ulysses' speech as a signal not that the fight has just begun, but that the fight has been in progress for some time and that Agamemnon will listen to Ulysses no longer. While the focus on Ulysses, Agamemnon, and Nestor suggests that the dialogue was given priority over the action of the combatants, the viewer was prompted to share Agamemnon's lack of interest in Ulysses' speech after the first "they call him Troilus" identified the heavy Trojan. With the options available to a video director, such as a close-up of Troilus during Ulysses' speech, Miller's choices seem to clearly opt for diverting attention away from Ulysses' speech and away from looking at Troilus. During Ulysses' speech there are noises of the fight heard, but while no action is seen, the anticipation of the fight becomes more important than Ulysses' speech about Troilus.

Mendes continued the RSC tradition of cutting and rearranging the moment. Ulysses' F only speech "They are opposed already" was moved to after the description of Troilus, again using it as a more immediate signal of the start to the fight. "They call him Troilus" was advanced to the beginning of Ulysses' speech, and was not repeated, creating a speech which read:

> They call him Troilus
> The youngest son of Priam, a true knight,
> Not yet mature, yet matchless; firm of word
> His heart and hand both open and both free;
> For what he has he gives, what thinks he shows,
> Manly as Hector, but more dangerous;
> For Hector in his blaze of wrath subscribes
> To tender objects, but he in heat of ~~action~~ [anger]
> Is more vindicative than jealous love.
> They are opposed.

Mendes' retaining the two lines describing the transparency of Troilus's state of mind is important in the confirmation of Agamemnon's ability to notice the heaviness of his disposition. While some of the comparison with Hector remains, the cuts eliminate the reference to Troilus as "a second hope, as fairly built as Hector," and along with the promotion of "they call him Troilus," the speech seems more clearly focused on Troilus. Perhaps this more singular focus is also served by the rearranging of "They are opposed," so that attention is only turned to Hector's fight after the description of Troilus.

Mendes offered an interesting staging of the movements following the fight. After the duel, Agamemnon, Menelaus, Ulysses, and Nestor gathered behind the upstage ladders to confer, and were joined by Diomedes after his speech (beginning "'Tis Agamemnon's wish,"

27. "The issue is embracement," Swan Theatre 1990, Mendes. Joe Cocks Studio Collection, Shakespeare Centre Library, Copyright Shakespeare Birthplace Trust.

28. "The issue is embracement," Swan Theatre 1990, Mendes. Joe Cocks Studio Collection, Shakespeare Centre Library, Copyright Shakespeare Birthplace Trust.

4.7.36, see illustration, where Agamemnon turns to go behind the ladders). Presumably, the conference was about the outcome of the fight, and what their reaction would be. At the point of the F only direction for "Agamemnon and the rest enter," Agamemnon and the others emerged from behind the ladders before Ajax's line "Great Agamemnon comes to meet us here" (4.7.43). Using the upstage area behind the ladders to remove themselves from the scene made it necessary for them to reenter the main playing space without ever having left the stage. Perhaps the staging is closer to Rowe's rewriting of the direction in which the group come forward rather than enter, as F, but Mendes' production depicted the advantage of having the Greeks reemerging as a group to greet Hector.

While Mendes' staging offered the audience a view of the Greeks as they gathered behind the ladders after the duel, the movement also suggests a point at which the Greeks could exit briefly, after the duel, before coming back onstage to greet Hector. While the point and purpose of their exit may not be crucial, their coming forward as a group does seem to have a significant impact on the scene. By increasing the distance they must travel as a group to come and meet Hector, the fact that another identity parade is taking place can be emphasized for the audience. The dramatic inventiveness and thematic resonance of Mendes' staging provides one of the best arguments for encouraging, in all kinds of readers, performers, and audiences, an open and inquisitive approach to textual ambiguity.

8
"Hence Broker, Lackey"

It is a measure of the heroic diction Troilus authentically achieves that his final speeches must be followed by Pandarus's scurrilous epilogue. If the force of Troilus's closing speeches were not so great, Shakespeare would not have to counteract it with an epilogue of such hostility. The juxtaposition of Troilus's report of the death of Hector, daring the sun to rise before he does, with Pandarus's "A goodly medicine for my aching bones!" forms the play's clearest moment of rhetorical bravado. Shakespeare pushes both chivalric heroism and scurrility to an extreme, and then insists that they be heard together.[1]

BARBARA BOWEN'S PERCEPTIVE READING REVELS IN THE RELATIONSHIP between Troilus's final speeches and Pandarus's final appearance, but many critics, bibliographers, and editors have argued that the QF ending may be only one of the ways the play ended. The theories of editors and bibliographers can be read alongside the play's theater history, revealing how the heroism and scurrility that Bowen describes have been emphasized and diminished in different literary, theatrical, and social climates. I am particularly interested in exploring the play's multiple and disruptive movements of closure, and the ways in which changing notions of an "authentic Shakespeare" have been evoked in the critical responses to originary and modern texts and performances.

Undoubtedly the most commented upon textual problem in *Troilus and Cressida* is F's near identical repetition of Pandarus's call to Troilus and Troilus's harsh reply. While Q prints the exchange only near the end of play, F has the dialogue as the last lines of 5.3 as well as near the end of the play. Since Steevens commented that "the poet would hardly have given us an unnecessary repetition of the same words, nor have dismissed Pandarus twice in the same manner,"[2] editors almost universally accept that a choice must be made between the two instances of the passage.[3] Steevens suggested that the entire passage of Pandarus delivering Cressida's letter (5.3.100–18) might be justifiably moved to the end of the play, and Capell (1767/8) and

My loue with words and errors ſtill ſhe feedes,
But edifies another with her deedes.　　　*Exeunt.*
　　　　　Enter Therſites ; excurſions.
Therſ. Now they are clapper-clawing one another : Ile

Q

My loue with words and errors ſtill ſhe feedes ;
But edifies another with her deedes.
Pand. Why, but heare you ?
Troy. Hence brother lackie ; ignomie and ſhame
Purſue thy life, and liue aye with thy name.
　　　A Larum.　　　　　　*Exeunt.*

Enter Therſites in excurſion.

Ther. Now they are clapper-clawing one another, Ile

F

29. "Hence brother," Q, F. Reproduced by permission of The Huntington Library, San Marino, California.

Rann (1789) followed his conjecture in their editions. Malone dismissed such a radical transposition, but agreed that F's repeated lines "do not constitute any part of the scene" (5.3).[4] Malone followed Q in omitting F's repeated lines, believing that "the players, or the editor of the folio, alone are responsible" for their inclusion at 5.3.

Twenty years after his initial comments about the variants were published, Steevens (in his 1793 edition) revised his speculation about the significance of F's repetition. He no longer believed that the dialogue between *Pandarus* and *Troilus* at the end of the play should be expanded to include the passage where Cressida's letter is torn, but instead suggested that Troilus's line, "Hope of revenge shall hide our inward woe" (5.11.31), marked the end of the play that Shakespeare wrote. Steevens proposed that either the ending of another Trojan war play was grafted onto Shakespeare's, or the "wretched buffoon who represented Pandarus" was responsible for adding Pandarus's final entrance, his second rejection by Troilus,

Ile haunt thee like a wicked conſcience ſtill.
That mouldeth goblins ſwift as fiienzes thoughts,
Strike a free march, to Troy with comfort goe
Hope of reueng ſhall hide our inward woe.

    Enter Pandarus,

Pan. But here you, here you.

 Troy. Hence broker, lacky, ignomyny, ſhame,
Purſue thy life, and liue aye with thy name.

    Exeunt all but Pandarus.

 Pan. A goodly medicine for my aking bones, Oh world,
world --- thus is the poore agent deſpiſ'd, Oh traitors and
bawds how earneſtly are you ſet a worke, and how ill re-
quited, why ſhould our endeuour bee ſo lou'd and the per-
formance ſo loathed, what verſe for it? What inſtance for it?
Let me ſee;
Full merrily the humble Bee doth ſing,
Till he hath loſt his hony and his ſting.
And being once ſubdude in armed taile,
Sweet hony, and ſweet notes together faile.
Good traiders in the fleſh, ſet this in your painted cloathes,
As many as be here of *Pandars* hall,
Your eyes halfe out weepe out at *Pandars* fall.
Or if you cannot weepe yet giue ſome grones,
Though not for me yet for my aking bones:
Brethren and ſiſters of the hold-ore trade,
Some two monthes hence my will ſhall here be made.
It ſhould be now, but that my feare is this,
Some gauled gooſe of Wincheſter would hiſſe.
Till then ile ſweat and ſeeke about for eaſes,
And at that time bequeath you my diſeaſes.

     FINIS.

30. Epilogue, Q, F. Reproduced by permission of The Huntington Library, San
Marino, California.

> Ile haunt thee, like a wicked confcience ftill,
> Th.t mouldeth goblins fwift as frenfies thoughts.
> Strike a free march to Troy, with comfort goe:
> Hope of reuenge, fhall hide our inward woe.
>
> *Enter Pandarus.*
>
> *Pand.* But heare you? heare you?
> *Troy.* Hence broker, lackie, ignomy, and fhame
> Purfue thy life, and liue aye with thy name. *Exeunt.*
>
> *Pan.* A goodly medcine, for mine akingbones: oh world,
> world, world! thus is the poore agent difpifde: Oh trai-
> tours and bawdes; how earneftly are you fet aworke, and
> how ill requited? why fhould our indeuour be fo defir'd,
> and the performance fo loath'd? What Verfe for it? what
> inftance for it? let me fee.
> Full merrily the humble Bee doth fing,
> Till he hath loft his hony, and his fting.
> And being once fubdu'd in armed taile,
> Sweete hony, and fweete notes together faile.
> Good tradersin the flefh, fet this in your painted cloathes;
> As many as be here of Panders hall,
> Your eyes halfe out, weepe out at *Pandar's* fall:
> Or if you cannot weepe, yet giue fome grones;
> Though not for me, yet for your akingbones:
> Brethren and fifters of the hold-dore trade,
> Some two months hence, my will fhall here be made:
> It fhould be now, but that my feare is this:
> Some galled Goofe of Winchefter would hiffe:
> Till then, Ile fweate, and feeke about for eafes;
> And at that time bequeath you my difeafes. *Exeunt.*
>
> ¶ ¶ ¶

F

and his "deliberate insult on his audience."[5] Steevens's view that the play originally ended with Troilus's couplet was supported in 1860 by William Sidney Walker, and Walker offered additional justification for F's inclusion of the lines in the earlier scene. Opposing Malone's defense of Q, Walker endorsed F's reading of 5.3, believing that 5.3 "is the proper place for these two speeches; for without them the [. . . scene] ends abruptly."[6] Walker suggested that Troilus's tearing of Cressida's letter leads naturally to Pandarus's rejection, and that "Pandarus' epilogue must, therefore, be an interpolation."[7] The first half of Pandarus's speech is, however, suspected of being Shakespeare's, and Walker proposed that "from 'A goodly medicine' to 'painted cloths' ought to be added to the end of V.3."[8] The following editorial and performance history will show how Walker's proposal to transfer part or all of Pandarus's final speech to the end of 5.3 has received significant theatrical and bibliographic support.

While nearly all editors follow Q (and Malone) in having the lines occur only near the end of the play, there has been much less agreement about the significance of the repetition, and commentators have constructed a vast array of explanations to account for the variant readings. Steevens, Malone, and Walker, in their opinions quoted above, all begin to speculate on theatrical and editorial interventions that distance F's repetition from the playwright. These theories have been continually recycled in an attempt to explain how the F only lines (at the end of 5.3) are a sign that Q, F, or both contain either textual corruption or theatrical interpolation. The questionable authority of F's repetition has also been particularly useful to commentators who have judged Pandarus's final address to the audience distasteful, supporting the opinion that Shakespeare would not end the play with such a scandalous speech.

Steevens's doubts about whether Shakespeare was responsible for having Pandarus enter after Troilus's rhyming couplet became a commonly expressed view in the nineteenth century, only occasionally advancing from a textual note to an emendation.[9] The Henry Irving edition's theatrical consideration of the play marked for deletion all the lines after Troilus says "Hope of revenge shall hide our inward woe." A. W. Verity also provided a note to the Irving edition, approvingly citing W. S. Walker's doubts about the placement and authorship of Pandarus's final speech: "I think there is much to be said for this view; at any rate, one would gladly believe that the ribald rubbish with which the play ends was not written by Shakespeare."[10] In 1907, however, Alfred Thiselton argued that Shakespeare originally wrote the ending in which Pandarus comes on to address Troilus and then the audience, but either when that version was being first rehearsed, or when the play was revived, it "was found convenient to end the play" with Troilus's rhyming couplet.[11] F therefore represents a later version, where Pandarus's role ends in the earlier scene. Thiselton explained F's repetition and its inclusion of the old ending by arguing that the Folio editors decided that "the author's original intention was deemed worthy of preserving for the benefit of the readers."[12]

While Thiselton may have been projecting onto the Folio editors a more modern desire for presenting readers with conflated texts that include original and revised intentions, his comments highlight the complex issues of authority and provenance that inform many of the views about how the play was written, and how it was or how it should be performed and edited. Thiselton implied that the actors were responsible for cutting Pandarus from the final scene without the playwright's authority, but Shakespeare was eventually, although slowly and reluctantly, given a more prominent role in the existence of alternative endings. Peter Alexander wrote in 1928 that "there can be little doubt that the passage belonged originally to the earlier

scene . . . and that it was transferred" to the end of the play. He cited
F's repetition as evidence that Q "gives a later draft of the play" than
F, perhaps revised when Shakespeare transcribed the play.[13]

Alexander's speculation about the first performance has been one
of the most influential in the critical and bibliographical history of
the play. Malone had proposed that the apparent contradiction between the 1603 Stationers' Register entry stating that the play was performed, and the claim in Qb's epistle that the play was not "clapper-
clawed with the palms of the vulgar," could be resolved if the play was
first performed at court. Alexander rejected this conjecture, asserting that *The Merry Wives of Windsor* represents the "right key for Elizabeth," but that

> in *Troilus* all is different: there is much scurrility and the audience are at
> times addressed directly and familiarly by the most scurril character in the
> most scurril terms; and the play concludes with an epilogue which pre-
> vents disapproval by implying that there will be no hissing except from
> bawds or panders or their unfortunate customers. This was obviously not
> for the ears of her Majesty. Nor can these particular addresses be de-
> tached from the play as a whole: they are in keeping with the rest.
>
> Shakespeare, however, may have written the play for some festivity at
> one of the Inns of Court. [. . . *Troilus and Cressida*] is excellent fooling for
> clerks. It is unlikely that this play was ever performed to an audience at
> the Globe.[14]

The impact of the theory is perhaps of more interest than the likely
truth of the theory itself. By positing a suitable occasion and audience
for the play's composition, Alexander seeks to judge, some three hundred years later, the expectations of audiences at court, public theaters, and the Inns, and the willingness of Shakespeare to write a play
specifically for such audiences. Alexander does not question Shakespeare's hand in the play or in Pandarus's speech, but the scurrilous
play is pardoned because he was pandering to the tastes of a special
audience.

When Chambers (in 1930) summarized the major theories about
the play, he dismissed the many proposals which suggested that
Shakespeare collaborated with, or was supplemented by another
playwright throughout the play. While Chambers left the authorship
theories to "cut each other's throats," he considered more carefully
the widely accepted doubts about the authorship of the battle scenes
(5.4–10).[15] R. A. Small's theory, supported "even outside the ranks of
professed disintegrators," argued that "the first occurrence of the repeated lines [. . . at the end of 5.3] marks the original end of the
play."[16] Chambers dismissed this possibility on the grounds that Hec-

tor's death was being "foreshadowed in 5.3," and must have always been included in the play, but Chambers did believe that 5.3 should mark "the end of Pandarus."[17] Although Chambers thought that F's repeated "they call him Troilus" (4.5.99, 111) preserved revisions made during composition, he felt that F's repeated passage at 5.3 and 5.11 "looks at first like a similar case, but here the real explanation may be different."[18] Chambers agreed with Fleay and others who doubted the authorship of the epilogue,[19] and attributed to an unknown source the decision to have Pandarus "incongruously brought back, on to the battlefield of all places," using the 5.3 lines to introduce the new ending.[20]

Like Chambers, Samuel Tannenbaum did not allow his bibliographical theory to override his critical judgment, and Tannenbaum admitted that his doubts about Shakespeare's authorship of the end of Pandarus's last speech (beginning "Good traders in the flesh") were "based purely on esthetic considerations."[21] Tannenbaum believed that F's repeated passage, and the large number of textual errors in the fifth act offer evidence that Shakespeare "worked upon (i.e., corrected and revised) the end of the play."[22] He offered two theories to explain F's repetition:

> (1) the lines may represent an addition made here (5.3) by Shakspere for the purpose of providing a natural and rueful exit for Pandarus, or (2) they represent an unsuccessful deletion which was made when it was decided (probably by Shakspere himself) to give the play a comic ending by assigning a closing speech to Pandarus. There can be hardly any doubt that the play originally ended with Troilus's poignant line, "Hope of revenge shall hide our inward woe." Pandarus's lines [at the end of 5.11, up until "Good traders in the flesh"] were, therefore, probably written during the revision of the play, not during its original composition.[23]

Greg concurred with Chambers on the implausibility of Pandarus's appearance on the battlefield, and believed that F's first dismissal of Pandarus is more appropriate, but like Tannenbaum he believed it was Shakespeare who was responsible for F's repeated lines. Greg seconded Chamber's view that F's repeated "They call him Troilus" was "an unquestionable false start," but unlike Chambers, Greg also explained the repeated dismissal of Pandarus as a similar printing error which allows reconstruction of the compositional process.

> There can be little doubt that the earlier was their original position and that they were intended to mark Pandarus's dismissal from the play. But later, when Shakespeare decided to have him speak the epilogue, and for that purpose brought him somewhat incongruously on to the field of bat-

tle, the lines were made to do duty and transferred to a later point in the text. If that is so F must somehow represent the foul papers in which the alteration was imperfectly made.[24]

Alice Walker agreed that the two instances of F's repetition ("They call him Troilus" and "Hence broker lackey") preserve "first and second thoughts in the process of composition. In both cases, the first thought was made use of later."[25] Walker's edition (of 1957) began to solidify support for the first shot theory, and many subsequent editors and commentators have accepted the theory and its editorial implications. With the common, though certainly not unanimous, acceptance of the Inns of Court and first shot theories, the main questions and conjectures that continue to be recycled were in place. Which of F's repeated dismissals of Pandarus came first, and what does that reveal about the way the play was written and performed? Did the decision to have Pandarus end the play come before or after the possibility of his role ending prior to the battle (in 5.3)? Were the two endings considered at the initial point of composition (as first and second shots), or was one ending the result of later revision? Was the addition or excision of Pandarus's final speech considered during the initial rehearsals, or for a revival? Does the nature of Pandarus's final address to the audience, especially when considered in relation to the claims of Q's title pages and epistle, or in relation to F's Prologue, suggest a place or occasion appropriate for different versions?

In 1964 and 1965 Nevill Coghill, J. M. Nosworthy, and E. A. J. Honigmann published books that included chapters offering extensive theories about the composition, printing, and first performances of *Troilus and Cressida*.[26] None of these critics fully supported the first shot theory, and all three suggested that Shakespeare at some point revised the end of the play. While Alexander's theory invites speculation on the occasion of the play's composition, critics have also used the Inns of Court theory as a starting point in speculations about revision and revivals. Nosworthy, for example, opposed the first shot theory, and revived the suggestion that the repeated exchange "provides for an alternative ending to the play."[27] After acknowledging that Alexander's theory of an Inns of Court performance "has won general acceptance," and indeed "commands acceptance," Nosworthy disputed Alexander's assumption that the play's only performance was at the Inns of Court. Pandarus's final speech would be without "any real meaning except in an Inn of Court," so that when the play was revived for the public theater, "Shakespeare dispensed with the now inappropriate Epilogue, resourcefully transferred the rejection of Pandarus to a suitable point in an earlier scene, and allowed the play to end on a tragic note."[28]

Like Nosworthy, Coghill also believed the play was performed at the Inns of Court with Pandarus's final speech, and at the Globe without it, but Coghill reversed the order of the first performances. He attempted to convince his readers that

> *Troilus and Cressida* was originally performed to public audiences at the Globe in 1602/3, and that it had neither the fierce Prologue nor the salacious "Epilogue" that are now an accepted part of its text. . . . It was revived for performance at one of the Inns of Court for the Christmas Revels of 1608, and . . . Shakespeare, who is known to have had trouble from undergraduate audiences at Christmas revels before, attempted to protect the play, by the addition of the Prologue and "Epilogue," from a bad reception by rowdy young cynics.[29]

Coghill's notion that a public performance preceded a private one was questioned in the *Times Literary Supplement* by Peter Alexander, and after a comment by J. K. Walton in *Shakespeare Survey* that Coghill's "arguments have been convincingly answered" by Alexander, a series of correspondences appeared in the *TLS* (in 1965, and more extensively in 1967) that debated the circumstances of composition, publication, and performance of *Troilus and Cressida*.[30] Coghill reaffirmed his belief that the prologue and epilogue were added for a private performance: "This protection was not needed at the Globe, but might help to control the rowdy audiences of the Inns of Court, from whom Shakespeare and his company had already suffered, when they presented *The Comedy of Errors* to them in 1594."[31] Alexander objected that the disturbance in 1594 occurred before the performance, and "has no significance whatever for an attempt to date the composition of the Prologue and Epilogue."[32] Alexander disputed Coghill's theory that the play would have been performed at the Globe, restating his view that it was not only performed at the Inns of Court, but written especially for it.

> The strongest evidence of the truth of the claim that *Troilus and Cressida* was written for private and not public performance is to be found in the play itself. . . . To treat the blatant scurrility of many passages in the play, and of the epilogue, as evidence of a production at a public theater ignores the tradition of "lewd and lascivious plays" and wittily obscene speeches associated with the Inns of Court.[33]

J. C. Maxwell contributed a more conservative, bibliographical view to the *TLS* debate, restating the first shot theory.

Most scholars would agree that the two lines preceding the epilogue were originally written for the end of V, iii, and that the decision to give Pandarus an epilogue was an afterthought. . . . The alteration can perfectly well have belonged to the original process of composition, with Shakespeare's first thoughts left undeleted in the manuscript which lies behind the Folio text of V, iii.[34]

Coghill replied by asking,

How came he to have this ragged "afterthought" for which he had to jettison a carefully constructed effect in a previous scene [5.3]? How is it possible to believe that such a total change of tone and direction, that is not even a true part of the play, but a piece of vaudeville chat, was "part of the original process of composition" as Mr. Maxwell suggests? It makes no sense. [. . . Shakespeare] was not one to bungle a carefully created effect for a sudden whim. That he was willing to do so later, for a particular and discernible purpose, and for a special audience, is another matter.[35]

In this final *TLS* letter, Coghill made clear the wider critical implications of the debate: "what is finally involved is our view of Shakespeare as an artist, his intention and his craftsmanship."[36] Coghill called attention to the way interpretations of bibliographic evidence can be colored by critical prejudices. Alexander's notion of what would or would not be appropriate for public and private theaters, and Maxwell's interpretation of bibliographical evidence are answered by Coghill's conception of dramatic construction, and the external forces that would require a violation of the play's original composition.

The critical prejudices involved in purportedly objective bibliographic theories were again highlighted in Gary Taylor's important essay of 1982.[37] The belief that F was set from foul papers had been one of the few commonly accepted points in many of the opposing theories, but Taylor questioned the "subjective judgements about the aesthetic superiority" of some variants, particularly

the two single pieces of evidence [F's repeated "they call him Troilus," and the repetition in F of Troilus' rejection of Pandarus] which form almost the entire basis for E. K. Chambers' claim—subsequently accepted and embellished by Alice Walker, W. W. Greg, J. M. Nosworthy, E. A. J. Honigmann, and G. B. Evans—that the Folio manuscript must have been foul papers.[38]

While Taylor argued that F's repetition of "they call him Troilus" is acceptable, or even desirable, he concurred with critical opinion about the repetition of Pandarus's rejection: "in this case, it cannot reasonably be claimed that both versions of the passage were intended to stand: . . . the exact repetition of Troilus' couplet would be pointless, ridiculous, and flat."[39]

Taylor not only accepted Alexander's Inns of Court theory, but stated, without much exaggeration, that it is a theory with which "almost all critics now agree."[40] He also approvingly cited Nosworthy's view that the epilogue was written especially for such an audience, and thus finds problematic, at least bibliographically, Coghill's belief that the Prologue and epilogue were added. Taylor did, however, still think that "Coghill's remarks on the dramatic function of the epilogue (88–91) are equally applicable if the Inns of Court performance was the play's premiere, and the epilogueless version used in subsequent performances at the Globe."[41] Coghill might object that his remarks about the epilogue were more closely wedded to his conviction that it was added rather than excised, but Taylor's point at least highlights the dialectical progression of the argument, with many theories precipitating a diametrically opposed conjecture.

Taylor proposed that if the Inns of Court performance was first, and the epilogue later cut, F would preserve not the foul papers, but a revised version, with Troilus's rejection of Pandarus appended to the scene where Pandarus delivers Cressida's letter (5.3). Q did not print the passage at 5.3 because it was not there in the first version, and thus there is no need to construct a theory explaining how Q rightly observed deletion marks that were not noticed in the printing of F.

> One need only presume that the Folio annotator ignored or did not see a signal to delete the Epilogue. Indeed, the signal may never have existed in the manuscript he was working from: as it came at the end of the play, and as the actors playing Pandarus and Troilus (and the rest of the company) can hardly have forgotten a change so fundamental, the promptbook may never have actually signalled the deletion at all; certainly, it could have signalled it very faintly and causally.[42] Even if the annotator saw the deletion, he might have ignored it; his doing so would at least be more plausible in these circumstances than in those envisaged by Walker, for here he need only passively let stand in his quarto copy lines marked for deletion in the manuscript, whereas in her reconstruction he must actively add to the quarto lines marked for deletion.[43]

Taylor's belief that the epilogue was excised by Shakespeare for a performance allows him to postulate removing it from modern editions: "There is nothing scandalous about omitting the epilogue; modern editors always omit the alternative version of the rejection of Pandarus, in V.iii, so that no more is at stake than a choice of omissions."[44] In bibliographical terms, the theory of copy-text and the conjecture about the revision must outweigh any critical or editorial desire to present the reader with the fuller text. While many editors have argued against the inclusion of Pandarus's final speech, questioning its authorship or its placement, few have used their arguments to justify eliminating the speech from their edition. Taylor's essay, however, coincided with his work as an editor, and the Oxford Shakespeare *Complete Works* printed the QF ending of the play, from Pandarus's entrance to his final speech, as Additional Passage B, which conveniently fit on the same page as Troilus's final speech, and Taylor's bracketed final stage direction, "[*Exeunt marching*]." The Norton Shakespeare, published about ten years after the Oxford using a text "based on the Oxford edition," prints the Oxford's additional passages in their QF position, but indents and italicizes them to "make it easier to see how the . . . passages functioned in a version of the play that Shakespeare also authored."[45]

Four years after the Oxford *Complete Works* was published, *Analytical and Enumerative Bibliography* dedicated an issue to the "New Oxford Shakespeare," including an essay by the general editors.[46] After indicating that they were not working on a revised version, Wells and Taylor offered the following parenthetic remark:

> (However, we do wish to endorse a conjecture made privately by Wilbur Sanders, who suggests that the Folio's addition of three lines at the end of 5.3 of *Troilus and Cressida* was intended as a cue for the addition of the whole passage which follows them, a passage placed by Q at the end of the play and by the Oxford edition as Additional Passage B. This suggestion both accounts for F's duplication, while permitting the retention—in a different place—of Pandarus' farewell to the audience. It also saves an editor from the embarrassment of omitting entirely a passage present in both substantive texts.)[47]

Sanders's suggestion is quite close to W. S. Walker's quoted above, but with perhaps a more bibliographic rationale. Walker believed only the first half of Pandarus's speech should end 5.3, but Sanders proposed the whole speech should be transferred. While it may seem like a logical objection that the epilogue-like quality of the speech would seem out of place before the end of the play, the theater history provides a number of examples where critics applauded the decision to have the speech as Walker and Sanders suggest.

Honigmann's influential book, *The Stability of Shakespeare's Text* (1965), challenged the tendency of the New Bibliography to "throw Shakespeare's words out of the canon through over-confidence regarding printing house practices."[48] Perhaps surprisingly, his chapter on *Troilus and Cressida* hardly mentions F's repeated dialogue between Troilus and Pandarus, or the possibility of a revised ending. Twenty-five years later, however, he considered the arguments put forward by Gary Taylor. Taylor's and Honigmann's articles contributed to another flurry of conjectures about the ending of the play, amid renewed interest in the possibility of Shakespearean revisions sparked by the work on *King Lear*.[49] Honigmann questioned Taylor's conclusions about *Troilus and Cressida*, admitting that Taylor's theory about the copy-texts of QF contradicts the conjectures about a different kind of revision that Honigmann proposed. Honigmann sided with Greg, Alice Walker, and those who believed that F's repeated dialogue preserved first thoughts, and that the original, more appropriate dismissal of Pandarus in the palace (5.3) was excised (or should have been) when Shakespeare wrote or revised the ending. Although Honigmann has some interesting speculations about the circumstances under which the play was written, revised, and performed, it is his theory about the change in the play's genre, and the possibility that a sequel was at one time contemplated, which relates most specifically to the present discussion of F's repeated dialogue.

Questions about the play's genre have been an issue since the first references to it as comedy (in Q's epistle), history (on Q's title page), and tragedy (in F). The textual ambiguity surrounding the ending has led to a number of theories about how the play's genre was modified either during composition or revision. Honigmann divorces his notion of a revised end from any speculation about the Inns of Court performance, but like Coghill and Nosworthy, is convinced that the play was started as a tragedy. The play that Honigmann believed Shakespeare set out to write, however, was a tragedy that would end with the death not only of Hector, but of Troilus as well.

> It seems that the lines were first written for V.3, the last opportunity for Troilus to renounce Pandar, if Troilus was to die in battle; then, when it was decided not to kill off Troilus, the lines were moved to V.10, thus creating an opening for Pandar and his "epilogue," where a sequel is promised.
>
>> Brethren and sisters of the hold-door trade,
>> Some two months hence my will shall here be made.
>
> This is an appetizer rather like the one offered at the end of *2 Henry IV:* "If you be not too much cloyed with fat meat, our humble author will continue the story with Sir John in it" (another promise of a sequel that could not be kept, it is believed, for fear of giving offence).[50]

The theory that Pandarus is alluding to a sequel in his final speech has a long history, and Hillebrand (in his New Variorum) nominated

Hertzberg as "one of the most vigorous proponents."[51] Honigmann is one of several more recent advocates, but there have also been many who have objected to the theory. Muir strongly asserted that "there is no evidence that Shakespeare ever intended to write a sequel or sequels."[52] Pandarus's declaration that he will make his will "some two months hence" is interpreted by Muir as a reference to the character's "approaching death, rather than to a sequel." Foakes similarly believed the notion of a sequel to be a "red herring," and like Muir believes that the lines should "more reasonably be interpreted as the character's final joke about impending death from the venereal disease he plans to bequeath to the audience."[53]

The editorial introduction and notes to *Troilus and Cressida* in *A Textual Companion* provided an opportunity for Taylor to reaffirm his theory of copy-text as set out in the *Shakespeare Studies* article, and to answer Honigmann's objections to it. Taylor did, however, agree with Honigmann's skepticism about the Inns of Court, and also accepted Honigmann's agreement with Nosworthy and others that Shakespeare at one time planned a sequel.

> Pandarus' intrusion at the end of the play therefore need not be explained as an anomalous extra-theatrical address to a specific audience for a single performance [at the Inns of Court], but as a more normal epilogue: alluding to the (notorious) presence of bawds and whores in the public playhouses on the South Bank (hence "Winchester"), and promising a sequel. "Some two monthes hence" is, on the evidence of Henslowe's records, not at all unreasonable as an interval between the première of a play and the première of its sequel. In this case (as in many others) the hoped-for sequel apparently never materialized.[54]

The Inns of Court theory, and its general acceptance, seemed crucial to Taylor's initial view of the occasion for composing and then excising Pandarus' appearance at the end of the play. Taylor did not, however, address in *A Textual Companion* how his new skepticism of the Inns of Court theory related to his belief that Pandarus should not appear in the last scene of F. Presumably, the specific circumstances of the first performance and first revival was a dispensable conjecture that related to, but did not form an integral part of the theory's bibliographical foundation.

The debate over whether Pandarus speaks of his impending death, or refers to a sequel, raises complex questions about how the final speech addresses the audience, and what kind of audience it addresses. Despite its detractors (including Harbage, Kimbrough, and more recently, Taylor and Honigmann) the Inns of Court theory continues to be cited as almost historical fact by a number of critics, editors, and reviewers. Kenneth Palmer, in his influential Arden edition, stated that

> the heirs of Pandar are hard to identify. No normal audience would be composed of *brethren and sisters of the hold-door trade* (and it is difficult to imagine one which was): one must therefore posit an audience which would find amusing such scurrilous abuse; and, to that extent, Alexander's theory of performance at an Inn of Court is very plausible.[55]

Palmer goes on to say that "presumably the young lawyers did not mind being called bawds," but the implication of Palmer's argument is that a "normal" (presumably Globe) audience would neither include bawds and whores, nor be expected to enjoy the scurrility of Pandarus's final speech. Assumptions about the makeup and expectation of the play's first audiences are, of course, problematic, but Pandarus's final speech has had the unique ability to lead critics to opposed conclusions.

In opposition to the many critics who cite Pandarus's speech as evidence that the play, or at least the speech, would not have been performed at the Globe, Baldwin remarked that Pandarus's final speech was "certainly calculated for a Bankside audience."[56] Ramsey similarly observed that "for a public theater audience, of course, these insults would have had good comic validity; but they do not square well with the guests assembled for an Inns of Court Revels."[57] Ramsey also objected to the Inns of Court theory because of Pandarus's two addresses specifically to women in the audience (at the end of 3.3 and 5.11). While women may have been present at an Inns of Court performance, it may seem less likely for women to be addressed specifically in such a setting.

Like Ramsey, Foakes also referred to Pandarus's two speeches to the audience as a way of arguing against the Inns of Court theory. As mentioned above, Foakes rejected the notion that Pandarus's final speech implies a sequel. He believed that the speech does not "refer to some particular time or event connected with the first performance, but rounds off the action by adding the impending fall of Pandarus to the impending fall of Troy."

> Once before, at the end of III.2, Pandarus stepped out of his individual part to address the audience in his symbolic role as pander. Then, flushed with success, he gleefully wished all maidens in the audience a pander's help; but now, in his epilogue in Act V, he appears as an ailing old bawd, riddled with the diseases of the profession, sardonically appealing to panders in the audience for sympathy. The effect is to project a play based on ancient legend startlingly into the audience's own world.[58]

Foakes recognized the possibility of the play at one point ending with Troilus's speech, but he preferred the QF ending as a way of reintroducing Pandarus's choric role.

> It seems to me that the sourly comic ending with Pandarus complaining to the audience is much the more appropriate to the general tone of the play, and the nature of its action; and the play falls naturally into two halves, one predominantly comic, and culminating in Pandarus's address to the audience at the end of III.2, the other harsher, and ending on a more bitter note, but also with Pandarus addressing the audience, so paralleling the first part.[59]

Foakes suggested that Pandarus's first speech directed at the audience may have been the point for some kind of interval, and virtually all modern productions have had their interval after Pandarus's couplet,

> And Cupid grant all tongue-tied maidens here
> Bed, chamber, and Pandar to provide this gear!
>
> (3.2.207)[60]

The symmetry of ending the play's two halves with Pandarus referring to the theater audience is certainly attractive, and will be returned to in the theater history which shows how productions have enhanced or diminished Pandarus's choric potential by the placement and staging of his final speech.

Foakes highlighted the desirability of the QF ending, but admitted that the textual evidence is inconclusive in determining whether Troilus or Pandarus should end the play. Robert Kimbrough and David Farley-Hills both offered theories that explore the alternative endings as possible points of revision, focusing not simply on the occasion or reason for the revisions, but on the way the changes alter the play, and especially the role of Pandarus. Kimbrough believed that Q represented a later version that excised the Prologue "after the topicality of the War of the Theatres was passé," and added a "new epilogue . . . directed at a public audience."[61] The new ending emphasized the role of Pandarus, and spurred Bonian and Walley into advertising on Qb's title page the large part Pandarus plays.

Farley-Hills argued that the play "shows unmistakable signs of two different endings, which strongly suggest two different audiences." Like Kimbrough, he connected Qb's title page and F's Prologue with the different endings, and a revision of Pandarus's character.

> Almost all commentaries are agreed that in one version the play was presented without the epilogue and that Troilus' lines in that version ap-

peared only at the end of V, iii. This suggests a version in which Pandarus was less prominent and would therefore be closer to the prologue's "argument" than to the quarto's second title-page.[62]

This seems one of the most fruitful arguments, connecting bibliographical details with a major character revision. How does Pandarus change, and how does the play itself change, with these different endings and beginnings? Much of the following stage history of the play's ending will concentrate on the steady increase in the emphasis of Pandarus, particularly his bawdiness and his metatheatrical potential. Farley-Hills intriguingly reads F's repetition as evidence that the first performances may have similarly adjusted the character's prominence.

Farley-Hills accepted Taylor's conclusion that Q derives from foul papers and F from a promptbook, but disagreed with Taylor's theory that the "private version preceded the public." Like Palmer and other supporters of the Inns of Court theory, Farley-Hills argued that Pandarus's reference to making his will suggests that the speech was written for an audience of law students. Farley-Hills also accepted, however, the remarks by Harbage, Baldwin, and Kimbrough that the Inns would not have been able to afford to commission the play.

> It is much more likely, on the evidence we have, that the play was written for the Globe in the normal course of events to add a Troy play to their repertoire. . . . The adaptation of Shakespeare's play for a "private" audience would make more sense as a salvaging operation after a "public" flop. The most likely venue for this revival, in view of Shakespeare's relationship with Marston at this time, would be Paul's playhouse, which seems always to have had a sizeable number of law students in its audience, and whose plays (especially Middleton's) are often characterized by their legal allusions.[63]

Bibliographers' quests to use textual evidence to fix the site of the original performances, whether it be at the Inns of Court, the Globe, or Paul's playhouse, suggest many interesting combinations of audience and version. Qualifying the play as specialist entertainment, or especially boys' entertainment, can, however, sanitize the play's philosophy, complexity, and lasciviousness.

Literary critics and theorists have also found Pandarus's address to the audience a rich source for speculation and commentary. René Girard, for example, has carefully considered the mimetic implications of Pandarus's final speech.

> It is fitting that the last word in this play should belong to Pandarus and deal with the mimetic contagion of the theater, symbolized by venereal

disease. . . . Pandarus bequeaths his illness to an audience entirely made up of people with the same calling as his own, bawds in other words, his own doubles and replicas, people at the same stage of the mimetic disease, people compelled to stage their own desires or, if it cannot be done, to watch them being staged by someone else.

If the theater puts the mimetic disease on the stage, it can only result in more contamination. The playwright is in league with the forces of chaos. Pandarus is a symbol of the theater and of those who live by the theater. The public would not go to the theater, it would not attend this kind of play, if it were not as predisposed to the mimetic illness as Pandarus himself. The theater provides voyeuristic gratification and frustration similar to those craved by Pandarus. The spectacle we most relish is that of furious desire playing havoc with the lives of our fellow men. The literary pander turns the spectators into addicts of mimetic representation. They will leave the place with a more acute case of the disease than when they entered.[64]

While it may seem problematic to speak of an audience reacting in a uniform way, Girard begins to unpack the complex exchange between the audience and Pandarus. The many critics who have speculated on the specific audience Pandarus addresses have relied heavily on the manner in which Pandarus engages with the audience. Without attempting to specify the kind of audience where Pandarus's speech would be most appropriate, Girard suggests a more general indictment of the experience of watching plays. His reading can also foreground the critical subtext present in the way theories like the Inns of Court create specialist audiences that diffuse the impact of Pandarus's speech. In Girard's poetics, Pandarus's diseases are bequeathed to all the audience, and all audiences, as the voyeurism involved in playgoing make us all "guilty creatures sitting at a play" (*Hamlet*, 2.2.591). The following stage history explores the way that the conjectures and concerns of editors and critics have been reflected in productions, and pays particular attention to the relationship between Pandarus and the audience.

Dryden ended his adaptation in a manner very different to *Troilus and Cressida,* but as with many of the passages discussed in this study, Dryden's alterations offer appropriate editorial and theatrical commentary. Dryden referred to Shakespeare's *Troilus and Cressida* as "the Tragedy which I have undertaken to correct" (Preface, 225), and as Barbara Bowen pointed out, Dryden attempted "to bring Shakespeare's play into line with the classicizing drama of Racine then paramount on the English stage. . . . Almost all his changes stem from the choice of genre."[65] The way Dryden set about correcting the tragedy specifically relates to the debate over the genre and alternative endings of *Troilus and Cressida*. Tannenbaum, Coghill, Nosworthy, and Honigmann all connected the possible alternative endings to the play's genre, but Joel Altman considered Shakespeare's use of sources to further explain how the play's genre and ending may have changed. Altman proposed that Shakespeare began writing a tragedy that would end with the death of Troilus. When Shakespeare decided to give Hector the death that Troilus suffers in the sources, at the hands of Achilles and his Myrmidons, the play began to move away from a tragic finale.[66] Dryden's decision to give back to Troilus the death by Achilles created the sort of tragic ending that Altman believed Shakespeare may have been contemplating.[67]

Although *Truth Found Too Late* does not end the play with Troilus's tirade, Dryden's decision to transpose Pandarus's final exit into an earlier scene anticipates the view of many commentators who would prefer the play to end on a more tragic note. As mentioned in the discussion of Cressida being kissed by the Greeks, in *Truth Found Too Late* Pandarus's final appearance comes soon after Troilus witnesses Cressida and Diomedes together in the Greek camp. As in *Troilus and Cressida*, Aeneas enters seeking Troilus, but as Troilus gives Ulysses "distracted thanks" and they move to exit, Pandarus interrupts Troilus with "Hear ye, my Lord, Hear ye" (*Truth Found Too Late*, 4.2.348). Pandarus tells Troilus of Cressida's arrival into the camp, delivers Cressida's letter to Troilus, and is immediately scorned and rejected by Troilus. Dryden then approximated what some directors of *Troilus and Cressida* will follow him in doing, and what W. S. Walker, Sanders, and Taylor believe Shakespeare did, which is to transfer Pandarus's speech which ends the play in QF (or, to be more precise, an altered, cut version of the speech), to the scene where Pandarus delivers Cressida's letter and makes his last appearance. With Troilus and Aeneas still onstage, Pandarus speaks his final lines in response to Troilus telling him to "Hence from my sight" (*Truth Found Too Late*, 4.2.286):

> O world, world; thou art an ungratefull patch of Earth! Thus the poor Agent is despis'd! he labours painfully in his calling, and trudges between parties: but when their turns are serv'd, come out's too good for him. I am mighty melancholy: I'le e'en go home, and shut up my doors; and dye o'th sullens like an old bird in a Cage! (*Truth Found Too Late*, 4.2.392)

Gone is the syphilitic Pandar and his bawdy song, but especially relevant to the present discussion, Dryden also eliminated the second half of Pandarus's speech. Maximillian Novak notes that "Dryden changes Pandarus' direct address to the audience (which he would have thought a technique of farce)."[68] Dryden did, however, include an epilogue that spoke directly to the audience, but Dryden's epilogue is delivered by Thersites, with only remote borrowings from Shakespeare.

> These cruel Critiques put me into passion;
> For in their lowring looks I reade damnation:
> Ye expect a Satyr, and I seldom fail,
> When I'm first beaten, 'tis my part to rail.
> You British fools, of the Old Trojan stock,
> That stand so thick one cannot miss the flock,
> Poets have cause to dread a keeping Pit,
> When Womens Cullyes come to judge of Wit.
> As we strow Rats-bane when we vermine fear,
> 'Twere worth our cost to scatter fool-bane here;   10
> And after all our judging Fops were serv'd,
> Dull Poets too shou'd have a dose reserv'd,
> Such Reprobates, as past all sence of shaming,
> Write on, and nere are satisfy'd with damming;
> Next, those, to whom the Stage does not belong,
> Such whose Vocation onely is to Song;
> At most to Prologue, when, for want of time,
> Poets take in for Journywork in Rhime.
> But I want curses for those mighty shoales,
> Of scribbling Chlorisses, and Phillis fools;   20
> Those Ophs shou'd be restraind, during their lives,
> From Pen and Ink, as Madmen are from knives.
> I cou'd rayl on, but 'twere a task as vain
> As Preaching truth at Rome, or wit in Spain:
> Yet to huff out our Play was worth my trying,
> John Lilburn scap'd his Judges by defying:
> If guilty, yet I'm sure o'th' Churches blessing,
> By suffering for the Plot, without confessing.

The decision to add to the choric element of Thersites' role, and the desire to have Thersites involved in the final image of the play, provide further examples of Dryden anticipating the performance interpretations of later productions.

Pandarus's last speech in *Troilus and Cressida*, as Stanley Wells has written, "wrenches the play into the time at which it is being performed,"[69] and *Truth Found Too Late* achieves a similar effect with Thersites' epilogue. The audience is directly implicated when referred to as "You British fools, of the Old Trojan stock" (5), and Thersites contemptuously rails against the "Womens Cullyes come to judge of Wit" (8) in the theater. When Dryden's Thersites condemns the "Dull Poets" (12), Novak notes that "Dryden is unlikely to be generalizing, since that was hardly the nature of epilogues," and offers two candidates for Dryden's criticism (Elkanah Settle and Thomas Shadwell).[70] There are also less veiled references to contemporary people ("Lilburn," 26) and events ("the [Popish] Plot," 28), conforming to the vogue of epilogues of the period.[71] The localized references that Dryden adds foreground part of his agenda in rewriting the play, and point forward to the way productions have staged the play's ending in a manner that is acutely aware of the audience.

When John Philip Kemble prepared *Troilus and Cressida* for his unrealized performance, he too, like Dryden, moved and cut Pandarus's speech that ends the play in QF. The edition Kemble used for his promptbook followed F in repeating Troilus's rejection of Pandarus, but Kemble would almost certainly have been aware of other options: he owned a copy of Q, which he marked "collated and perfect,"[72] and as James Boaden, Kemble's friend and biographer noted, Kemble "was intimate, according to their different habits, with Mr. Steevens, Mr. Malone, and Mr. Reed, the editors and commentators of Shakespeare."[73] Boaden also recorded that when Kemble "prepared, and rendered prodigiously attractive" a stage version of *The Tempest,* he introduced "in a temperate way some of the additions of D'Avenant and Dryden."[74]

Jeanne Newlin observed that Kemble's alterations "made the siege of Troy his heroic main plot and relegated the unhappy love affair to a tragic subplot."[75] It is not surprising then that Kemble's production would have ended with Troilus's final speech (somewhat cut, but ending, as QF, "Hope of revenge shall hide our inward woe"). Kemble did not, however, dispose entirely of Pandarus's lines. Like Dryden, Kemble not only wanted Pandarus's role to end in the scene where he delivered Cressida's letter, but he wanted Pandarus to have a final speech lamenting the role of the pander.

> A goodly medicine for my aching bones! ~~O world, world, world!~~ Thus is the poor agent despised! O traitors and bawds, how earnestly are you set a-work, and how ill requited! ~~Why should our endeavour be so loved and the performance so loathed? What verse for it?~~ What instance for it? Let me see:
>
> > "Full merrily the humblebee doth sing
> > Till he hath lost his honey and his sting,
> > And being once subdued in armèd tail,
> > Sweet honey and sweet notes together fail."
>
> Good traders in the flesh, set this in your painted cloths.[76]

Kemble ended the speech and the scene with this cut version of the speech, and signalled a scene change from "Priam's Palace" to "The field of battle between Troy and the Grecian tents." By cutting the final half of Pandarus's speech, Kemble, like Dryden, can only offer limited support to the conjecture (of W. S. Walker, Sanders, and Taylor) that Pandarus's speech should be delivered at the end of the palace scene. Dryden's and Kemble's decisions to cut the direct address to the audience may be related to its lascivious content and aggressive tone, but the cuts also imply that the final half of the speech may have seemed inappropriate before the play had finished.

Like Dryden's adaptation and Kemble's aborted production, Poel also rejected the QF ending, and rearranged Troilus's final encounter with Pandarus and the end of the play in a way that comments directly on the editorial concerns. The Cassell National Library edition that Poel marked for performance follows Q by printing Troilus's rejection of Pandarus only at the end of the play, but the Cassell edition also omitted Pandarus's final speech, concluding the play with Troilus telling Pandarus to "Live aye with thy name." Poel reinstated, with a pencilled addition in his promptbook, the F only lines at the end of the palace scene, and cut the same lines at the end of the play. Whether his decision was influenced by the bibliographical evidence, or based more purely on dramatic considerations, Poel offered a production that approximated the conjecture of how F should have been printed, with Pandarus rejected before the battle, and Troilus's mourning of Hector ending the play.

After Hector's reaction to Cassandra's prophecy ("You are amazed . . . at night," 5.3.94), Poel had Troilus exit with Priam and Hector as the inner stage curtain was closed. Troilus and Pandarus then re-entered in front of the curtain for their exchange, which in the promptbook is entitled the "Letter" scene.[77] Just as many commentators have objected to the intrusion of Pandarus onto the battlefield, Poel may have wanted to distance Pandarus from the tragedy of Hector. Poel's staging pushed the scene closer to the audience, and outside the "frame like contrivance at the back of the stage" which R. T. Rundle Milliken described as "giving the artificial effect of the grouping in a painted picture."[78] Troilus's rejection of Pandarus could have been especially poignant in contrast to Hector's more remote, perhaps formalistic, rejection of his family's warning.

Poel staged Pandarus's final exit as many critics believe Shakespeare at one time intended, but he also created a finale that was more purely his own invention, while still giving the final lines to Troilus. After Agamemnon says "Great Troy is ours, and our sharp wars are ended" (5.10.9), and the Greeks exit, Poel's promptbook has the following direction:

> Re open tableau curtain
> Hector slain, Troilus weeping, discov[ere]d
> Final Tableau Blue
> (1) Music starts, (2) Cassandra's cry off, (3) low drum, (4) close tableau, up, House lights up

All of the final scene was cut, with the exception of four lines for Troilus, presumably spoken through his tears.

> Frown on, you heavens, effect your rage with speed!
> Sit, gods, upon your thrones, and smile at Troy!
> I say at once let your brief plagues be mercy,
> And linger not our sure destructions on!
>
> (5.11.6)[79]

The tableau was described by John Palmer as

> the lit figure of Troilus mourning Hector upon the inner stage; seen through the purple gloom of the tragic scene; the faint cry of Cassandra floating in the air.[80]

Without Aeneas's comment to Troilus ("My Lord, you do discomfort all the host," 5.11.10), and without Troilus's enraged reaction to Hector's death, Poel significantly alters the end of the play and Troilus's character, presenting a submissive mourning that would seem to leave the audience with a more traditional tragic end.

Poel's tableau both emphasizes and distinguishes some differences between the possible endings with or without Pandarus's final address to the audience. Although endorsing the desirability of ending the play with the tragic and heroic finale of Hector's death and Troilus's reaction, Poel's cuts also highlight the complex dialogue and dramatic situation he eliminated from the final scene. Even without Pandarus's salacious attack on the audience, the play ends not with submissive mourning, but with anger and defiance. Perhaps Poel's introduction of Cassandra's cry adds some of the discomfort eliminated with Troilus's and Pandarus's speeches, but Poel's ending would seem to have left an impression far less bitter than either the QF or the conjectured end. Since Poel himself played Pandarus, an interesting relationship would have been set up between playwright, director, actor, character, and audience if Pandarus's final speech was delivered. The reviewer for the *Pall Mall Gazette* wrote that "Pandarus it is true does have his ugly significance—though last night he had none."[81] Poel cut the greatest opportunity to assert Pandarus's "ugly significance," and it would seem that as director and actor, he opted for a very different relationship with his audience than that set up in Pandarus's final speech.

George Bernard Shaw's oft-quoted remark, that in *Troilus and Cressida, All's Well That Ends Well,* and *Measure for Measure* Shakespeare was "ready and willing to start at the twentieth century if the seventeenth would only let him,"[82] is especially appropriate for the stage history of Pandarus's last speech. The first two major British productions to bring Pandarus on at the end of the play were Macowan's and Guthrie's, and both directors set their productions in the twentieth century. While Poel cut all but five lines of the last scene, Macowan spoke of the importance of the scene, stressing Troilus's metamorphosis and its juxtaposition with Pandarus's appearance.

> One of the chief themes of the play is the gradual degeneration of Troilus from someone hopeful, idealistic, full of love, to a man entirely embittered and giving himself over to a future of the thought of nothing but revenge. . . . And then Shakespeare does an amazing thing which is, as it were, to send all that up and finish the play on a note of utter triviality.[83]

Macowan included all of Troilus's final speech (beginning "You understand me not" and ending "our inward woe"), but followed it not with Pandarus's entrance, but with a stage clearing exeunt. It is unclear whether Troilus rejected Pandarus in the earlier scene, but the dialogue between Troilus and Pandarus was entirely cut at the end of the play, and Pandarus entered alone to deliver a cut version of his final speech.

> [~~A goodly medicine for my aching bones.~~] O world, [~~world,~~] world! Thus is the poor agent despised. O traders and bawds, how earnestly are you set awork, and how ill requited! [~~Why should our endeavour be so desired and the performance so loathed?~~] What verse for it? What instance for it? Let me see.

> > Full merrily the humble-bee doth sting,
> > Till he hath lost his honey and his sting;
> > And being once subdued in armèd tail,
> > Sweet honey and sweet notes together fail.

> Good traders in the flesh, set this is [*sic*] your painted cloths.
>
> > > > > > > > > [*Exit*][84]

This ending of the play is printed as an appendix to James Christy's doctoral dissertation, and while Christy had a personal interview with Macowan, and presumably consulted a copy of the promptbook,

Christy seems to be mistaken about a crucial aspect of the final lines.[85] In a review that Christy does not cite, a different ending is described. It was to Thersites,

> and not to Pandarus, [that] this production gives the last word in the play. "Good traders in the flesh, set this in your painted cloths," he snarls, and you go home thinking of "Idiot's Delight" and "For Services Rendered."[86]

No mention of Thersites is made in Christy's version of Macowan's script for the last scene, and when speaking to Christy about the ending, Macowan was unclear about other matters. Macowan could not remember if Pandarus entered "in front of the barbed wire battlefield set or in front of the traverse curtain. He hoped he had done the former."[87] These two options present very different stage images, which both support and refute the critical opinion that Pandarus's entrance is an incongruous intrusion on the battlefield. Macowan's favored option puts Pandarus on the battlefield, but by cutting the dialogue with Troilus, Pandarus was separated from the action rather than entering into its midst. If Pandarus's rejection did occur in the earlier scene (5.3), Macowan supports the critics who believe that Pandarus's rejection most appropriately follows from his delivering of Cressida's letter, but Macowan also showed a desire for Pandarus to end the play. In the space before a curtain, or even on the deserted battlefield, Pandarus's choric presence would be heightened by eliminating the dialogue with Troilus, but Macowan also diminished the metatheatricality of the moment by cutting Pandarus's direct address to the audience.

Dryden, Kemble, and some later directors cut the last half of the speech when it was given in the scene where Pandarus delivers Cressida's letter, but Macowan, as the director of the first major production to have Pandarus enter at the end of the play, similarly did not want Pandarus to predict that he will bequeath the audience his diseases. It was not, however, prudishness that caused Macowan to excise the second half of the speech. He explained to Christy that he cut the speech because the "references to brothels and venereal disease were too Elizabethan for the context of his [modern dress] production."[88] Macowan also spoke of the way Max Adrian helped create an ending that combined seemingly disparate qualities.

> Max Adrian brought something quite wonderful to this because, while one despises Pandarus and he's a ridiculous character and so on, there's something exceedingly lovable always about Max Adrian's personality, and this end had a kind of pathos from the Pandarus angle which gave it another dimension. It made a very strange end to this very strange play.[89]

If Thersites did speak the final line, his presence might have achieved some of the choric scurrility that was cut from the second half of Pandarus's speech. As discussed in the chapter on the play's opening, Thersites delivered the Prologue leaning on the proscenium dressed as a war correspondent. His final admonishment to "set this in your painted cloths" would end the play, as it began, with Thersites addressing the audience.

Throughout this study it has been shown how productions react, directly or indirectly, to the editions they use, especially when editions used for promptbooks take unusual action, either in the text or in the notes. One of the clearest examples of this dialogue between editors and directors is the way that the first three productions of *Troilus and Cressida* originating at the Shakespeare Memorial Theatre all reacted to the note in Ridley's New Temple Edition about F's repeated lines:

> Q omits their earlier occurrence, probably rightly. One would say certainly rightly if the play has its intended conclusion. But it has been held that the play should end at line 31 with Troilus' couplet, that the epilogue is an intrusion and that the lines were transferred to this point [near the end of the play] to introduce [Pandarus' final speech].[90]

Ridley does not seem fully supportive of the view he cites that the epilogue is intrusive, but Payne, Quayle, and Shaw all used Ridley's edition for their promptbooks, and all agreed with the conjecture that "the play should end at line 31 with Troilus' couplet." Ridley repeated Pandarus's rejection, as F, but bracketed the F only lines at the end of 5.3. Payne, Quayle, and Shaw all disregarded Ridley's brackets and included Troilus's rejection of Pandarus in the earlier scene. All three directors also transposed to the end of 5.3 differently cut versions of Pandarus's speech from the end of the play.

Payne's promptbook has the note "insert speech from end of play" at the end of 5.3, and at the end of the play the speech is untouched until after "set this in your painted cloths." The rest of the speech is crossed out, again denying Pandarus his ten lines of rhyming couplets. For the final scene, Payne had the Trojans enter onto his "inner above" space, but Troilus entered below. The promptbook notes that after the first rhyming couplet in Troilus's final speech, "{But march away: / Hector is dead;} there is no more to say,"[91] he was "going up steps" to join the other Trojans. This movement would seem to coincide aptly with the sense of a false ending to the play, and while some other promptbooks note a pause after the couplet, Payne's offered an action that further highlighted the sense of an aborted ending. The movement could also indicate the shift in mood from mourning to revenge, with Troilus walking up the steps to join the other Trojans as his failure to find anything "more to say" about his brother's death is superseded by the warrior's "hope of revenge."

While Payne's reviewers did not mention the transposition of Pandarus's speech or the effect of the ending, Quayle's production did spur some comments. Brian Harvey thought that Quayle left himself "open to criticism" by moving Pandarus's speech, which should "seal the mood of nausea."[92] J. C. Trewin seemed more sympathetic:

> When Troilus (Paul Scofield), already stricken, mourns at the last for Hector, his low, charged voice rising from a hell of grief and anger, the play wears transiently the tragic mask. At Stratford now we leave with this in our minds instead of the wry epilogue of Pandarus, transferred to an earlier scene.[93]

Without seeming to judge the transferal as desirable or undesirable, Trewin indicated the tragic effect achieved by ending with Troilus. The fact that Pandarus speaks his "wry epilogue" earlier was given even less critical comment, leaving the reader to wonder if its wry character was more appropriate or effective before the battle scenes.

Quayle's promptbook is virtually unmarked for Pandarus's entrance and dialogue in 5.3, and Pandarus delivered Cressida's letter and spoke of his "whoreson tisick" in an uncut version of the passage. While Payne had crossed out the direction for Troilus to tear the letter, Quayle left the direction untouched, but included a note for Troilus to hit Pandarus with the letter as he said "ignomy and shame."[94] The promptbook has Pandarus's speech from the end of the play pasted in at the end of 5.3. After "set this in your painted cloths," there is an erased line through the rest of the speech, presumably indicating that the lines were at one time cut, but subsequently reinstated. Some individual lines were cut in this reinstated passage, so that after being uncut through Pandarus' song, the speech concluded,

> ~~Good traders in the flesh, set this in your painted cloths:~~
> As many as be here of Pandar's hall,
> Your eyes, half out, weep out at Pandar's fall;
> ~~Or if you cannot weep, yet give some groans,~~
> ~~Though not for me, yet for your aching bones.~~
> Brethren and sisters of the hold-door trade,
> Some two months hence my will shall here be made:
> ~~It should be now, but that my fear is this,~~
> ~~Some galled goose of Winchester would hiss:~~
> Till then I'll sweat and seek about for eases,
> And at that time bequeath you my diseases. (Ridley's edition)

Despite the five lines that were cut, Quayle presented a version of the speech that directly addressed the audience, and a direction in the promptbook for Pandarus to cross to the center of the stage apron for the latter half of the speech could have emphasized his implicating the audience as potential members of "Pandar's hall." Although some of the references to venereal disease were cut, many were retained, and the speech lost little of its bawdiness. Quayle's decision to keep a relatively full version of the speech is especially relevant for the present discussion, supporting the conjecture that the epilogue-like speech could be spoken before the end of the play.

Like Payne's direction for Troilus to join the Trojans after his first rhyming couplet, Quayle less emphatically indicated a false sense of the play ending by marking pauses before and after Troilus says,

> {But march away:
> Hector is dead;} there is no more to say.[95]

Ralph Berry commented that for the end of the play,

> Pandarus' epilogue vanishes, leaving Troilus to end on "Hope of revenge shall hide our inward woe." This is the "Romantic" way of ending the play, and the promptbook confirms the speculation: on "inward," Aeneas and the Trojans exeunt, and the directions call for "lights, music," with "on high violin note, Lights 42 IN BLACKOUT, FAST CURTAIN." This is typical of late forties theater (the period of, for example, Cocteau's *The Eagle Has Two Heads*), a heroic, gestural conclusion.[96]

Linking the ending to a theatrical trend of the production's era, Berry establishes a justification for the director's departure from the QF ending without recourse to bibliographical arguments. Berry also emphasizes the importance of understanding decisions about the script within the context of the entire experience the production offered, with the music and blackout as essential as the rearrangement of the text in creating the play's finale.

Quayle played Pandarus in the next Shakespeare Memorial Theatre production, directed by Byam Shaw, and some similarities between the two productions may be expected. Pandarus's speech was again transposed to the end of 5.3, but there were many differences between the productions' cuts and the actions in both the palace and battlefield scenes. Pandarus spoke all but five lines of his final speech when Quayle directed the play, but when Quayle played Pandarus the speech ended with "set this in your painted cloths."[97] Some discussion between actor and director may have occurred about the success of Quayle's production, and the desirability of transposing a nearly full version of Pandarus's speech into the earlier scene may have been questioned.

Critics began to notice the juxtaposition of Pandarus's speech in Quayle's production, but the reviewers of Shaw's production were much more outspoken in their assessment of the arrangement. Claude Westell wrote that

> Mr Shaw's way with his groups and his handling of the big moments, as always, excites one's admiration, and he has devised a masterly ending with the defeated Trojans dragging their dejected way homewards to lick their wounds, leaving disillusioned Troilus standing sword in hand looking to the sky and the stars.
>
> THE LAST WORD
>
> We were relieved that the last word was not as the poet would have had it, with Pandarus. This nasty old goer-between, as played by Anthony Quayle, took on an even nastier aspect than usual.[98]

Westell was pleased with the spectacle of the end, and the denial of a more prominent role for Pandarus. His comparing how "the poet would have had it" with Shaw's arrangement suggests a lack of awareness of the editorial argument that Shaw's arrangement is quite close to how "the poet would have had it." Westell's judgment of the desirability of Shaw's ending therefore offers support for the conjectured end based more purely on dramatic preference.

Harold Hobson also applauded Shaw's ending as dramatically effective, and similarly expressed concern over its lack of authority.

> Disillusion and disgust hang over the play which Shakespeare concludes with one of Pandarus's characteristically sweaty, and bawdy speeches. But Mr. Byam Shaw chooses to strike a grander note, and leaves us with Troilus, a lone figure on an empty stage, with drawn sword, amid the deepening gloom, facing in desperate defiance, but with will still unbroken, the naked night. I cannot see what justification there is for this, except that it succeeds. It may make nonsense of the general drift of the play; but it is in itself fine. It would be a superb conclusion—to some other drama.[99]

Both Hobson and Westell acknowledge the success of Shaw's ending, but deny Shakespeare any of the credit. A more scholarly review appeared in *Shakespeare Quarterly*, where Richard David recognized the connection between the editorial conjectures and the director's ending.

> Quayle [as Pandarus] managed to suggest that Pandarus' passion derived not from any anxiety to gratify a taste of his own but from a desperate so-

licitude that others (especially the young) should gratify theirs, in the only terms that he knew. Perhaps this was part of the attempt to domesticate Pandarus within the chosen pattern of the production, but Pandarus cannot be so tamed. His envoy, exquisitely prepared for with a sudden rounding on the audience, the ferocious "Good traders in the flesh, set *this* in your painted cloths!"—this envoy bursts open any convention. Nor can there be much doubt that, however muddled the last scene of the play, this was intended to be the final sting, the last ten lines of our text being but a doggerel epilogue. Byam Shaw taking advantage of the muddle, and of the fact that Pandarus' last entry is made to almost the same words as his previous one, ran the two together, and Pandarus' parting shot was made (more plausibly, it must be admitted) within the gates of Troy, leaving the stricken battlefield entirely to Troilus and his despair. But this was pure anti-climax after Pandarus' blow in the face; the play trailed off on an unresolved discord; the audience shifted uneasily, wondering if there was more to come, and departed feeling somehow cheated.[100]

David stresses how Pandarus's final speech is integral in the progression of the character, and how any attempt to "tame" Pandarus diminishes the character's complexity. While he strongly believes that the bibliographical "muddle" cannot deprive the play of the ending he feels is "prepared for" and undoubtedly "the final sting," David supports fully Shaw's cutting of the final ten lines, and is sympathetic to the way the transposition presents a more "plausible" setting for the speech. David usefully critiques how the transposition created an anticlimactic finale, but his view of an unresolved ending may also have positive critical and performance value. Whether Troilus rejects Pandarus before or after the battle, the unresolved aspects of the war and the love plots are crucial to the play's ending. Agamemnon's final lines,

> If in his death the gods have us befriended,
> Great Troy is ours, and our sharp wars are ended
>
> (5.10.8)

are highly interpretive and speculative. Troilus's resolve to keep fighting, and indeed the fact that Troilus is left alive, allows the play to end more or less "in the middle," as the Prologue describes it beginning. While Pandarus's final speech does present some sort of dramatic and theatrically conventional sense of closure, the way the speech looks forward to "some two months hence" still retains an openness which can also lead an audience into "wondering," in David's words, "if there was more to come."

The complex reactions to Shaw's staging, with critics praising and blaming playwright and director for the placement of Pandarus's speech and the effectiveness of the play's ending, are given a further

dimension in Trewin's review, where he laments the weak performance of Laurence Harvey as Troilus.

> I waited hopefully to the last; surely something must make me change my
> opinion. Nothing did, though I agree that at the curtain—the Pandarus
> passage is now spatchcocked in earlier—it was, for the moment, an heroic
> stage picture when Troilus, in the thickening light, gazed defiantly to-
> wards the Greek tents and the far-set plain. The end crowned all, but it
> was the producer's work, not Mr. Harvey's.[101]

Shaw is praised for the stage image, which was powerful despite the
actor. David's view that Quayle as Pandarus stole the show, and
Trewin's view that Harvey as Troilus could not spoil the effectiveness
of Shaw's ending, show the actors and director working at times
against each other. In his brief stage history of the play, Ralph Berry
also acknowledged the textual problems of the scene, while assessing
the authority of Shaw's transposition of Pandarus's speech.

> This is an acceptable piece of theatrical engineering, in view of the ir-
> regularities of the original text, but it makes the play end on a note quite
> different from Shakespeare's design. For now the ending, as in the 1948
> production [directed by Quayle], is on Troilus' "Hope of revenge shall
> hide our inward woe," at which, to a despondent trumpet, all the Trojans
> exeunt save Troilus, who is left outlined against the walls of the doomed
> city.[102]

While Berry feels the textual problems can justify the transposition
in the theater, he has a sense of Shakespeare's design that requires
Pandarus to deliver his speech at the end of the play. The "irregular-
ities of the original text" are not considered enough to allow for the
possibility that Shakespeare may have had more than one design, or
that "theatrical engineering" can expand our sense of what the dramatic implications of these designs might be.

Like Payne, Quayle, and Shaw, Tyrone Guthrie also marked Ridley's edition for his promptbook. Unlike the Stratford directors, however, Guthrie eliminated Pandarus's being rejected at the end of 5.3,
as Q, and in the final scene left virtually intact both Troilus's rejection of Pandarus, and Pandarus's final speech. The chapter on the
opening of the play discusses how Guthrie cut the Prologue and began the play as Q with Pandarus and Troilus. His following Q, by having Pandarus only rejected at the end of the play, created a production which supports the theory (proposed by Kimbrough and
Farley-Hills) that Q presents a version which may emphasize Pandarus by beginning and ending with him. The support must be lim-

ited, and while the framing of the play may change in the proposed versions, the potential for the war plot or the love plot to dominate has as much to do with performance choices as textual choices. For example, although Shaw roughly followed the conjectured F version, by beginning with the Prologue and ending with Troilus, many reviewers still considered Quayle's portrayal of Pandarus one of the successes of Shaw's production.

Without overstating the relationship between Guthrie's textual choices and the prominence of Pandarus, it should still be noted that Paul Rogers's Pandarus received considerable praise, with several reviewers particularly mentioning the final speech.

> Paul Rogers, as the man-about-Troy, Pandarus the Panderer, steals the show. His final scene, in which he sings a twentieth century, off-beat dirge full of Noel Coward nostalgia of the passing of the good old days, sets a golden seal on the whole play.[103]

The reviewer for *Truth* likened Pandarus's song to a different tradition, but similarly found the ending successful, despite the gimmickry.

> And even the last exhibitionist fling—with Pandarus, in floppy roué's hat, in the extremities of melancholic disposition, sitting on two richly-labelled travelling-bags, croaking his final speech as a negro "blues"—can be forgiven for the panache with which it is carried out.[104]

Pandarus's potential to be a show-stealing exhibitionist is certainly aided by his role at the end of the play. His rejection, and his address to the audience, give directors and actors the opportunity to create many different relationships between Pandarus and Troilus, and between Pandarus and the audience. Guthrie had cut nearly half of Troilus's final speech,[105] and along with Paul Rogers's dynamic performance, and Guthrie's decision to have Pandarus enter with his suitcases, the audience may be forgiven for thinking more about the fate of Pandarus than of Hector's tragedy or Troilus' plight.

Although the stage history from 1960 until 1998 does not provide further examples of directors following editorial conjectures about the transposition of Pandarus's final speech, the way that productions have staged the speech can provide insight into many of the issues debated by editors. Reviewers and critics have often commented on the chaos of the final scenes, and the transition and balance between the battlefield scenes and the lasciviousness of Pandarus can reveal much about a production's vision of the play. While Guthrie sought opportunities to enhance or invent comic moments, the Hall/Barton production was praised for achieving a more balanced approach. Guthrie had set the play just before the first world war, the last time that he believed war could be seen as a "sport, a gallant, delightful employment,"[106] but Hall and Barton established a more serious approach to the fighting. Robert Speaight wrote that Hall and Barton were

> under no temptation to turn a Shakespearian battle into a Bolshoi ballet. . . . Your whole company has got to fight, and the way they did so in this production was not in the least reminiscent of a ball game. I have never seen anything more sinister than the slaying of Hector. And the playing of different lights through the smoke of a pardonably anachronistic cannon gave a lurid chiaroscuro to the scene. . . . Mr. Max Adrian's Pandarus had matured in subtlety with the years [since he played Pandarus in Macowan's production]. His last, decrepit entrance was the perfect counterpart to the spiritual decomposition of the play.[107]

A number of critics similarly praised Max Adrian's Pandarus, calling him "the triumph of the production,"[108] and relished the way he was "rightly on close terms with the audience."[109] There did not, however, seem to be the danger of Pandarus undermining the seriousness of the play. Trewin wrote that

> Mr. Hall and Mr. Barton spare us nothing, and wisely so. You cannot compromise with *Troilus and Cressida*. The battle scenes, which we have known to tail off raggedly, have now an astonishing effect on a stage overcast by wreathing, fuming smoke so that Greeks and Trojans are seen as figures wrapped in cloud, sometimes emerging from it sharply-defined, at other times almost spectral in this hell where the great names ring and shine ("Renew, renew! The fierce Polydamus hath beat down Menon") and where, as "ugly night comes breathing" behind the setting sun, the Myrmidons close on Hector at Achilles' word. Presently, when Hector is dead, and at the horse's tail "dragged through the shameful field," first Troilus and then Pandarus come to end the tale of wars and lechery.[110]

The Hall/Barton promptbook notes that during Troilus's final speech, Pandarus entered (at about "Go in to Troy"), and stood upstage watching Troilus. There is no other indication of movement, and although many critics commented on the final moments, none mentioned Pandarus's early entrance. The decision to have Pandarus onstage during Troilus's speech shows the directors' creating an image that directly contradicts the critics who believe that Pandarus's appearance on the battlefield is inappropriate.

Trewin wrote of "a death's hand that finally haunted the Phrygian field,"[111] and Christy described a "Pandarus, who comes onto the now bloodstained sand in white with an ashen face visibly decaying from his diseases."[112] Despite this haunting image, Michael Green-wald characterized Adrian's Pandarus as "broadly comic" when compared with the "more cynical" Pandarus of David Waller in Barton's 1968 production: "where Max Adrian was a lean, macabre, dangerous Pandarus, Waller was more effete, vulgar, portly, and lethargic."[113] Pandarus's entrance in the final scene was taken even further from the text than the early entrance in the Hall/Barton production. The promptbook notes that as Pandarus entered in the final scene, Thersites also entered and observed Pandarus's rejection. Troilus pushed "Pandarus to the floor" as he told him to go "hence," making some sense of the contradiction of Pandarus remaining onstage after being told to go "hence." Although silent, Thersites' presence during this brief encounter adds the kind of voyeurism that debased Cressida's encounter with Diomedes, and the battle scenes, inviting the audience at least to be aware, if not entirely to concur with Thersites' reductive view.

John Barton remembered that Pandarus's final speech was presented as a "mad dance of death," with Pandarus's rhyming couplets accompanied by Thersites playing a tambourine.[114] Irving Wardle likened the scene to "a pair of buskers," and Rosemary Say described how "the two old parasites huddle together chanting their litany of despair.[115] Norman Rodway, who played Thersites, recalled that there was not any recognition between Thersites and Pandarus, and remembers that Thersites' presence was used to suggest the similar viewpoint of the two characters by the end of the play.[116] Michael Greenwald speculated that Barton's decision to have Thersites onstage may have been influenced by Barton's theatrical and academic experience at Cambridge.

> Rylands had taught him [Barton] that there are two choruses for *Troilus and Cressida*, Thersites and Pandarus. Both Kott and Rossiter have suggested that these two "clowns" are but two sides of the same coin, which may explain Barton's innovative linking of the two vile characters in the Epilogue. Pandarus was accompanied by Thersites' drum-playing and dancing to a chantlike rhythm that underscored the old pimp's speech.[117]

In Barton's "notes to the company at rehearsal," quoted in the program, he remarked that "Shakespeare keeps modifying our view of" all the characters.

> Troilus, Cressida, Pandarus and even Hector coarsen as the action proceeds. Others grow in strength. . . . Thersites is at first frustrated, beaten, cowed: by the end of the play, his philosophy achieves a monstrous domination.[118]

Rodway's Thersites appeared "physically scabrous, poxy and putrefy-
ing, the mordancy of his sick, abusive wit is mocked by a monstrous
phallus which lolls from a cod-piece shaped like a mask."[119] This
phallus, a thick red rope attached to the mouth of the cod piece
mask, was left onstage after Thersites and Pandarus exited. Like Macowan's decision to have Thersites speak the last line, Barton heightened the choric and scurrilous potential of Pandarus's final speech
by having Thersites present. As the role of Cressida has rad◆ally
changed with society's views of women, so too has there been more
acceptance and emphasis of the darker side of Pandarus's character,
particularly evident in the increase in stage business surrounding
Pandarus's final lines.

John Barton was criticized in some reviews for overloading the production with images of depravity, but in an interview he explained
that this was not his intention. He felt the play requires balance, and
that the heroism and tragedy need to be presented seriously.[120]
While the emphasis on the darker, satiric elements of the play is present in the decision to have Thersites onstage with Pandarus at the
end, Troilus's speech before Pandarus entered was an example of the
way the irony is set up by a more somber and tragic image. Greenwald noted that "Michael Williams' Troilus evolved from a high-spir-
ited youth to an angry, more knowledgeable young man. His eulogy
for the slain Hector was delivered defiantly, an outburst to an un-
yielding cosmos."[121] Greenwald also detailed some of the thinking
that went into Troilus's speech for Barton's next production, with
Michael Gwilym as Troilus.

> Several critics questioned the smile that Gwilym employed during
> Troilus's speech about Hector's death. The actor says that Barton in-
> structed him to find occasion to smile, to inject humor, albeit cynical, into
> a speech to minimize the emotional heaviness and self-pity. In the 1984
> television series, "Playing Shakespeare," Barton repeated his instructions
> concerning the speech for the viewers' benefit:

> > Try it as if you've decided that, because everything is so grievous, you
> > can only survive by shutting off your grief. Try *enjoying* discomforting
> > the other Trojans who don't realize the horror of things as you do.
> > When you get to the "who shall tell Priam so" show that you have
> > changed. You are not the emotional young man of the rest of the play,
> > but you have grown up and are grimly self-controlled. Make it an *objec-
> > tive* prophecy.[122]

The feelings and motives of Troilus's speech are crucial in a discussion of the play's ending, especially when considering whether

31. Norman Rodway as Thersites, with his death mask codpiece, RST 1968, Barton. Thos F. and Mig Holte Collection, Shakespeare Centre Library. Copyright Shakespeare Birthplace Trust.

Troilus should reject Pandarus before or after the battle. Barton's view that Troilus's most profound change occurs during the speech raises questions about how Troilus's rejection of Pandarus is motivated and judged, and how the placement of that rejection alters the dramatic possibilities. When Pandarus enters with Cressida's letter, Troilus greets him with "What now?," implying that he has no more interest in the pander and his niece. With the Q ending of 5.3, Troilus does not respond directly to Pandarus again in the scene, and Troilus's speech, as he presumably tears the letter ("Words, words"), has more to do with his jealous rage than with any resentment at the messenger. The conjectured reading of F couples the reaction to Cressida's letter with the rejection of Pandarus, denying any further progression of the love story, and sending Troilus into battle even more embittered. Although Troilus's jealous rage significantly contributes to his actions in the battle, it is primarily as a warrior that he would end the play if Pandarus did not reappear. With dialogue between Troilus and Pandarus framing the battle, the final rejection of

Pandarus is something reserved until the end, not only dramatically or narratively, but also in terms of the progression of the individual characters. Q deprives Troilus of a final abuse of Pandarus until the end, where Hector's death influences, or at least informs, Troilus's rejection of Pandarus.

As in Barton's 1968 production, in 1976 Barton and Kyle had Thersites onstage with Pandarus at the end of the play. There was, however, a much more elaborate staging than the tambourine accompaniment from the earlier production. Richard David offered the most complete description of the Barton/Kyle finale, where David Waller, as in Barton's 1968 production, played Pandarus.

> The directors bravely gave us the complete text including Pandarus' extraordinary last will and testament. The scene was presented as a macabre pantomime with Pandarus, now decked as a corpse, making his exit through the trap into his promised grave (Barton now regularly signs his production with an entombment). But someone must open the trap and provide the grave-clothes. Who more fitting than Thersites, whom Shakespeare himself modelled on the Vice of the Moralities, and whom the directors had prepared us to see as a circus clown? With him he brought the dummy Helen with which Achilles had earlier teased Menelaus and whose presence, as part of Diomed's luggage, at the assignation with Cressida had created a quite superfluous puzzle for the audience. She now, as an emblem of the prostitute, joined the pandar in the grave. To bring off Pandarus' final harlequinade was a triumph, besides which Hector's bloody execution was a mere *coup de théâtre;* but I doubt whether even the triumph was worth all that mumbo-jumbo.[123]

Irving Wardle thought the "final transformation of this Pandarus into a death's head spectre is extremely unlikely,"[124] but others were more convinced. John Peter wrote of David Waller's Pandarus,

> I can pay him no greater compliment than to say that his final, incongruous appearance on the battlefield and his horrible dismissal by Troilus becomes one of the rare occasions when Shakespeare is seen to be both unfair and clumsy. The humanity of Waller's performance shows up the momentary harshness of his author.[125]

Macowan's description of Max Adrian's Pandarus, quoted above, referred to a similar element of humanity and charisma that increased the complexity of the audience's reaction to the dying Pandarus. By comparing the staging of Pandarus's extra-textual death with Hector's death, David highlights some of the important dramatic decisions that must be made in staging the end of the play. Troilus's reactions to Hector's death may begin as a somewhat conventional mourning at the end of a tragedy, but Troilus's anger, and his unresolved situation provide a director and actor with the opportunity to create sympathy for Troilus, alienate Troilus from the audience, or leave the moment and the character more ambiguous. Pandarus's final appearance has a similar range of possibilities. John Peter's view that Shakespeare is being unfair shows how the audience's enjoyment of Pandarus in the early part of the play can present an opportunity to alter the affections for the character. Audiences can be provoked into questioning their earlier enjoyment of Pandarus, as his endearing bawdiness turns to confrontational vituperation.

The notion that Pandarus's appearance on the battlefield is inappropriate was given two very different responses by two directors in 1981, with Hands's RSC production embracing the incongruity, while Miller's BBC production sought to remedy it. The rehearsal notes for Hands's production concisely report the final image the director devised: "*End of Play:* The idea was that a coil of barbed wire is run quickly from left Prosc[enium] to Right at a certain point. Pandarus gets caught in it."[126] Michael Coveney praised the finale for the way it provided a fitting merger of the worlds of love and war: "Tony Church makes more of Pandarus's songs than anyone I can remember and his farewell, hands trapped in the vicious wire, movingly summarizes the lovers' tragedy."[127] The battlefield was considered a particularly apt place for Pandarus's rejection and final speech, stressing how the war had destroyed the relationship which Pandarus nurtured. Michael Billington, however, did not see the "sense in Pandarus being finally impaled on [the designer] Farrah's barbed wire fence since he says 'some two months hence my will shall here be made'."[128] This observation can be related to the other death images directors have given to Pandarus, such as the death's head (Hall/Barton and Barton) and the grave (of Barton/Kyle). Critics and editors have focused on what Pandarus means by declaring "my will shall here be made," proposing theories about the place of performance and the possibility of a sequel. Productions are more naturally concerned with what the lines can mean in terms of Pandarus's condition, how close he is to death, and how images of his impending or more immediate death can help create the final moments.

Henry Fenwick, in his introduction to the edition that accompanied Jonathan Miller's BBC production, offered some insight into the decisions made for the final scene. Fenwick reported that Charles Gray, who played Pandarus, told Miller

"I don't know what happens to him in the end: I said to Jonathan, "I don't know how to do it." That last speech is awfully peculiar. I think you could play it in a bouncing-back way: "Back to the house and pack; we're get-ting out of here." In fact, Gray plays it with a terrifying, self-absorbed mad-ness. As Troy falls apart, so too does Pandarus. The news of Hector's death, usually played on the battlefield, is played in Troy as the soldiers retreat back within the walls. "There's no reason for Pandarus to wander out on to the battlefield," Miller points out. "It must be at the moment when the whole war is disintegrating and people are retreating back into the walls of Troy, weary soldiers, lying propped against the walls, and this decaying old man trying to make his way through the jostling ruined crowds to identify his young protégé, who rejects him—much as Prince Hal rejects the old Falstaff. Those scenes of the repudiation of an older person who has been the cause of distress by bringing about an apparent satisfaction are very important in Shakespeare."[129]

There were two primary sets used for the production, and all the scenes within Troy were filmed before the Greek camp scenes. Miller's decision to have the final scene staged in Troy meant that it was filmed as the last scene in the Troy set, immediately after the scene where Hector is warned against fighting, and Pandarus deliv-ers Cressida's letter to Troilus (5.3). Susan Willis, who was present during the filming, noted some of the unexpected connections that resulted from filming the scenes in succession.

> During camera rehearsal as he watched how Troilus's exit and talk with Pandarus [at the end of 5.3] worked, Miller had an inspiration; he mo-bilized all the extras dressed as soldiers, who were standing in and near the studio waiting to tape the play's last scene, and sent them jostling past Troilus and Pandarus to give a sense of chaos. Miller commented that this was very nice as an elegiac scene, against the flow, and told Charles Gray (Pandarus) to be lost in the crowd at the end. The soldiers streaming past made the scene more effective as transition to the battlefield scenes and also provided a stark contrast to the soldiers' return down that same colonnade in the last scene, which was taped immediately afterward.[130]

Near the end of 5.3, as Hector told Priam that he will "Do deeds of praise, and tell you them at night" (5.3.96), extras began to move out of the palace room. After Priam took his final farewell of Hector, the scene switched to the colonnade, a hallway with the sky partially visi-ble. The space was crowded with soldiers moving to battle, and as Troilus turned a corner to join those heading out to fight, he delivered his speech beginning "They are at it" (98). As Willis describes above, it is during this march to battle that Pandarus intercepted Troilus.

Miller's shift of place for the dialogue between Troilus and Pan-darus is similar to Poel's staging, since both directors presented the dialogue as a separate scene. While Poel seemed to create a more intimate scene played before the closed inner stage curtain, Miller's populating the scene with soldiers made it more public, and more overtly connected with Troilus heading for battle. QF both have directions for an "Alarum" after Priam's final line, and F also has a direction for "A Larum" after the F only passage which ends the scene (see illustration on page 193). Both texts have Thersites enter for the next scene "in excursion" (Q reads "Thersites: excursions," F reads "Thersites in excursion"). Pandarus's entrance and his dialogue with Troilus is therefore surrounded by the impending war, and Miller increased this effect by having the soldiers' presence add to the sense that Pandarus is interrupting Troilus during the mobilization of troops. The scene ended with Pandarus attempting to pick up the pieces of Cressida's letter that Troilus had torn and discarded. Pandarus's attempt to reassemble the letter was frustrated by the soldiers' rushing past, and the scene faded out with Pandarus scrambling around on the floor. This image emphasized that even without the F only lines, the scene can be played as a rejection of Pandarus, leaving him visually scorned and humiliated, and can make even more pathetic Pandarus' attempt at the end of the play to speak with Troilus.

For the end of the play, Miller cut the Greeks' reaction to Hector's death (5.9), allowing Achilles' declaration, "Along the field I will the Troyan trail" to be followed immediately by the Trojans' reaction (5.11). The final scene began with Aeneas walking down the colonnade against the flow of soldiers, trying to convince them not to give up fighting as they retreated into Troy. Troilus interrupted Aeneas with the news of Hector's death, and directed his first speech and the first part of his second speech mostly to Aeneas. For the first couplet ("away"/"say"), Troilus stepped a bit closer to the camera, and as Aeneas began comforting the wounded soldiers, Troilus's ranting became more crazed. This allowed Troilus's final lines to be directed more toward a general public, as a kind of aside shouted to the world.

For the last two lines of Troilus's final speech ("Strike a free march . . . inward woe") the scene shifted, with Troilus following the flow of soldiers along the colonnade into a more enclosed, darker part of the palace, where a stretcher carried Hector's mangled body. From within a doorway Pandarus called out to Troilus, and Troilus hardly stopped as he shouted his rejection. Like the palace scene before the battle, the very public setting for Pandarus's attempt to speak with Troilus connected the scene more emphatically to the events of the war. Willis observed that the

context of Troy allowed Miller to finish the story, as one might consider it, by showing Hector's body brought in and the family mourning, a moment important to feel the full impact of his death. In discussing the appropriateness of that concluding shot, Miller said he liked Pandarus staggering past the mourners, ignoring the genuine tragedy, the real loss.[131]

Pandarus's intrusion on the family's mourning made him no less out of place than if he had been on the battlefield. His delirious stumbling and rambling did not, however, distract the viewer's attention away from the tragedy, but added to it. The audience was left with a striking juxtaposition between the mangled warrior and the diseased Pandar, widening the scope of those destroyed in the course of the play.

Both Davies' (1985) and Mendes' (1989) RSC productions were praised for the different ways they presented the descent of Pandarus from his comic beginning to his diseased end. Michael Billington wrote that in Davies' production,

> if any one performance encapsulates the theme of shifting decadence it is Clive Merrison's brilliant Pandarus. He changes visibly from a snickering, sleazy emotional and military parasite (Shakespeare always had a dislike of camp-followers) to a syphilitic, cream-suited wreck picking out a piano-tune like a brothel-musician in a revolution.[132]

In a similar way that Miller's setting of the end of 5.3 and the end of the play in the colonnade went outside the text to provide a strong visual parallel between the moments, Davies used his ever-present piano as a link between the two moments. As Troilus read and tore Cressida's long letter (the rehearsal notes call for a 6–10 page letter, and the video confirms that Troilus read many of the pages), Pandarus did not become violently upset, but simply stared distractedly ahead as he stood by the piano. As Troilus tore the letter, Pandarus sank onto the piano stool, physically weak and emotionally exhausted. Troilus tossed the bits of paper in a shower over Pandarus's head and ran out, while gunshots, explosions, and flashes of light signaled the approaching war. Pandarus simply swiveled round in his chair and began to bang a discordant melody on the piano.

Pandarus remained onstage throughout the ensuing scenes, occasionally playing as the characters entered, fought, and exited. Thersites climbed on the piano, and the piano stool, while Pandarus remained sitting, hunched over with a shawl around his shoulders to help indicate his sickly condition. After observing Achilles and his Myrmidons slay Hector, Pandarus turned to the piano again, but only resumed playing after Troilus entered and began his final speech. Troilus's first couplet ("away"/"say") was followed by the Trojans wearily moving offstage, leaving Troilus and Pandarus alone, and ne-

32. Hector threatens Thersites, RST 1985, Davies. Joe Cocks Studio Collection, Shakespeare Centre Library. Copyright Shakespeare Birthplace Trust.

33. Hector and Achilles fight, RST 1985, Davies. Joe Cocks Studio Collection, Shakespeare Centre Library. Copyright Shakespeare Birthplace Trust.

cessitating the cut of "Strike a free march towards Troy," as there was only Pandarus left to heed such an order. As Pandarus called from his stool, Troilus quickly rejected him, and moved swiftly offstage, leaving Pandarus sitting at the piano to begin his final speech facing the audience. He turned to the piano as he wondered, "what verse for it, what instance for it." Nicholas Shrimpton observed that Pandarus "accompanied himself on the piano, with a Kurt Weill–like tune, for the song in his final speech."[133] After the song, Pandarus picked up his cane and staggered downstage to warn the audience that he planned to bequeath them his diseases. His final exit up the winding staircase was accompanied by the piano, playing by itself.

The critical concern about Pandarus's incongruous appearance on the battlefield was somewhat defused by the decaying mansion which provided the permanent set, but the decision to keep Pandarus onstage for the entire battle still provides an important statement about the desirability of linking, despite any loss of realism, the destruction of Troy with the devastation of Pandarus. It has already been noted, in the chapter on the Prologue, that Davies had Pandarus appear onstage at the beginning of the play, reading his newspaper from the time the audience walked into the theater until after the Prologue was spoken. As an interested but inactive bystander of the war, Pandarus's appearance and complacency was contrasted with the soldiers who carried on their dying comrade and spoke the Prologue. This image also sets up Pandarus's dramatic transformation in the course of the play. While the Prologue speaks only of the war, and nothing of Troilus, Cressida, and Pandarus, Pandarus's final speech mentions nothing of the war. Part of Pandarus's wretchedness is undoubtedly caused by the war that destroyed the love he attempted to nurture, but his diseases are more directly associated with his activity as the "bawd" that Cressida recognizes in her first scene, and as the "broker" that Troilus rejects.

The different subject matter and tone of the Prologue and epilogue might support the theory that they were not meant to be part of the same version, but Davies' decision to have Pandarus onstage for the Prologue suggests the positive value of emphasizing the incongruity. Mendes' production made a similar argument for the connection between the Prologue and epilogue by having Pandarus speak both. As with Merrison's Pandarus in Davies' production, several critics enjoyed the transformation of Norman Rodway's Pandarus: Peter Holland wrote of Mendes' "economically linking the beginning and the end of the play together, making the diseased Pandarus of the epilogue a distorted image of the dapper figure at the start."[134] Elizabeth Beroud described the image of Rodway's Pandarus at the end in terms of how he differed from his first appearance: "half dressed with no traces of coat, hat or cane—his shirt is half unbuttoned and he is barefoot."[135] Once before Pandarus had taken his shoes off, to paddle in a pool with Cressida in the second scene, and in Helen's scene he was humiliatingly relieved of his jacket and hat by her servants. This final transformation of Pandarus was altogether different.

When told about the editorial argument and the theatrical precedents for having Pandarus deliver his final speech before the battle, Norman Rodway replied, "You'd have a hard job talking someone into playing Pandarus if the epilogue was cut or moved. I'd be very unhappy with that, and I shan't tell Sam [Mendes] about it either."[136] While Rodway's comments self-consciously reflect his agenda as an actor, rather than any bibliographical or critical judgment, they highlight the importance of the speech not only to the play, but to the character and actor. The stature of the role, and the ability of the role to move the audience, is greatly enhanced by both the speech and its placement.

I did not feel that I was betraying Rodway's confidence when I asked Mendes, as they were re-rehearsing the production for its London transfer, whether he knew of the editorial debate about the play's conclusion.[137] Mendes was adamant that "Shakespeare would not miss such a trick" as Pandarus's final speech, but perhaps it still could be asked if he did miss it the first time, and added it during a revision. It is a testament to the changing nature of directors' and editors' understanding of Shakespeare and his plays that Mendes believes the final speech an integral part of Shakespeare's composition, when early editors questioned its authorship and many early directors concurred with the editorial view that the speech should be either cut altogether, or partially cut and placed earlier.

For the first time in over fifty years, Boyd's production returned to the earlier performance tradition of having Pandarus's final speech given before the battle. In a production that had more than a few significant cuts and rearranged passages, as illustrated below, this alteration had some editorial rationale. Roy Hanlon, who played Pandarus, recalled that the decision to end Pandarus's role before the battle happened late in rehearsals with an awareness of editorial conjecture. In contrast to Rodway's remarks that ending the play was a vital aspect of the role, Hanlon felt there was a good deal of narrative and dramatic sense in having Pandarus depart before the battle.[138]

Boyd's production was the first I attended that transposed Pandarus's speech. Perhaps I was too eager to notice how it worked as I self-consciously watched the performance, watched the audience, and questioned friends and colleagues about their reactions. While

I remain skeptical about the theory that Shakespeare or his company placed Pandarus's speech before the battle, Boyd's production effectively staged the early exit by Pandarus and the play ending with Troilus. What was most surprising, in my reactions and in the reactions of some I spoke with, is that it did not seem out of place in the early position. The power of a production to tell its own story can create narrative momentum and make sense of the placement of a speech in the context of that production, and Pandarus's addressing the audience before the battle had few traces of the incongruity I expected from an epilogue-like speech coming before the end of the play. I looked to other audience members in vain for indications of confusion: there were no obvious signs that anyone thought the play was over as Pandarus bequeathed us his diseases.

John Peter, who called Boyd's production "dreary, confusing and undercast," wrote that "as the play goes on, you start noticing phrases and lines being left out: a case either of inept cutting or sloppy speaking."[139] In his short review he did not specify whether Pandarus's final exit or the end of the play was "confusing" as a result of "inept cutting," but his views do suggest that this arrangement, along with other textual alterations, was not successful. Charles Spencer, while agreeing in some respects with Peter's sense of confusion, firmly placed his perplexity in "fretting about exactly where and when the action was supposedly taking place," World War I, the Balkans, or Ireland. Spencer did, however, urge audiences to "forget about the setting and concentrate instead upon the narrative and performances, which are both impressive and harrowing."[140] Without making reference to the arrangement of Pandarus's and the play's final scenes, the review contrasts Peter's judgment to allow a more positive view of the production's choices.

While the early placement of Pandarus' final speech has the support of some scholars, perhaps most interesting about the conclusion of Boyd's production was his unique staging and adaptation of Troilus's speech which ended the play, worth quoting in full with brackets and braces added to indicate: <words cut from the text>, {words added to the text}, and [my notes].

> But march away; {march away}
> Hector is dead; there is no more to say.   [*Enter Cressida*]
> Stay yet. You vile abominable <tents> {Greeks},
> Thus proudly pitched upon our Phrygian plains,
> Let Titan rise as early as he dare,
> I'll through and through you! And thou <great sized coward>
>   {despised Achilles},

No space of earth shall sunder our two hates;
I'll haunt thee like a wicked conscience still,
That mouldeth goblins swift as frenzy's thoughts.
<Strike a free march! To Troy with comfort go:
Hope of revenge shall hide our inward woe.>

> {Fate, hear me what I say!   [from 5.6.26]
> I reck not though thou end my life today.
> I reck not though thou end my life today.
> End my life today.}[141]

Boyd's transposed lines that ended the production are taken from within the battle, when Troilus vows to be taken himself rather than let Ajax keep the captured Aeneas (5.6.26). In the midst of the fighting the lines reaffirm the reckless abandon of Troilus's fighting, as well as asserting a dedication to a homosocial ideal of heroic camaraderie. Transposed to the end of the play, and repeated with increasing vengeance and self-destructive doom, the lines offer a bleak vision that is more self-absorbed and nihilistic than the lines they replace ("with comfort go, / Hope of revenge shall hide our inward woe.")

Perhaps most original in the ending was not the adapted text, but the decision to bring Cressida onstage at "Stay yet," where she remained, silent, for Troilus's final speech. One effect of moving Pandarus's final rejection by Troilus and Pandarus's speech to the earlier position is that the play ends with the image of Troilus as a warrior reacting to Hector's slaughter. Boyd's arrangement, however, juxtaposes the warrior's response to Hector's death with the silent Cressida, offering a number of possible ways of understanding the destructiveness and cost of war. Even without Pandarus's speech ending the play, Boyd provided the audience with a final image that did not minimize the personal tragedy of the lovers.

Cressida also appeared at the end of the play in Nunn's production in the following year, but unlike Boyd's finale with a silent unseen Cressida on the battlefield, Nunn added a moment where Pandarus, Cressida, and Troilus all spoke, and Pandarus's speech did end the play. Nunn also added to the earlier productions' desire to have Thersites onstage at the end of the play by giving Thersites a short speech. The elaborate rewriting of the end of the play, perhaps the most excessive but certainly not the only example of the significant rearranging of the text in Nunn's production, deserves to be quoted in full. As the Trojans exited after Troilus's speech ending "With comfort go / Hope of revenge shall hide our inward woe," Pandarus entered through the central aisle of the stalls, bringing Cressida with him. Troilus responded to their appearance:

TROILUS.	Hector is dead; there is no more to say.	[taken from 5.11.22]
CRESSIDA.	Poor our sex! This fault in us I find: The error of our eye directs our mind.	[5.2.111]
TROILUS.	My love with words and errors still she feeds, But edifies another with her deeds.	[5.3.114]
CRESSIDA.	What error leads must err. O then conclude: Minds swayed by eyes are full of turpitude.	[5.2.113]
TROILUS.	Come, wind, to wind: there turn and change together.	[5.3.109]
PANDARUS.	A goodly medicine for my aching bones.	[Add. B.4]
TROILUS.	Hence, broker-lackey. Ignomy and shame Pursue thy life, and live aye with thy name. Exit	[Add. B.2]

THERSITES *[who had been watching from the side, comes forward]*
After this, the vengeance on the whole camp—or rather,   [2.3.17]
the Neapolitan bone-ache, for that methinks is the curse
dependent on those that war for a placket.   *[Kicks Pandarus]*
Now the dry serpigo on the subject, and war and lechery   [2.3.73]
confound all.[142]

Pandarus then continued with his final speech, from "O world, world, world" to the end, with four lines cut and with actions described below. Without providing any neat resolutions, Nunn's final scene did offer some sense of closure that the play denies. Bringing the characters together allowed Cressida to offer some explanation for her actions to Troilus, and allowed Troilus to reject not just her letter, and not just Pandarus, but Cressida herself.

While Troilus's couplet, "march away / Hector is dead, there is no more to say," has been a point at which some believe the play may have ended, and while for others it provides one of several false endings, in Nunn's final dialogue it is shortened to a single line about the death of Hector, used to try to silence Cressida and Pandarus. With the loss of Hector comes a loss of value, a loss of care, and a loss of the need for further talk about relationships.

Nunn's use of Thersites was innovative in a number of ways. Bringing Thersites on near the end, before Pandarus's final speech, allowed him to comment directly to the audience on the adapted scene of Troilus's rejection of Cressida and Pandarus. His curse of "the Neopolitan bone ache," in such proximity to Pandarus bequeathing the audience his diseases, adds to the infectiously corrupt and degraded state of love at the end of the play. Before he exited, Thersites kicked the rejected Pandarus, adding another statement of violent revulsion for the bawd. Thersites then thrust his hand down his own trousers to retrieve Cressida's glove (that Troilus had discarded and Thersites had picked up and used to masturbate after Cressida pledged herself to Diomedes in 5.2). Thersites returned the glove to a dazed Cressida, who was sitting on the stage giving only a distracted sense of recognition as Thersites exited and Pandarus began his final speech.

Even after Thersites and Troilus had exited, Pandarus's speech still did not revert to its usual address to the audience. Nunn's staging not only appropriated part of Cressida's final soliloquy to make it a direct speech to Troilus, but most of Pandarus's final lines were delivered to Cressida, or in a distracted way to himself, but not directly to the audience. As Pandarus somewhat recovered from having been kicked by Thersites, and while he spoke the verse, "Full merrily the humble-bee doth sing," Pandarus applied lipstick to Cressida in a garish and careless fashion that produced a disturbing image of Cressida with red lipstick smeared across her face. When Pandarus finally turned to the audience, at "Good Traders in the flesh," it was with this reinforced view of him as a bawd. But even as he spoke to the audience, he was still on the ground wrapped up in an embrace with Cressida, moaning about his state and the state of the lovers rather than confronting or implicating the audience. When he finally did raise himself and bequeath the audience his diseases, he led Cressida by the hand, as he had led her into the scene, but as he exited, she let his hand go and moved away from him. Cressida, in a state of shock, did not know where to turn. She slowly spun around, distraught and disoriented, without any sense of where she belonged, and exited as the sounds of gunshots and warfare raged in the background.

The image of her alone is a performance rhyme with several moments in Nunn's production: immediately after the Prologue, Cressida entered alone (discussed in chapter 1). After a Prologue that began with the whole cast onstage and ended with the warriors clashing in one of the many early extra-textual battle scenes, Cressida's silent appearance alone on the vast Olivier stage gave the impression of a woman looking lost and isolated amid the chaos of war. In addition to her appearance alone for her soliloquy that ends the second scene (1.2.278, somewhat altered in placement by Nunn), Cressida was again isolated after her scene with Diomedes, when she delivered her lines that were, in Nunn's production, reduced to the couplet, "Troilus farewell, one eye looks on thee / But with my heart the other eye doth see" (5.2.109). Despite the brevity of the cut speech (the rest of the speech was used near the end of the play, as quoted above), Nunn provided another extended image of Cressida alone. As Troilus and Ulysses moved from their peripheral position, where they watched Diomedes and Cressida, to center stage, Cressida slowly walked straight back, beyond the open doors near the back of the stage to an area that was lit with a soft blue glow. She stood for a while before slowly moving offstage, and was available for the audience to watch through the first part of Troilus's dialogue when he asks Ulysses, "Was Cressid here?" (126).

Many reviewers commented upon these images of Cressida alone, which were given prominence not only by being repeated but also by being the last image of the production. Macaulay considered it "a novel touch . . . [to have] her alone, lost onstage as if cut off from her moorings," and Butler wrote that a "daringly . . . emphatic Cressida is left alone, silhouetted against the Trojan walls. An individual victim stands emblematically for her entire sex." Peter observed that "Nunn clearly thinks she is the main victim of the play," and Gross also noted that sympathy for Cressida "is pushed about as far as it can go. She is far more a victim than usual, far less a wanton." Several critics found fault with Nunn's ending. Nightingale called it a "last, spurious glimpse of Cressida," Peter considered "bringing her on at the end, wandering alone on the battlefield, . . . a piece of banal melodrama," and Gross thought it "rewriting the play to end it with an image of her in grieving isolation."[143]

The reviewers who stressed the production's emphasis on the victimization of Cressida show how the decisions about staging the ending, and altering the ending, contribute to a production's interpretative agenda. Issues of authority and textual manipulation were again raised in a rewriting of the play, and while Nunn's choices adapted the text, they provide another example of how the ambiguity and importance of the play's ending seems to invite radically different interpretations. In terms of the editorial debate, Nunn offers a performance choice that clearly finds no problem with bringing Pandarus (and even Cressida) on the battlefield, and maximizes to the point of supplementation an ending that returns from the war to the love story.

Peter Hall, who had Thersites speak the Prologue, added to the tradition of having Thersites onstage for Pandarus's final speech. What was most inventive about Hall's Pandarus delivering his final speech is that, although he referred to making his will some two months hence, he actually died onstage. After he literally keeled over upon bequeathing the audience his diseases, Thersites came from his peripheral position to center stage, inspected Pandarus's corpse, and, in a reversal of the start of the play, began scavenging some of the remnants of war strewed about the stage. After pausing for a few moments to take it all in, and offer a silent satirical expression, he reached up as if to turn the lights off, creating a Brechtian moment of closing the production. His presence and final actions added to Pandarus's framing device, stepping somewhat outside the play to offer a direct engagement with the audience. As Pandarus's speech arguably makes reference to the theatrical present, "as many as be here of Pandar's hall," Thersites' actions at the end of Hall's production mirrored his actions at the beginning of the play (discussed in chapter 1), making the audience aware of a theater space and of a performed (and satirized) legend.

Nunn's and Hall's endings offered experimental and inventive conclusions, but such an approach is probably appropriate for a play whose ending has been the subject of such controversy and conjecture. Whether in the rhymed couplets that do not end the play, the lack of staged resolution to the war or the title characters, or the epilogue-like speech that defies the convention of self-conscious deference to the audience, *Troilus and Cressida* seems to be engaging with expectations of closure. The way productions have experimented with the metatheatricality of the play's end, from reducing Pandarus's choric role by cutting or moving his final speech or expanding the choric quality of the conclusion by adding Thersites to the final image, speaks at least for the potential the play has for raising questions about the relationship between the audience and the drama.

Conclusion

"All's done my lord.

It is.

Why stay we then?"

WHEN IT WAS ANNOUNCED THAT IAN JUDGE WOULD BE DIRECTING *Troilus and Cressida* for the RSC (at the RST) in 1996, I wrote to him requesting an interview, and planned to ask him about his initial preparations of the text. I told him of the play's many textual questions, and of my interest in the theatrical interpretation of these moments. He thought that it might be useful for him and the actors if I attended rehearsals, especially for the first two weeks when the company sat around a table discussing the play. I would then be welcome to occasionally attend subsequent rehearsals. The opportunity to move my work on the editorial issues from theater history to theater practice was obviously very attractive, and I conclude this study with some reflections on that experience.

During the first two weeks of rehearsals, the actors that appeared in a scene came to read and discuss nearly every line. All had Muir's Oxford edition; a few, including the director, had Palmer's Arden, and I had half a dozen recent editions, the New Variorum, and my QF parallel text with its corresponding selective collation of editions and productions. Table rehearsals began with the cast reading a scene before they discussed the text in some detail. I was called on in several ways; either I was asked to go over my choice of textual options after the first read-through, or I would tell them of variants and emendations when the passages were being discussed. Most of the staging matters were addressed at subsequent rehearsals, when there were additional opportunities to suggest alternative readings.

I mentioned about half of the substantive variants, and many of the emendations in the dialogue and stage directions over the course of the eight-week rehearsal period. There were times when the director

242

or the actors immediately preferred one reading to another for reasons of meaning, scansion, or verbal resonance, and other times when there was some discussion and a good bit of vocal toying with the choices before a decision was made. Many decisions differed from Muir's edition, and all around the table (the director, actors, the assistant stage manager with the promptbook, and myself) altered their texts when such decisions were made. Judge and many of the actors expressed enthusiasm for the choices I offered them, and for the chance to make the text their own in a variety of ways. They were surprised at the sheer number of variants and emendations, but also at the quality of the choices, the significance of the differences, and at the number of times that the decisions made by editors were, in their view, obviously the weaker choice. Several of the actors asked for some guidance in learning to read the collation with a greater scholarly awareness of the potential authority or lack of authority for certain readings.

Some of the passages written about in this study were decided in an instant, others were thoroughly investigated, and still others were evolved throughout the initial rehearsal period, the rerehearsal prior to the production's transfer to London's Barbican Theatre, and during the run of performances in both Stratford and London. It was not only the decisions made about these moments (some of which have been described in the preceding chapters), but the decision-making process that confirmed and expanded my belief in the desirability of a dialogue between editorial and theatrical concerns. Observing and contributing to the rehearsals of Judge's production showed some of the ways that theatrical interpretations can perceptively interrogate editorial issues, but it also revealed the way in which editorial debate can provoke valuable theatrical exploration. The textual ambiguity provided a rich source of options for the dialogue and the stage directions, and led to debate, experimentation, and choices that added to the production's unique interpretation of the play. A mutual exchange of approaches and ideas is not only beneficial to scholars and theater professionals, but a merging of textual and performance concerns can lead to a range of interpretive possibilities on a variety of pedagogical levels. Editing assignments used in conjunction with performance exercises and research into performance history can help capitalize on textual ambiguity as a way of encouraging complementary approaches to produce insights.

Appendix A

EDITIONS OF *TROILUS AND CRESSIDA*

This appendix is a selective chronological list of the editions of *Troilus and Cressida* that have been consulted. Each entry begins with the name (in uppercase letters) by which the edition is referred to throughout the book. In most cases this is the editor's surname. The titles of collected works by Shakespeare are not named, unless relevant, and single volume editions are named by series. Collected, single volume, and acting editions are listed separately. The collations in New Variorum and other editions were used as a guide to the editorial history of passages, but when a specific editor is discussed or cited, the original edition was consulted to confirm the reading. Editions were consulted at The Shakespeare Institute Library, The University of Birmingham Main Library, The Birmingham Shakespeare Library, The British Library, The University of London Library (Senate House), The Folger Shakespeare Library, The New York City Public Library, and The Library of Congress.

COLLECTED EDITIONS OF SHAKESPEARE

F (1623), *Mr William Shakespeare's Comedies, Histories, Tragedies,* First Folio
ROWE, Nicholas (1709, 1709b, 1714)
POPE, Alexander (1723–5, 1728)
THEOBALD, Lewis (1733, 1740)
HANMER, Thomas (1743–4, 1770)
JOHNSON, Samuel (1765)
CAPELL, Edward (1767–8)
STEEVENS, George (1773, 1778) with Samuel Johnson
    (1785) with Johnson and Isaac Reed
    (1793) with Reed
RANN, Joseph (1786–94)
MALONE, Edmond (1790)
REED, Isaac (1803, 1813)
SINGER, Samuel Weller (1826, 1856)
KNIGHT, Charles (1838–43, 1842–4, 1867)
COLLIER, J. Payne (1842–4, 1853, 1858)

244

DELIUS, Nicolaus (1854–[61])
DYCE, Alexander (1857, 1864–7, 1875–6)
WHITE, Richard Grant (1857–66, 1883)
STAUNTON, Howard (1858–60)
CAMBRIDGE, W. G. Clark and W. Aldis Wright (1863–6)
  William Aldis Wright (1891–3)
KEIGHTLY, Thomas (1864)
HUDSON, H. N. (1851–6, 1881)
PORTER AND CLARKE, Charlotte and Helen (1910)
TATLOCK, J. S. P. (1912)
KITTREDGE, G. L. (1936)
ALEXANDER, Peter (1951)
SISSON, C. J. (1954)
MUNRO, John (1958)
TAYLOR, Gary, prime responsibility for editing *Troilus and Cressida* in *The Complete Works*, Stanley Wells and Gary Taylor, general editors, Oxford Shakespeare (1986), with notes in *A Textual Companion* (1987). All citation of Shakespeare's plays are to this edition.
EVANS, G. Blakemore, textual ed., Riverside Shakespeare (second edition, 1997)
NORTON Shakespeare: Based on the Oxford Edition, Stephen Greenblatt, general editor (1997)

Single Volume Editions
of *Troilus and Cressida*

Q (1609), Quarto; Qa, first state; Qb, second state
DEIGHTON, K. (1906), Arden [First Series]
RIDLEY, M. R. (1935), New Temple
NEW VARIORUM, edited by H. N. Hillebrand, supplemented by T. W. Baldwin (1953)
WALKER, Alice (1957), New [Cambridge]
WHITAKER, Virgil K. (1958), Pelican
SELTZER, Daniel (1963), Signet Classic
PALMER, Kenneth (1982), Arden [Second Series]
MUIR, Kenneth (1982) Oxford, also published as World's Classics (1994)
WALTER, J. H. (1982), The Players'
FOAKES, R. A. (1987), New Penguin
BEVINGTON, David (1998), Arden Third Series

Acting Editions

BELL'S ACTING EDITION (1774), Bell's Edition of Shakespeare's Plays—
  As they were performed at the Theatres Royal in London, Regulated from

the promptbooks of each House by permission with notes critical and il-
lustrative By the Author of the Dramatic Censor [Francis Gentleman]
CUMBERLAND'S BRITISH THEATRE (ca. 1852), arranged by Thomas
Lacy [?]
HENRY IRVING SHAKESPEARE (1888), ed. by Irving and F. A. Marshall,
with annotations by A. W. Verity
PAPP, Joseph, and Bernard Beckerman (1967), The Festival
MILLER, Jonathan, director (1991), BBC TV, Donald Snodin, script editor,
based on Peter Alexander's text.

Appendix B

THEATER HISTORY

This appendix notes the source material consulted for the theater history of *Troilus and Cressida* and guides the reader to theater histories with a broader scope than the present study. All the promptbooks, videotapes, and audiotapes listed have been studied firsthand. There is a list of interviews conducted and productions that I have attended. The cast lists are selective, but include most of the productions referred to in the book. Programs are the main source for the cast lists, and when a program does not list a part, the entry is left blank. A blank entry does not necessarily imply that the part was cut.

SELECTED THEATER HISTORIES

Editions of Troilus and Cressida

Harold Hillebrand, ed., T. W. Baldwin, supplemental ed. A New Variorum, 505–18.
Kenneth Muir, ed., Oxford Shakespeare, 9–12.
Barbara Bowan, *"Troilus and Cressida* on the Stage," in Signet Classic, revised edition, edited by Daniel Seltzer, 265–87.
David Bevington, ed. Arden Shakespeare Third Series, 87–117

Books And Periodicals

Jeanne T. Newlin, "The Modernity of *Troilus and Cressida:* The Case for Theatrical Criticism." *Harvard Library Bulletin* 17 (1969): 353–73.
J. C. Trewin, *Going To Shakespeare* (London: G. Allen & Unwin, 1978), 177–82.
Ralph Berry, *Changing Styles in Shakespeare* (London: G. Allen & Unwin, 1981), 49–65.
Samuel L. Leiter, ed., *Shakespeare Around the Globe* (New York: Greenwood Press, 1986), 747–65.
James Shaw, *"Troilus and Cressida,"* in *Shakespeare in Performance,* ed. by Keith Parsons and Pamela Mason (London: Salamander, 1995), 221–27.

Unpublished Works

Michael Kimberley, "*Troilus and Cressida* on the English Stage" (Master's thesis, Shakespeare Institute, University of Birmingham, 1968).
James Christy, "Five Twentieth-Century Productions of *Troilus and Cressida*" (Ph.D. diss., Stanford University, 1972).

COLLECTIONS OF REVIEWS

Shakespearean Criticism 18, ed. by Joseph C. Tardiff and others (1992).
Shakespeare Institute of the University of Birmingham, Stratford-upon-Avon.
Shakespeare Centre Library, Shakespeare Birthplace Trust, Stratford-upon-Avon.
Birmingham Shakespeare Library, Birmingham Central Library, United Kingdom.
Theatre Museum Library, London.
Lincoln Center Performing Arts Library, New York City Public Library.
Review articles regularly appear in *Shakespeare Survey* and *Shakespeare Quarterly*.
"World Shakespeare Bibliography" in *Shakespeare Quarterly* lists reviews and review articles.

PRODUCTION ARCHIVES

The Shakespeare Centre Library houses archives from productions at the Shakespeare Memorial Theatre, and productions by the Royal Shakespeare Company (founded 1960), including promptbooks, stage manager's scripts, photographs, rehearsal notes, archival videotapes, and programs. Specific materials consulted are cited in the following list of productions, as are other repositories of production archives.

The British Library National Sound Archive (NSA), London, has audiotapes of West End productions from the 1960s to the present, including the RSC productions directed by Barton, Barton/Kyle, Hands, Davies, and Mendes (see production details for recording information).

The Theatre Museum Library houses the promptbooks of productions directed by William Poel and Tyrone Guthrie. It also contains programs, playbills, and other ephemera connected with some of the productions discussed.

The Lincoln Center Performing Arts Library holds reviews, photographs, and ephemera connected to some of the productions discussed, especially the American productions.

INTERVIEWS WITH ACTORS AND DIRECTORS

Joseph Papp, 12 August 1990, director of 1965 New York Shakespeare Festival

John Barton, 24 October 1991, director of RSC 1968, joint director of RSC 1960, 1976

Norman Rodway, 25 January 1991, Thersites in RSC 1968, Pandarus in RSC 1990

Anton Lesser, 8 August 1991, Troilus in BBC 1981 and RSC 1985

Sam Mendes 31 May 1991, director of RSC 1990

Amanda Root, 14 December 1990, Cressida in RSC 1990

Ralph Fiennes, 10 December 1990, Troilus in RSC 1990

Roy Hanlon, 4 January 1999, Pandarus in RSC 1998

Andrew French, 10 March 1999, Aeneas in Royal National Theatre, 1999

I also had many informal talks with the cast of Mendes' RSC 1990 production. The director, assistant director, and actors (including Simon Russell Beale, Amanda Root, Ralph Fiennes) also participated in a number of question-and-answer sessions and workshops at The Shakespeare Institute that I attended. As a teacher I led class discussions with Richard McCabe (Thersites, RSC 1998) and most of the cast of Hall's 2001 production.

MAJOR PRODUCTIONS ATTENDED

1985 RSC, Howard Davies, Royal Shakespeare Theatre

1990 RSC, Sam Mendes, Swan Theatre and The Pit

1995 New York Shakespeare Festival, Mark Wing Davies, Delacorte Theatre

1997 RSC, Ian Judge, worked as textual advisor for 10 weeks of rehearsals and previews

1998 RSC, Michael Boyd, Swan Theatre

1999 Royal National Theatre, Trevor Nunn, Olivier Theatre

2001 Theatre for a New Audience, Peter Hall, American Place Theatre

Director: William Poel
Company: Elizabethan Stage Society
First Performance: 10 December 1912, King's Hall, London
Revived: 12 May 1913, Shakespeare Festival Theatre, Stratford-upon-Avon, with some cast changes
Promptbooks: The Theatre Museum holds two promptbooks, without any identification of what they represent. It may be that one was for London and the other for the Stratford revival, or that one was Poel's private copy and the other used as a promptbook. Both are in Poel's hand, and both have a combination of ink and pencil markings. There are many differences between the promptbooks.
Promptbook edition: Cassall's National Library; one promptbook uses the 1889 printing, the other uses the 1893 printing

Prologue	Richard Neville
Priam	Desmond Brannigan
Hector	P. L. Eyre
Deiphobus	
Helenus	Gabrielle Harris
Paris	May Carey
Troilus	Esmé Percy
Margarelon	
Cassandra	Hermione Gingold
Andromache	Muriel Dole
Aeneas	Madge Whiteman
Antenor	
Pandarus	William Poel
Cressida	Edith Evans
Calchas	Desmond Brannigan
Helen	Enid Lorimer
Alexander	Grace Laurence
Agamemnon	G. P. Twyman
Menelaus	Archibald McLean
Nestor	H. B. Barwell
Ulysses	Henry Doughty
Achilles	William H. Baker
Patroclus	Robert Carey
Diomedes	Herbert Ranson
Ajax	P. K. Merredew
Thersites	Elespeth Keith

Director: Henry Herbert
Designer: Charles B. Falls
First Performance: 6 June 1932, Moss's Broadway Theater, New York City
Promptbook and other production archives: Player's Club Library, New York
    City
Promptbook edition: Typescript, edition unknown, but reference is made
    to Israel Gollancz's Temple Edition.

Prologue	Augustin Duncan
Priam	F. Sayre Crawley
Hector	Herbert Ranson
Deiphobus	Alan Cambell
Helenus	Philip Leigh
Paris	Charles Brokaw
Troilus	Jerome Lawler
Margarelon	John Kramer
Cassandra	Elieen Huban
Andromache	Ivah Coburn
Aeneas	Leo G. Carroll
Antenor	Gordon Hart
Pandarus	Eugene Powers
Cressida	Edith Barrett
Calchas	Howard Kyle
Helen	Blanche Yurka
Alexander	Burford Hampden
Agamemnon	Elliot Cabot
Menelaus	P. J. Kelly
Nestor	Robert Le Sueur
Ulysses	Willian Sams
Achilles	Reynolds Evans
Patroclus	George Gaul
Diomedes	Allyn Joalyn
Ajax	Charles Coburn
Thersites	Otis Skinner

Director: Ben Iden Payne
First Performance: 24 April 1936, Shakespeare Memorial Theatre, Stratford-
upon-Avon
Promptbook and other performance archives: Shakespeare Centre
Promptbook edition: M. R. Ridley, ed., New Temple

Prologue..
Priam... Eric Maxon
Hector... Peter Glenville
Deiphobus.. Leigh Crutchley
Helenus... John Rudling
Paris.. Trevor Howard
Troilus .... Donald Eccles
Margarelon .... John Rudling
Cassandra.. Rosalind Iden
Andromache... Valerie Tudor
Aeneas... Dennis Roberts
Antenor... David Russell
Pandarus... Randle Ayrton
Cressida... Pamela Brown
Calchas.. Roy Byford
Helen... Valerie Hall
Alexander.. Donald Layn-Smith
Agamemnon .... Gerald Kay Souper
Menelaus... Stanley Howlett
Nestor.. Geoffrey Wilkinson
Ulysses .... Donald Wolfit
Achilles.. Norman Wooland
Patroclus .... Basil Langton
Diomedes.. Raymond Raikes
Ajax.. Alexander Gauge
Thersites.. James Dale

Director: Michael Macowan
First Performance: 21 September 1938, Westminster Theatre, London
Company: London Mask Theatre Company
Promptbook: unknown
Promptbook edition: unknown
Program and other ephemera at the Theatre Museum, London
Interview with Macowan, and details about cuts in James Christy, "Five Twen-
   tieth-Century Productions of *Troilus and Cressida*"

Prologue	Stephen Murray
Priam	Robert Enhardt
Hector	Colin Keith-Johnston
Deiphobus	
Helenus	
Paris	Michael Denison
Troilus	Robert Harris
Margarelon	Reginald Lockwood
Cassandra	Rosanna Seaborn
Andromache	Mary Alexander
Aeneas	Claude Bailey
Antenor	
Pandarus	Max Adrian
Cressida	Ruth Lodge
Calchas	Robert Enhardt
Helen	Orial Ross
Alexander	Elspeth Currie
Agamemnon	Arthur Ridley
Menelaus	David Marsh
Nestor	John Garside
Ulysses	Robert Speaight
Achilles	George Woodbridge
Patroclus	Frank Lonson
Diomedes	Harry Andrews
Ajax	Richard George
Thersites	Stephen Murray

Director: Anthony Quayle
First Performance: 2 July 1948, Shakespeare Memorial Theatre, Stratford-upon-Avon
Promptbook and other performance archives: Shakespeare Centre
Promptbook edition: M. R. Ridley, ed., New Temple

Prologue	Paul Hardwick
Priam	Julian Amyes
Hector	Anthony Quayle
Deiphobus	
Helenus	Harold Kasket
Paris	John Justin
Troilus	Paul Scofield
Margarelon	Alan Dipper
Cassandra	Ena Burrill
Andromache	Lorna Whitehouse
Aeneas	Manfred Priestley
Antenor	
Pandarus	Noel Williamson
Cressida	Heather Stannard
Calchas	Arnold Diamond
Helen	Diana Wynyard
Alexander	Clifford Williams
Agamemnon	Michael Gwynn
Menelaus	John Van Eyssen
Nestor	John Kidd
Ulysses	William Squire
Achilles	Douglas Wilmer
Patroclus	Edmund Prudom
Diomedes	Michael Godfrey
Ajax	William Monk
Thersites	Esmond Knight

Director: Glen Byam Shaw
First Performance: 13 July 1954
Shakespeare Memorial Theatre, Stratford-upon-Avon
Promptbook and other performance archives: Shakespeare Centre
Promptbook edition: M. R. Ridley, ed., New Temple

Prologue	James Grout
Priam	Geoffrey Bayldon
Hector	Raymond Westwell
Deiphobus	Timothy Parkes
Helenus	David King
Paris	Basil Hoskins
Troilus	Laurence Harvey
Margarelon	John Turner
Cassandra	Jean Wilson
Andromache	Jan Bashford
Aeneas	Powys Thomas
Antenor	Ian Mullins
Pandarus	Anthony Quayle
Cressida	Muriel Pavlow
Calchas	Edward Atienza
Helen	Barbara Jefford
Alexander	Peter Duguid
Agamemnon	William Devlin
Menelaus	Philip Morant
Nestor	Mervyn Blake
Ulysses	Leo McKern
Achilles	Keith Mitchell
Patroclus	Jerome Willis
Diomedes	Bernard Kay
Ajax	James Grout
Thersites	Tony Britton

Director: Tyrone Guthrie
First Performance: 3 April 1956, Old Vic Theatre, London
Transferred: 26 December 1956, Winter Garden Theater, New York City, with several cast changes
Promptbook and other performance archives: Theatre Museum, London
Promptbook edition: Alice Walker, ed., New [Cambridge]

Prologue	cut
Priam	Job Stewart
Hector	Jack Gwillim
Deiphobus	John Woodvine
Helenus	John Wood
Paris	Ronald Allen
Troilus	John Neville
Margarelon	
Cassandra	Rachel Roberts
Andromache	Margaret Courtenay
Aeneas	Denis Holmes
Antenor	James Villiers
Pandarus	Paul Rogers
Cressida	Rosemary Harris
Calchas	Gerald Cross
Helen	Wendy Hiller
Alexander	Margaret Courtenay
Agamemnon	Derek Francis
Menelaus	Edward Harvey
Nestor	Dudley Jones
Ulysses	Richard Wordsworth
Achilles	Charles Gray
Patroclus	Jeremy Brett
Diomedes	Anthony White
Ajax	Laurence Hardy
Thersites	Clifford Williams

Directors: Peter Hall and John Barton
Designer: Leslie Hurry
First Performance: 26 July 1960, Shakespeare Memorial Theatre, Stratford-upon-Avon
Revived for Edinburgh Festival, tour, and London in 1962, with many cast changes (from 15 October at the Aldwych Theatre, London)
Company: Royal Shakespeare Company
Promptbook and other performance archives: Shakespeare Centre
Promptbook edition: Alice Walker, ed., New [Cambridge]

Prologue	Paul Hardwick
Priam	Clifford Rose
Hector	Derek Godfrey
Deiphobus	Don Webster
Helenus	Walter Brown
Paris	David Sumner
Troilus	Denholm Elliot
Margarelon	Roger Bizley
Cassandra	Frances Cuka
Andromache	Diana Rigg
Aeneas	Donald Douglas
Antenor	Roy Dotrice
Pandarus	Max Adrian
Cressida	Dorothy Tutin
Calchas	Stephen Thorn
Helen	Elizabeth Sellars
Alexander	Clive Swift
Agamemnon	Peter Jeffery
Menelaus	Walter Brown
Nestor	James Bree
Ulysses	Eric Porter
Achilles	Patrick Allen
Patroclus	Dinsdale Landen
Diomedes	David Buck
Ajax	Paul Hardwick
Thersites	Peter O'Toole

Director: John Harrison
First Performance: 19 February 1963, Birmingham Repertory Theatre
Promptbook and other performance archives: Birmingham Shakespeare Library
Promptbook edition: A. Harbage, ed., Pelican Shakespeare

Prologue	Arthur Pentelow
Priam	Terence Greenidge
Hector	Paul Carson
Deiphobus	
Helenus	Peter Dennis
Paris	Robert Robinson
Troilus	Derek Jacobi
Margarelon	Peter Dennis
Cassandra	Lesley Nunnerley
Andromache	Elspeth Duxbury
Aeneas	Michael Latimer
Antenor	Peter Price
Pandarus	Ralph Nossek
Cressida	Jennifer Hilary
Calchas	Peter Miles-Johnson
Helen	Georgine Anderson
Alexander	
Agamemnon	Colin Pinney
Menelaus	Ronald Harvi
Nestor	Frank Ellis
Ulysses	Desmond Gill
Achilles	Philip Voss
Patroclus	Michael May
Diomedes	William Ingram
Ajax	Roy Patrick
Thersites	Arthur Pentelow

Director: John Barton
Designer: Timothy O'Brien
Company: Royal Shakespeare Company
First Performance: 8 August 1968, Royal Shakespeare Theatre, Stratford-
  upon-Avon
Transferred: 19 June 1969, Aldwych Theatre, London, tour of Europe,
  Japan, New York, and return to Aldwych Theatre, with some cast changes
Promptbook and other performance archives: Shakespeare Centre
Promptbook edition: Alice Walker, ed., New [Cambridge]
AudioTape: 8 August 1970, Aldwych Theatre, NSA

Prologue	various
Priam	
Hector	Patrick Stewart
Deiphobus	
Helenus	
Paris	Bernard Lloyd
Troilus	Michael Williams
Margarelon	
Cassandra	Susan Fleetwood
Andromache	Diane Fletcher
Aeneas	Ben Kingsley
Antenor	
Pandarus	David Waller
Cressida	Helen Mirren
Calchas	
Helen	Sheila Allen
Alexander	
Agamemnon	Bryan Robson
Menelaus	Ted Valentine
Nestor	Clifford Rose
Ulysses	Sebastian Shaw
Achilles	Alan Howard
Patroclus	Richard Jones Barry
Diomedes	Bruce Myers
Ajax	Richard Moore
Thersites	Norman Rodway

Director: John Barton and Barry Kyle
Designer: Chris Dyer
Company: Royal Shakespeare Company
First Performance: 17 August 1976, Royal Shakespeare Theatre, Stratford-upon-Avon
Transferred: 15 September 1977, Aldwych Theatre, London, with some cast changes
Promptbook and other performance archives: Shakespeare Centre
Promptbook edition: Alice Walker, ed., New [Cambridge]
Audiotape: 25 October 1977, Aldwych Theatre, NSA

Prologue	David Lyon or
	John Nettles or
	Keith Taylor or
	Jacob Witkin
Priam	Dennis Clinton
Hector	Michael Pennington
Deiphobus	Peter Woodward
Helenus	Paul Whitworth
Paris	Richard Durden
Troilus	Mike Gwilym
Margarelon	David Lyon
Cassandra	Barbara Shelly
Andromache	Meg Davies
Aeneas	Nickolas Grace
Antenor	Leonard Preston
Pandarus	David Waller
Cressida	Francesca Annis
Calchas	Clyde Pollitt
Helen	Barbara Leigh-Hunt
Alexander	Paul Brooke
Agamemnon	Ivan Beavis
Menelaus	Jacob Witkin
Nestor	Norman Tyrrell
Ulysses	Tony Church
Achilles	Robin Ellis
Patroclus	Paul Moriarty
Diomedes	Paul Shelly
Ajax	Brian Coburn
Thersites	John Nettles

Director: Terry Hands
Designer: Farrah
First Performance: 6 July 1981 Aldwych Theatre, London
Company: Royal Shakespeare Company
Promptbook: reported lost
Stage manager's script and other performance archives: Shakespeare Centre
Stage manager's script edition: Daniel Seltzer, Signet Classic
Rehearsal notes: Shakespeare Centre
Audiotape: 27 July 1981, Aldwych Theatre, NSA

Prologue	Joe Melia
Priam	Raymond Llewellyn
Hector	Bruce Pruchase
Deiphobus	Johnathan Tafler
Helenus	Timothy Walker
Paris	Bille Brown
Troilus	James Hazeldine
Margarelon	Abraham Osuagwu
Cassandra	Catherine Riding
Andromache	Patricia Shakesby
Aeneas	Paul Whitworth
Antenor	Peter MacKriel
Pandarus	Tony Church
Cressida	Carol Royale
Calchas	John Darrell
Helen	Barbara Kinghorn
Alexander	Rolf Saxon
Agamemnon	Trevor Baxter
Menelaus	Richard Cordery
Nestor	Oliver Ford Davies
Ulysses	John Carlisle
Achilles	David Suchet
Patroclus	Chris Hunter
Diomedes	Pip Miller
Ajax	Terry Wood
Thersites	Joe Melia

Director: Jonathan Miller
Designer: Colin Lowrey
Script editor: Donald Snodin
Literary consultant: John Wilders
Recorded between 28 July and 5 August 1981
First Broadcast: 7 November 1981, BBC 2
Performance edition: *The BBC TV Troilus and Cressida* (1991)
Text used: Peter Alexander

Prologue	Benjamin Whitrow
Priam	Esmond Knight
Hector	John Shrapnel
Deiphobus	Peter J. Cassell
Helenus	Tony Portacio
Paris	David Firth
Troilus	Anton Lesser
Margarelon	Cornelius Garrett
Cassandra	Elayne Sharling
Andromache	Merelina Kendall
Aeneas	Tony Steedman
Antenor	
Pandarus	Charles Gray
Cressida	Suzanne Burden
Calchas	Peter Whitebread
Helen	Ann Pennington
Alexander	Max Harvey
Agamemnon	Vernon Dobtcheff
Menelaus	Bernard Brown
Nestor	Geoffrey Chater
Ulysses	Benjamin Whitrow
Achilles	Kenneth Haigh
Patroclus	Simon Cutter
Diomedes	Paul Moriarty
Ajax	Anthony Pedley
Thersites	The Incredible Orlando (Jack Birkett)

Director: Howard Davies
Designer: Ralph Koltai
First Performance: 20 June 1985, Royal Shakespeare Theatre, Stratford-upon-Avon
Company: Royal Shakespeare Company
Transferred: Barbican Theatre, London, with some cast changes
Promptbook and other performance archives: Shakespeare Centre
Promptbook edition: Virgil Whitaker, ed., Pelican
Rehearsal notes: Helen Lovat-Fraser, Deputy Stage Manager, Shakespeare Centre
Videotape: 20 November 1985, RST, Shakespeare Centre
Audiotape: 1 August 1986, Aldwych Theatre (with Emma D'Inverno as Cressida)
Attended: August 1985.

Prologue	Gerard Logan
Priam	Colin Douglas
Hector	David Burke
Deiphobus	
Helenus	Paul Spence
Paris	Sean Baker
Troilus	Anton Lesser
Margarelon	Paul Spence
Cassandra	Mary Jo Randle
Andromache	Janet Dale
Aeneas	Alexander Wilson
Antenor	
Pandarus	Clive Merrison
Cressida	Juliet Stevenson
Calchas	Richard Conway
Helen	Lindsay Duncan
Alexander	Roger Hymans
Agamemnon	Joseph O'Conor
Menelaus	Brian Horstead
Nestor	Mark Dignam
Ulysses	Peter Jeffrey
Achilles	Alan Rickman
Patroclus	Hilton McRae
Diomedes	Bruce Alexander
Ajax	Clive Russell
Thersites	Alun Armstrong, then Christopher Wright

Director: Sam Mendes
Designer: Anthony Ward
First Performance: 18 April 1990, Swan Theatre, Stratford-upon-Avon
Company: Royal Shakespeare Company
Transferred: 18 June 1991, The Pit, London
Promptbook and other performance archives: Shakespeare Centre
Promptbook edition: R. A. Foakes, ed. New Penguin
Videotape: 20 November 1985, Shakespeare Centre
Attended: April, June 1990, July 1991.

Prologue	Norman Rodway
Priam	Griffith Jones
Hector	David Troughton
Deiphobus	
Helenus	Michael Bott
Paris	John Warnaby
Troilus	Ralph Fiennes
Margarelon	
Cassandra	Linda Scott Kerr
Andromache	Julie Saunders
Aeneas	Mike Dowling
Antenor	Simon Austin
Pandarus	Norman Rodway
Cressida	Amanda Root
Calchas	Richard Avery
Helen	Sally Dexter
Alexander	Lloyd Hutchinson
Agamemnon	Sylvester Morand
Menelaus	Michael Gardiner
Nestor	Alfred Burke
Ulysses	Paul Jesson
Achilles	Ciaran Hinds
Patroclus	Patterson Joseph
Diomedes	Grant Thatcher
Ajax	Richard Ridings
Thersites	Simon Russell Beale

Director: Ian Judge
Designer: John Gunter
First Performance: 19 July 1996, Royal Shakespeare Theatre, Stratford-upon-Avon
Company: Royal Shakespeare Company
Transferred: 4 December 1997, Barbican Theatre, London
Promptbook and other performance archives: Shakespeare Centre
Promptbook edition: K. Muir, ed. Oxford Shakespeare
Worked as Textual Advisor.
Attended July, September 1996, January 1997.

Prologue...	
Priam...	Griffith Jones
Hector...	Louis Hilyer
Deiphobus...	Mark Gillis
Helenus...	Alisdair Simpson
Paris..	Ray Fearon
Troilus	Joseph Fiennes
Margarelon	Stephen Billington
Cassandra..	Sara Weymouth
Andromache	Martina Laird
Aeneas...	David Pullan
Antenor...	Simon Westwood
Pandarus	Clive Francis
Cressida...	Victoria Hamilton
Calchas..	Raymond Bowers
Helen...	Katia Caballero
Alexander..	Paul Ritter
Agamemnon	Edward de Souza
Menelaus..	Colin Farrell
Nestor..	Arthur Cox
Ulysses	Philip Voss
Achilles..	Philip Quast
Patroclus	Jeremy Sheffield
Diomedes...	Richard Dillane
Ajax...	Ross O'Hennessy
Thersites..	Richard McCabe

Director: Michael Boyd
Designer: Tom Piper
First Performance: 28 October 1998, The Pit, London
Company: Royal Shakespeare Company
Transferred: 8 December 1998, Swan Theatre, Stratford-upon-Avon
Promptbook and other performance archives: Shakespeare Centre
Promptbook edition: R. A. Foakes, ed. Penguin
Attended: December 1998.

Prologue	
Priam	Michael Loughan
Hector	Alistair Petrie
Deiphobus	
Helenus	Stephen Armstrong
Paris	Jack Tarlton
Troilus	William Houston
Margarelon	
Cassandra	Catherine Walker
Andromache	Jane Macfarlane
Aeneas	Rory Murray
Antenor	
Pandarus	Roy Hanlon
Cressida	Jayne Ashbourne
Calchas	Robert Calvert
Helen	Sara Stewart
Alexander	
Agamemnon	Sam Graham
Menelaus	Sam Cox
Nestor	
Ulysses	Colin Hurley
Achilles	Darrell D'Silva
Patroclus	Elaine Pyke
Diomedes	Robert Willox
Ajax	Paul Hamilton
Thersites	Lloyd Hutchinson
Hecuba	Janet Whiteside

Director: Trevor Nunn
Designer: Rob Howell
First Performance: 15 March 1999, Olivier Theatre, London
Company: Royal National Theatre
Promptbook and other performance archives: Royal National Theatre Archive and Press Office
Promptbook edition: David Bevington, ed. Arden Third Series (program misidentifies editor as Clifford Leech)
Attended: March, July 1999.

Role	Actor
Prologue	David Weston
Priam	Oscar James
Hector	Dhobi Oparei
Deiphobus	Mark Springer
Helenus	Vernon Douglas
Paris	Chu Omambala
Troilus	Peter de Jersey
Margarelon	Michael Wildman
Cassandra	Jax Williams
Andromache	Sara Powell
Aeneas	Andrew French
Antenor	
Pandarus	David Bamber
Cressida	Sophie Okonedo
Calchas	Ruddy L Davis
Helen	Aislinn Sands
Alexander	Gilz Terera
Agamemnon	Oliver Cotton
Menelaus	David Burt
Nestor	Denis Quilley
Ulysses	Roger Allam
Achilles	Raymond Coulthard
Patroclus	Daniel Evans
Diomedes	Alex Hanson
Ajax	Simon Day
Thersites	Jasper Britton

Director: Peter Hall
Designer: Douglas Stein
First Performance: 2 April 2001, American Place Theatre, New York City
Company: Theatre For a New Audience
Promptbook edition: David Bevington, ed. Arden Third Series
Attended: April 2001.

Prologue	Andrew Weems
Priam	Frank Raiter
Hector	David Conrad
Deiphobus	Luke Kirby
Helenus	Andrew Elvis Miller
Paris	Lorenzo Pisoni
Troilus	Joey Kern
Margarelon	Thomas M. Hammond
Cassandra	Vivienne Benesch
Andromache	Tari Signor
Aeneas	Thomas M. Hammond
Antenor	Matt Semler
Pandarus	Tony Church
Cressida	Tricia Paoluccio
Calchas	Frank Raiter
Helen	Cindy Katz
Alexander	Jordan Charney
Agamemnon	Terence Rigby
Menelaus	Jordan Charney
Nestor	Nicholas Kepros
Ulysses	Philip Goodwin
Achilles	Idris Elba
Patroclus	Luke Kirby
Diomedes	Michael Rogers
Ajax	Earl Hindman
Thersites	Andrew Weems

Notes

INTRODUCTION:
"SHALL I NOT LIE IN PUBLISHING A TRUTH?"

1. Editions of Troilus and Cressida are listed in Appendix A and generally referred to by the editor's name. Details of productions and promptbooks are given in Appendix B and generally referred to by director's name.

2. Twenty-fifth International Shakespeare Conference, 24 August 1992.

3. Kenneth Muir, ed., 3.

4. Three essays that discuss moments in the theatrical and editorial history of *Troilus and Cressida* are David Bevington, "Editing Informed by Performance History: The Double Ending of *Troilus and Cressida*," in *Shakespeare: Text and Theater: Essays in Honor of Jay L. Halio,* edited by Lois Potter and Arthur F. Kinney (Newark: University of Delaware Press, 1999), 298–309; Barbara Hodgdon, "He Do Cressida in Different Voices," *English Literary Renaissance* 20 (spring 1990): 254–286; and Peter Holland, "*Troilus and Cressida* and the Rate of Exchange," in *Surprised by Scenes: Essays in Honour of Professor Yasunari Takahashi,* edited by Yasunari Takada (Tokyo: Keyusha, 1994), 86–104. A more general consideration of the relationship between editors and performers is the chapter "Suiting the Word to the Action?: Scholarship and Stage Direction" in Charles H. Frey, *Experiencing Shakespeare: Essays on Text, Classroom, and Performance* (Columbia: University of Missouri Press, 1988), 94–103. See also the essays about *King Lear* by Roger Warren and Stanley Wells discussed below, and Ralph Berry, "The Editing and Staging of Shakespeare's Plays," *Queen's Quarterly* 88 (1981): 536–43.

5. Introduction to *Shakespeare Reread,* edited by Russ McDonald (Ithaca, N.Y.: Cornell University Press, 1994), 11.

6. *Shakespeare Quarterly* 44 (1993): 255.

7. See Stephen Orgel, "The Authentic Shakespeare," *Representations* 21 (1988): 1–26 and Terence Hawkes, *That Shakespeherian Rag* (London: Methuen, 1986), esp. 77–78.

8. For a history of the New Bibliography see F. P. Wilson, *Shakespeare and the New Bibliography,* revised by Helen Gardner (Oxford: Clarendon, 1970). For a critique of the goals of the New Bibliographers see Laurie E. Maguire, *Shakespearean Suspect Texts: The "Bad" Quartos in Their Contexts* (Cambridge: Cambridge University Press, 1996); Marion Trousdale, "Diachronic and Synchronic: Critical Bibliography and the Acting of Plays" in *Shakespeare: Text, Language, Criticism. Essays in Honor of Marvin Spevack,* edited by Bernhard Fabian and Kurt Tetzeli von Rosador (Hildesheim: Olms-Weidmann, 1987): 307–14; and "A Second Look at Critical Bibliography and the Acting of Plays," *Shakespeare Quarterly* 41 (1990): 87–96.

9. Jerome J. McGann, *A Critique of Modern Textual Criticism* (Chicago: University of Chicago Press, 1983) and *The Texual Condition* (Princeton: Princeton University

Press, 1991); D. F. McKenzie, "Printers of the Mind: Some Notes on Bibliographical Theories and Printing House Practices," *Studies in Bibliography* 22 (1969): 1–77; Paul Werstine, "'Foul Papers' and 'Prompt-books': Printer's Copy for Shakespeare's *Comedy of Errors*," *Studies in Bibliography* 41 (1988): 232–46.

10. See, for example, Paul Werstine, "Narratives about Printed Shakespearean Texts: 'Foul Papers' and 'Bad' Quartos," *Shakespeare Quarterly* 41 (1990): 65–86.

11. "The Shakespearean Editor as Shrew-Tamer," *English Literary Renaissance* 22 (1992): 198.

12. "Introduction: The Once and Future *King Lear*," in *The Division of the Kingdoms*, edited by Gary Taylor and Michael Warren (Oxford: Clarendon, 1983), 20.

13. Roger Warren discusses the treatment of the scenes in three modern productions (1956, 1962, and 1968), 53–56.

14. "The Folio Omission of the Mock Trial," in *Division of the Kingdoms*, ed. Taylor and Warren, 53.

15. *Shakespeare Studies* 15 (1982): 99–136.

16. Taylor (113) cites Anthony Quayle's 1948 production that kept Cressida onstage, as F, for Ulysses' speech about her (4.6.55), as discussed below in chapter 6: "I'll bring you to your father."

17. "Textual Problems, Editorial Assertions in Editions of Shakespeare," in *Textual Criticism and Literary Interpretation*, edited by Jerome J. McGann (Chicago: University of Chicago Press, 1985), 27.

18. Some recent articles about the texts of *Troilus and Cressida* include Phebe Jensen, "The Textual Politics of *Troilus and Cressida*," *Shakespeare Quarterly* 46 (1995): 414–23; and Karen Bjelland's two articles, "The Cultural Value of Analytical Bibliography and Textual Criticism: The Case of *Troilus and Cressida*," *Text* 7 (1994): 272–95; "Variants as Epistemological Shifts: A Proposed Methodology for Recovering the Two Texts of Shakespeare's *Troilus and Cressida*," *Papers of the Bibliographical Society of America* (1994): 53–78. See also John Jones, *Shakespeare at Work* (Oxford: Clarendon, 1995).

19. The most recent textual introductions are in the editions of Bevington, Foakes, Taylor (*A Textual Companion*), and Muir.

20. Appendix B lists some theater histories.

21. I am particularly attracted to the possibilities of electronic editions, such as the *Internet Shakespeare Editions* (http://web.uvic.ca/shakespeare/index.html).

22. Alan Dessen, "Shakespeare's Scripts and the Modern Director," *Shakespeare Survey* 36 (1983): 57–64 is just one example. For a discussion of Dessen's work, see Cary Mazer, "Historicizing Alan Dessen: Scholarship, Stagecraft, and the 'Shakespeare Revolution,'" in *Shakespeare, Theory, and Performance*, edited by James C. Bulman (London: Routledge, 1996), 149–67.

23. Alan Dessen, "Modern Productions and the Elizabethan Scholar," *Renaissance Drama* 18 (1987): 206.

24. Laurie E. Osborne explores performance editions as a "convergence of editorial and theatrical approaches to Shakespeare" in her book *The Trick of Singularity: "Twelfth Night" and the Performance Editions* (Iowa City: University of Iowa Press, 1996). See the list of performance editions in Appendix B.

25. Jeanne Newlin believes that Kemble probably consulted the Bell edition. See "The Darkened Stage: J. P. Kemble and *Troilus and Cressida*," in *The Triple Bond*, edited by Joseph Price (University Park: Pennsylvania State University Press, 1975), 192.

26. See the essays collected in *Textual and Theatrical Shakespeare: Questions of Evidence*, edited by Edward Pechter (Iowa City: University of Iowa Press, 1996), especially Barbara Hodgdon, "'Here Apparent': Photography, History, and the Theatri-

cal Unconscious," 181–209; and W. B. Worthen, "Invisible Bullets, Violet Beards: Reading Actors Reading," 210–29.

27. Appendix B lists archives consulted and productions attended by the author.

28. John Barton, interview by author, London, 24 October 1991.

29. "Playing *King Lear:* Donald Sinden Talks to J. W. R. Meadowcroft," *Shakespeare Survey* 33 (1980): 81.

30. See Janet Adelman, *Suffocating Mothers* (New York: Routledge, 1992), and Linda Charnes, *Materializing the Subject in Shakespeare* (Cambridge: Harvard University Press, 1993).

31. See Harry Berger Jr., "*Troilus and Cressida:* The Observer as Basilisk," *Comparative Drama* 2 (1968): 122–36, and Hodgdon, "He Do Cressida in Different Voices."

1. "THE VAUNT AND FIRSTLINGS"

1. Philip Williams, "The 'Second Issue' of Shakespeare's *Troilus and Cressida, 1609,*" *Studies in Bibliography* 2 (1949): 25–33.

2. See *Reader-Response Criticism: From Formalism to Post-Structuralism,* ed. Jane Tompkins (Baltimore: Johns Hopkins University Press, 1980).

3. "A never writer to an ever reader: news," in *Troilus and Cressida* (London, 1609), second state [Qb], reprinted in modern spelling in *William Shakespeare: The Complete Works,* ed. by Stanley Wells and Gary Taylor (Oxford: Clarendon, 1986), xliii. All citations of Shakespeare's plays are from this edition.

4. See, for example, Leah Marcus, *Puzzling Shakespeare* (Berkeley and Los Angeles: University of California Press, 1988), and Margreta de Grazia, *Shakespeare Verbatim* (Oxford: Clarendon, 1991).

5. John Heminges and Henry Condell, in William Shakespeare, *Comedies, Histories, & Tragedies* (London, 1623), [First Folio], sig. A3, reprinted in modern spelling in *William Shakespeare: The Complete Works,* xlv.

6. Heminges and Condell.

7. Charlton Hinman, *The Printing and Proof-Reading of the First Folio of Shakespeare* (Oxford: Clarendon, 1963), 2:328–29.

8. Muir, 3.

9. E. K. Chambers, *The Elizabethan Stage* (Oxford: Clarendon, 1923), 3:542–47.

10. Pandarus tells Cressida, when they watch Hector return home from battle, to "Look you what hacks are on his helmet" (1.2.200), and later asks her to notice that Troilus's helmet is "more hacked than Hector's" (230). Nestor remarks that although he has "oft" seen Hector fight, but his "countenance" was "locked in steel" (4.7.67, 79). Diomedes will wear the sleeve Cressida gives him (and he later forcefully takes) on his "helm" (5.2.96).

11. Thomas Heywood, *The Second Part of The Iron Age* (London, 1623), E4v, F1r.

12. For an analysis of the Peacham drawing, see *Titus Andronicus,* Oxford Shakespeare, edited by Eugene M. Waith (Oxford: Clarendon, 1984), 20–27.

13. Eric S. Mallin, *Inscribing the Time: Shakespeare and the End of Elizabethan England* (Berkeley and Los Angeles: University of California Press, 1995), 25–62.

14. Johnson, Malone, and Theobald are just some of the editors who placed the prologue before the dramatis personae.

15. John Dryden, *Troilus and Cressida, or Truth Found Too Late,* ed. Maximillian E. Novak, in *The Works of John Dryden* (Berkeley and Los Angeles: University of California Press, 1984), 13:217–355. First performed in 1679, with Betterton also playing

Troilus. For convenience, Dryden's play will be referred to throughout this book as *Truth Found Too Late*, which Novak argues "may have been Dryden's preferred title" (497).

16. *Bell's Edition of Shakespeare's Plays—As they were performed at the Theatres Royal in London, Regulated from the prompt books of each House by permission with notes critical and illustrative By the Author of the Dramatic Censor,* vol. 6 (London, 1774).

17. Ibid. 163.

18. Ibid. 171.

19. For a discussion of Kemble's aborted production see Jeanne T. Newlin, "The Darkened Stage: J. P. Kemble and *Troilus and Cressida*."

20. Kemble's copy of Qa is in the Huntington Library.

21. *The Henry Irving Shakespeare,* edited by Henry Irving and F. A. Marshall, with annotations by A. W. Verity (London, 1888), 4:312.

22. Kemble reassigns three speeches, Nestor's "And in the imitation . . . with danger" (1.3.185–96) to Diomedes, Ulysses' "They tax our policy . . . his execution" (1.3.197–210) to Nestor, and Nestor's "Let this be granted . . . Thetis' sons" (1.3.211–12) to Agamemnon, and adding to this speech the scene's concluding lines:

> But you, grave pair
> Like time and wisdom marching hand in hand,
> Must find some stop to these increasing evils;
> You, who could tell whence the distemper springs,
> Must vindicate the dignity of kings. *Exeunt–Flourish*

23. The booking slip for the Elizabethan Stage Society performances at the King's Hall, London, October 1912, in the Poel Collection, Theatre Museum, London.

24. Poel's essay, "Shakespeare's *Troilus and Cressida*," originally appeared in two parts, "Shakespeare and Ben Jonson," *New Age,* 28 November 1912, 82–83; and "Shakespeare and Essex," *New Age,* 5 December 1912, 106–7.

25. E. M. Moore, "William Poel," *Shakespeare Quarterly* 23 (1972): 33.

26. Two reviews that disapproved of the setting were "Elizabethan Dresses of Greek Heroes," *News Chronicle,* 23 April 1936, and "Trojans Clad as Elizabethans," *Birmingham Gazette,* 23 April 1936.

27. Sidney Charteris, "Faults of *Troilus and Cressida*," *Evening Dispatch,* 25 April 1936.

28. *Evening Dispatch,* 23 April 1936.

29. Our Dramatic Critic, "Shakespeare at His Bitterest," *Morning Post,* 25 April 1936.

30. Correspondent, "Shakespeare in Munich," *Times* (London), 30 December 1936.

31. Michael Macowan, Preface in 1938 program, in the Theatre Museum, London.

32. James Christy, "Five Twentieth-Century Productions of *Troilus and Cressida*" (Ph.D. diss., Stanford University, 1972), 98.

33. *Birmingham News,* 17 July 1954.

34. *Birmingham Weekly Post,* 16 July 1954.

35. *Nottingham Guardian Journal,* 15 July 1954.

36. Tyrone Guthrie, "This is Shakespeare?" *New York Herald Tribune,* 23 December 1956. A typescript of the article, with cuts and corrections by Guthrie, is in the Lincoln Center Performing Arts Library, New York.

37. *Illustrated London News,* 14 April 1956.

38. The chapter on Pandarus's final speech explores some of the debate concerning the play's genre and a possible change in genre either during or after the initial composition.

39. *Birmingham Post*, 27 July 1960.

40. Eric Keown, *Punch*, 10 August 1960, 208.

41. An impression recalled by Stanley Wells in a conversation with the author, September 1992.

42. *The Festival Shakespeare Troilus and Cressida*, edited by Bernard Beckerman and Joseph Papp (New York: Macmillan, 1967), 203.

43. Hilary Spurling, *The Spectator*, 16 August 1968.

44. John Barton, interview by author, London, 24 October 1991.

45. Ralph Berry, *Changing Styles in Shakespeare* (London: Allen & Unwin, 1981), 60.

46. Robert Cushman, *Observer*, 22 August 1976.

47. Irving Wardle, *Times* (London), 19 August 1976.

48. Muir, 52.

49. John Nettles, who played Thersites, is only one of several actors listed in the program as "playing" the Prologue. See cast list in Appendix B.

50. Robert Cushman, *Observer*, quoted in *London Theatre Record*, 2–15 July 1981.

51. Muir, 38.

52. Susan Willis, *The BBC Shakespeare Plays* (Chapel Hill: University of North Carolina Press, 1991), 243.

53. Ibid., 256.

54. Stanley Wells, *Times Literary Supplement*, 20 November 1981.

55. Garry O'Connor, *Plays and Players*, August 1990, 29.

56. Irving Wardle, *Independent on Sunday*, 6 May 1990.

57. Norman Rodway, interview with author, Stratford-upon-Avon, 25 January 1991.

58. Judge is referred to as a "feelgood" director by Michael Billington, *Guardian*, 25 July 1998, Paul Taylor, *Independent*, 26 July 1996, and Jeremy Kingson, *Times* (London), 7 December 1996, and as "Cheeky Chappie" by Robert Gore-Langton, *Daily Telegraph*, 26 July 1996.

59. "Shakespeare in Stratford-upon-Avon: The Royal Shakespeare Company's 'Half Season,' April–September 1996," *Shakespeare Quarterly* 48 (1997) 213.

60. Benedict Nightingale, *Times* (London), 26 July 1996.

61. John Gross, *Sunday Telegraph*, 28 July 1996.

62. Jack Tinker, *Daily Mail*, 25 July 1996, Nicholas de Jongh, *Evening Telegraph*, 5 December 1996, Michael Billington, *Guardian*, 25 July 1998.

63. John Peter, *Sunday Times*, 12 January 1997, Robert Hewison, *Sunday Times*, 28 July 1996.

64. Charles Spencer, *Daily Telegraph*, 9 November 1998.

65. My understanding of the opening was informed by a discussion with the production's assistant director, Ron Russell, New York, 29 April 2001.

66. Personal interviews with Anton Lesser (Troilus in the 1981 BBC and 1985 RSC productions), John Barton, Norman Rodway (Thersites in the RSC 1968, and Pandarus in the RSC 1990 productions), Sam Mendes, Roy Hanlon (Pandarus in RSC 1998), Ron Russell (assistant director to Peter Hall, 2001), and my observation of Judge's rehearsals, revealed not only late decisions about the prologue, but several last minute changes. See Appendix B for interview dates.

67. The debate is discussed at greater length, with full references, in chapter 8.

68. Nevill Coghill, *Times Literary Supplement*, 19 January 1967.

2. "WHO WERE THOSE WENT BY?"

1. Hodgdon, "He Do Cressida in Different Voices," 263–64. As discussed below, Hodgdon is writing specifically about Cressida questioning the identity of soldiers (1.2.185, 214, 223).

2. Muir, 57. The only edition besides Muir's which I found that suggests a possible appearance by Helen and Hecuba includes the note that "if Helen and Hecuba appear, they would be in Elizabethan costume, and wearing masks to protect their complexion." *Troilus and Cressida*, The Players Shakespeare, edited by J. H. Walter (London: Heinemann Educational Books, 1982), 60.

3. Adelman, *Suffocating Mothers*, 43.

4. Compare Alexander's report of Hector chiding Andromache (1.2.6), and Hector's forceful dismissal of Andromache's plea not to fight (5.3). But also compare Paris listening to Helen's desire for him not to fight, where female dominance is also destructive since it damages the heroic image of Paris (3.1.133–34).

5. Carol Chillington Rutter, *Enter the Body: Women and Representation on Shakespeare's Stage* (London: Routledge, 2001), 116–17.

6. Payne, Quayle, Shaw, and Herbert began the scene with Helen and Hecuba crossing the stage. One of Poel's promptbooks (1889) has the note, "Helen and Hecuba cross stage." While the other promptbook has the same note, "Hecuba" is crossed-through in pencil and "Helenus" written in, but Helenus was one of several male parts played by an actress. Since 1954, the only major production to include Helen and Hecuba walking together is Miller's BBC video, discussed below. Miller also added Helen to the Trojan council scene (2.2).

7. The more common practice of adding women to Helen's scene will be discussed in chapter 5. Charles Fry's 1907 staged reading included women attending Helen and Hecuba as part of a final tableau depicting the mourning of Hector, but no mention is made in the program or reviews of Hecuba in earlier scenes.

8. Stephen Rathbun, "The Summer Season," *New York Sun*, 13 June 1932.

9. Stephen Rathbun, "Poor Shakespeare," *New York Sun*, 20 June 1932.

10. Bevington also makes the connection between the two pairs of spectators in a long note on the location of the scene, 356.

11. Kemble's rewriting of the direction is followed by the Henry Irving Shakespeare (without mentioning Kemble). Kemble's direction would seem to imply a raised place, but the main stage itself may be meant to suggest "the walls."

12. The "plot" is in the British Library (MS. Add 10449), and transcribed by Greg in *Dramatic Documents from the Elizabethan Playhouses* (Oxford: Clarendon, 1932). The assignment of the play to the Admiral's Company and Dekker and Chettle is discussed in G. Bullough, "The Lost *Troilus and Cressida*," *Essays and Studies* 17 (1964): 24–40. See also David Bradley, *From Text to Performance in the Elizabethan Theatre: Preparing the Play for the Stage* (Cambridge: Cambridge University Press, 1992).

13. Thomas Heywood, *The Iron Age*, edited by Arlene W. Weiner (London: Garland, 1979).

14. For a relevant discussion of the use of "above" spaces, see Leslie Thomson, "'Enter Above': The Staging of *Women Beware Women*," *Studies in English Literature* 26 (1986): 331–44.

15. Richard Hosley, "Shakespeare's Use of a Gallery Over the Stage," *Shakespeare Survey* 10 (1957): 78.

16. Translated and quoted in New Variorum, 30.

17. New Variorum, 30–31.

18. Muir, 63.

19. Bevington, 357.

20. Wells et al., *A Textual Companion,* 427.

21. Hosley lists and discusses many instances of descents within scenes in "Shakespeare's Use of a Gallery Over the Stage."

22. Leslie Thomson, "Broken Brackets and 'Mended Texts," *Renaissance Drama* 19 (1988): 190.

23. Hosley, "Use of a Gallery," 84. Hosley includes only generally accepted aloft scenes, and does not mention *Troilus and Cressida* in his analysis of Shakespeare's use of the gallery.

24. Peter Thomson, *Shakespeare's Theatre* (London: Routledge, 1983), 52.

25. Ibid., 51.

26. *A New Variorum Edition of Shakespeare: Antony and Cleopatra,* edited by Marvin Spevack (New York: Modern Language Association of America, 1990). Spevack's summary and conclusions of the proposed stagings for the scene appear on 777–93.

27. Bevington, 357.

28. The Inns of Court theory, and the possibility of the play being written or revised for a particular audience, is discussed in chapter 8.

29. Allardyce Nicoll, "Passing Over the Stage," *Shakespeare Survey* 12 (1959): 48. For a more recent and extensive list of examples and a brief description of "passing" directions, see Alan Dessen and Leslie Thomson, *A Dictionary of Stage Directions in English Drama, 1580–1642* (Cambridge: Cambridge University Press, 1999), 158–59.

30. Nicoll, "Passing Over," 53.

31. Bevington, 149.

32. Michael Hattaway, *Elizabethan Popular Theatre* (London: Routledge, 1982), 117–18. Hattaway is specifically discussing the stage directions in *The Spanish Tragedy,* where an army is given an entrance and after only one line of dialogue another direction reads: "They enter and pass by" (1.2.109–10).

33. The many references to the soldiers as "yonder" might indicate they are still in the yard, and Troilus could be exiting through the audience as Pandarus says "Look . . . how he goes." This staging would also provide action to fill up the time of the descriptions, and allow Cressida to see the warriors at a distance without recognizing them when she asks their names.

34. Hodgdon, "He Do Cressida," 265–6.

35. Ibid., 269.

36. Norman Rodway (Pandarus in Mendes' production) confirmed in a personal interview that the decision to change the word was conscious. Interview by author, Stratford-upon-Avon, 25 January 1991. While some changes to the Peter Alexander text are noted in Miller's published BBC script, the change from "here" to "there" is not, making it difficult to determine if the change was consciously or unconsciously made by director and/or actor.

37. Dryden also changed the line to allow Cressida and Pandarus not to move for the passing of the soldiers, changing the line to "shall we stay and see 'em as they come by" (1.2.168).

38. Davies' text reads:

PANDARUS: Hark, they are coming from the field. Shall we ~~stand up here and~~ see them as they pass toward Ilium? Good niece, do; sweet niece, Cressida.

CRESSIDA: At your pleasure.

PANDARUS: ~~Here, Here, Here's an excellent place; here we may see most bravely.~~ I'll tell you them all by their names as they pass by; but mark Troilus above the rest.

39. Willis, *The BBC Shakespeare Plays,* 247.

40. The end of Miller's production showed Pandarus, in his struggle to speak with Troilus, having to fight his way through the warriors who carried Hector's body home. This moment will be discussed in the final chapter. Another production which made an explicit connection between the soldiers' procession in the second scene and their marching home at the end of the play was David Williams's 1987 Stratford, Ontario production that played the same music (Handel's march from *Judas Maccabaeus*) for both. See Alexander Leggatt's review in *Shakespeare Bulletin* (September/October 1987): 10–11.

41. Hodgdon ("He Do Cressida," 269) describes Hands's staging of Troilus exiting "backward, gazing at Cressida" also in terms of Ophelia's description of Hamlet.

42. Hosley, "Use of a Gallery," 78.

43. Miller, for example, had trumpet blasts for each entrance over a continual drum beat, and Mendes had a drum beat throughout. The use of offstage noises is discussed below.

44. Alexander is present to begin the scene, and is not given an exit, but most editions and productions, although certainly not all, have him leave soon after Pandarus arrives.

45. Hands also had Paris fix his hair, but with a mirror a servant handed him. Hodgdon, "He Do Cressida," 269.

46. Terry Hands, speaking at the RSC Summer School, 12 August 1990.

47. Norman Rodway (Pandarus), interview.

48. Even more of the audience lost sight of Pandarus and Cressida when the production transferred to The Pit, where they stood on a platform directly behind approximately one quarter of the audience.

49. *A Theatre of Envy* (Oxford: Oxford University Press, 1991), 124.

50. *Times*, (London) 4 April 1956 "The Old Vic *Troilus and Cressida*."

51. "The 1960 Season at Stratford-upon-Avon," *Shakespeare Quarterly* 11 (1960): 451.

52. Ralph Berry, *Shakespeare and the Awareness of the Audience* (London: Macmillan, 1985), 116; Joel B. Altman, "The Practice of Shakespeare's Text," *Style* 23 (1989): 480.

53. The stage direction, "Enter common soldiers" only appears in F.

54. E. A. J. Honigmann, "Re-enter the Stage Direction," *Shakespeare Survey* 29 (1976): 118.

55. Dryden anticipated, and perhaps influenced, Capell by rearranging the stage direction to come before Cressida's questions about Helenus, Troilus and the common soldiers (*Truth Found Too Late*, 1.2.201, 210, 223).

56. Hodgdon "He Do Cressida," 263–64. Hodgdon cites the Pelican, Arden, and Oxford editions, but she does not mention that Capell (perhaps following Dryden) initiated the change. Although she does not indicate which Oxford edition she uses, she is citing Muir's and not Taylor's text. Hodgdon is surely mistaken in saying that "Although it is Pandarus who notices Aeneas . . . Cressida's language calls up the rest of the spectacle." Her point is an insightful and valid one, but only applicable to Antenor, Helenus, Troilus, and the common soldiers. Hector and Paris, like Aeneas, are introduced by Pandarus without any indication that Cressida has seen them first.

57. There is the seemingly pointless possibility that Pandarus thinks Cressida is asking about Deiphobus, who may be offstage and never enter, or may be onstage though not given a stage direction.

58. The scenes are in some ways a mirror of each other, with Troilus being presented by Pandarus as a war hero, and Cressida being presented as a whore by Ulysses (to Troilus) and Thersites (to the audience).

59. Paris later wonders why Troilus is absent from battle (3.1.135), presumably an-

other instance when he did not fight for personal reasons. Perhaps again he is lovesick, for Helen notices that "he hangs the lip at something" (3.1.136).

60. Pandarus's earlier "Hark" (1.2.173) is preceded in QF by a direction "Sound a retreat" (after 1.2.170).

61. Compare Criseyde's private, swooning reaction to Troilus' passing, "'Who yaf me drynke'" (2.651) to Cressida's sober "What sneaking fellow comes yonder" (1.2.223).

62. Rodway interview.

3. "ENTER CASSANDRA"

1. See "Attributions to Compositors of the First Folio" in *A Textual Companion*, 148–54.

2. Ophelia later enters "as before" in Q1 where F and Q2 have only "Enter Ophelia" (4.5.154).

3. See *A Textual Companion* for recent theories of copy texts, and Paul Werstine, "Compositor B of the Shakespeare First Folio," *AEB* 2 (1978): 241–63.

4. *Elizabethan Stage Conventions and Modern Interpreters* (Cambridge: Cambridge University Press, 1984), 36. Dessen indicates the range of possible interpretations of hair down by citing examples from the manuscripts of *Dick of Devonshire* and *The Swisser, A Warning for Fair Women*, and Massinger's *The Unnatural Combat*, where a signal for hair down indicates the effects of violence or rape. Dessen goes on to give examples of how "hair about the ears can indicate public shame (*2 Edward IV, The Insatiate Countess, The Bloody Banquet, The Emperor of the East*) or high passion (*Northward Ho*) or mourning (*Swetnam the Woman-Hater Arraigned by Women*) or madness (*I The Iron Age, Tom a Lincoln*)," 36–37.

5. Dessen, *Elizaebethan Stage Conventions*, 34.

6. Determining the priority of Shakespeare's or Heywood's play is problematic, and arguments have been proposed for influence in both directions (see the introduction to Weiner's edition, especially xxiii–xxvii). There is, however, no surviving edition of *The Iron Age* before 1632, making any knowledge Shakespeare would have had of Heywood's play most likely from watching a performance of *The Iron Age*, though the circulation of a private manuscript or a lost earlier edition of Heywood's play must remain a possibility. If Shakespeare's play preceded Heywood's, the influence could have been both in performance and print.

7. Palmer's gloss on "a more temperate fire," 112.

8. For an excellent discussion of the way the play evokes legend, see Elizabeth Freund, "'Ariachne's broken woof': the rhetoric of citation in *Troilus and Cressida*," in *Shakespeare and the Question of Theory*, edited by Patricia Parker and Geoffrey Hartman (New York: Methuen, 1985), 19–37.

9. The RSC programs for 1968 (Barton), 1976 (Barton/Kyle), and 1990 (Mendes) printed essentially the same "Who's Who."

10. The quotation is the gloss of "fool of fantasie" in *The Riverside Chaucer*, ed. Larry D. Benson (Oxford: Clarendon, 1988), 581.

11. Raole Lefevre, *The Recuyell of the Historyes of Troye*, translated by William Caxton (London, c. 1474), 2.2.97–112, in Bullough, 191–92, hereafter referred to as "Caxton."

12. Editors who print the conflation include Ridley, Walker, Seltzer, Muir, Taylor, and Foakes. Of the recent scholarly editions, only Palmer (following Q) and Bevington (following F) keep the directions separate.

13. Willis, *BBC Shakespeare Plays*, 238–39, 241–42.

14. J. C. Trewin, *Birmingham Post*, 20 February 1963.

15. *Stratford-upon-Avon Herald*, 22 February 1963.

16. Harbage, Seltzer, and Bevington are exceptions in following the QF placement. Harrison's use of Harbage's edition, Hands's use of Seltzer's edition, and Nunn's and Hall's use of Bevington's edition for their promptbooks are the only instances I found where an edition used as a promptbook did not follow Theobald's emendation.

17. Alan C. Dessen, *Recovering Shakespeare's Theatrical Vocabulary* (Cambridge: Cambridge University Press, 1995), 73.

18. The notes in Quayle's promptbook read: "Cassandra enters u/r through doorway" after her first speech, and "Cassandra enters R to bottom of stairs" after "Cry Trojans cry" in her third speech.

19. The promptbook notes "P. Wood, Troilus scare her," and the program lists P. Wood as Margarelon. The promptbook does not indicate any change from "What shriek," but "What start" is on the NSA audio tape of 1977.

20. Willis, *BBC Shakespeare Plays*, 239

21. Ibid., 247.

22. Poel cut Pandarus's last speech in 3.2, replacing it with Cressida's "Well, uncle, what folly I commit I dedicate to you" (3.2.99).

4. "GOOD THERSITES COME IN AND RAIL"

1. New Variorum, 112. Italics are Hillebrand's.

2. Walker, 173.

3. Palmer, 171.

4. Muir, 99.

5. Foakes, 186.

6. My proposal for an added direction was influenced by Stanley Wells's arguments for an increase in directions to help readers visualize actions implied by dialogue. See *Re-editing Shakespeare for the Modern Reader*, 75–77, and the general introduction to *William Shakespeare: The Complete Works*, xxxvii.

7. Thersites' second speech is 90 words in Q (89 in F) and 66 in Dryden (*Truth Found Too Late*, 3.1.10–16). Dryden cut the sentence "Let thy blood . . . lazars," but otherwise followed Shakespeare fairly closely, altering only the odd words, most notably "a gilt counterfeit" becomes "an Asse with gilt trappings."

8. Program to 1968 RSC *Troilus and Cressida*.

9. National Sound Archives (NSA) audiotape of 27 July 1981 at the Aldwych Theatre.

10. The promptbook actually has Thersites' second speech and the three speeches after it cut, but a video from the RST (20 November 1985) includes the lines and the business described above. The NSA audiotape of a performance at the Barbican Theatre follows the promptbook's cuts, suggesting that the cuts were made when the production transferred from Stratford to London.

11. Taylor, "Bibliography, Performance, Interpretation," 112.

12. Wells et al., *A Textual Companion*, 430.

13. Sam Mendes, interview with author, London, 31 May 1991.

14. Simon Russell Beale, "Thersites in *Troilus and Cressida*" in *Players of Shakespeare 3*, ed. by Russell Jackson and Robert Smallwood (Cambridge: Cambridge University Press, 1993), 163.

15. Mendes, in an interview with the author, said that he did not consult Taylor's edited text in *The Complete Works*. When I told Mendes of Taylor's proposed arrangement, he said, "I completely concur with Gary Taylor that Patroclus comes out because he says 'come in and rail,' and he then goes back in again."

16. The production changed "lazars" to "lepers."

17. See especially the discussion of the Trojans marching home (1.2) in chapter 2, the variants surrounding Ulysses' description of Cressida's "wanton spirits" (4.6.57) in chapter 6, and Ulysses' description of Troilus (4.6.98–115) in chapter 7.

18. Beale, "Thersites," 167.

5. "Who Play They To?"

1. R. A. Foakes, "*Troilus and Cressida* Reconsidered," *University of Toronto Quarterly* 32 (1963): 146.

2. Jan Kott, *Shakespeare Our Contemporary*, translated by Boleslaw Taborski (London: Methuen, 1965), 61–62.

3. Q has far fewer stage directions than F, and the lack of an entrance for the servant and the direction for music are two of the many unquestionable oversights.

4. Other editors following Capell include Dyce, Delius, and Deighton.

5. Bevington (221) notes nine possible meanings of Pandarus's repeated "fair," and concludes that the word "chiefly conveys (as does the repeated word *sweat* also) the enervation of this courtly scene."

6. Wells et al., *A Textual Companion*, 431.

7. The Oxford Shakespeare uses broken brackets, which are brackets without the lower horizontal line, to "indicate directions (and speech prefixes) whose substance and/or location are, in the editors' opinion, not confidently to be inferred from the dialogue, however likely they may appear" (Wells et al., *A Textual Companion*, 155). I silently replace broken brackets with regular brackets, and indicate the use of broken brackets where required.

8. Bevington, 225.

9. *Troilus and Cressida*, Harvester New Critical Introductions to Shakespeare (Boston: Twayne Publishers, 1987), 77.

10. Dessen, *Elizabethan Stage Conventions and Modern Interpreters*, 86. There are many other relevant scenes, perhaps the most famous being when King Henry commands from his deathbed, "Into some other chamber," and the scene continues without a break from a different room (*2 Henry IV*, 4.3.133).

11. After "you shall piece it out with a piece of your performance" (3.1.51–52), the promptbook has the note: "All: Yes—sing to us Pandarus."

12. QF read "disposer," as does Ridley, which was the prompt-book edition. Taylor has "dispenser."

13. *Theater Arts Monthly* (1932): 739.

14. *The Sketch*, 21 September 1938, 592.

15. Christy, "Five Twentieth-Century Productions," 124.

16. Christy notes that in the scene "cutting was limited to trimming Elizabethan phrases like 'i'faith' and 'prithee now'" ("Five Twentieth-Century Productions," 125). Therefore, the line "give me an instrument" was presumably not cut.

17. *Scotsman*, 5 April 1956.

18. *Kensington Post*, 13 April 1956.

19. *Times* (London), 4 April 1956.

20. *Evening News,* 4 April 1956.

21. *Truth,* 13 April 1956.

22. *Illustrated London News,* 14 April 1956.

23. *The Saturday Review,* 12 January 1957.

24. Christy, "Five Twentieth-Century Productions," 125.

25. "Mr Guthrie puts Shakespeare in Fancy Dress," *Evening Standard,* 4 April 1956.

26. *Music in Shakespearean Tragedy* (London: Routledge, 1963), 132.

27. A note in New Variorum lists several of the proposed meanings of "broken music" (135–36). Walker, Palmer, Muir, and Bevington agree with the most common interpretation of broken music as "employing different families of instruments" (Walker, 232).

28. T. McAlindon, "Language, Style, and Meaning," *PMLA* 84 (1969): 29–41, reprinted in *Troilus and Cressida: A Casebook,* ed. Priscilla Martin (London: Macmillan, 1976), 214.

29. The soldiers are not present in production photographs, and may have been cut, but their mention in the promptbook at least shows that they were considered.

30. Pandarus's speech to the entering Paris and Helen is trimmed on the 1970 audiotape to "Fair be to you, my lord, and to you fair queen, fair thoughts be your fair pillow!" but the lines are unmarked in the promptbook. Both the promptbook and audiotape of the 1976 production have the line altered as on the 1970 tape.

31. RSC program for 1968 production of *Troilus and Cressida* directed by John Barton.

32. "Sex and Warfare at Stratford," *Times* (London), 9 August 1968.

33. Examples of the dichotomy between the private and public self runs throughout the play, perhaps most clearly seen when the war conflicts with the men's love interests. Troilus's first lines (1.1.1–3), Achilles' reaction to Hecuba's letter (5.1.34–39), and Hector's argument with Andromache (5.3) are three instances.

34. All quotes are taken from essays in *Troilus and Cressida: A Casebook,* ed. by Priscilla Martin. Kenneth Muir, "The Fusing of Themes," 90; A. P. Rossiter, "*Troilus* as 'Inquisition'," 113; Arnold Stein, "The Disjunctive Imagination," 189; T. McAlindon, "Language, Style, and Meaning," 214.

35. John Nettles interviewed by Stephen Greenwald, 15 February 1980, quoted in Greenwald, *Directions by Indirections: John Barton of the Royal Shakespeare Company* (Newark: University of Delaware Press, 1985), 72.

36. Richard David, *Shakespeare in the Theatre* (Cambridge: Cambridge University Press, 1978), 119–20.

37. Stanley Wells, "Speaking for Themselves," *Times Literary Supplement,* 20 November 1981, 1366.

38. John Barber, *Daily Telegraph,* reprinted in *London Theatre Record,* 2–15 July 1981, 339.

39. Michael Coveney, *Financial Times,* reprinted in *London Theatre Record,* 2–15 July 1981, 340.

40. Milton Shulman, *New Standard,* reprinted in *London Theatre Record,* 2–15 July 1981, 342.

41. Roger Warren, "Interpretations of Shakespearian Comedy, 1981," *Shakespeare Survey* 35 (1982): 203.

42. Michael Billington, *Guardian,* reprinted in *London Theatre Record,* 2–15 July 1981.

43. Stanley Wells, "Speaking for Themselves."

44. Vivian Thomas, *The Moral Universe of Shakespeare's Problem Plays* (London: Routledge, 1987), 135–36.

45. Ralph Berry, *Shakespeare and the Awareness of the Audience,* 119.

46. Different seats in the theater had different views, partial views, or no view at all, of the musicians.

47. R. V. Holdsworth, *Times Literary Supplement,* 4–10 May 1990, 474.

48. Elizabeth Beroud, "Scrutiny of a Mask," *Cahiers Elisabethains* 39 (1991): 65.

49. Interviews with Sam Mendes and Norman Rodway.

50. Michael Billington, *Guardian,* 19 June 1991.

6. "I'LL BRING YOU TO YOUR FATHER"

1. For a "survey of literary criticism concerning Cressida from the late 1940s to the mid 1980s" see Sharon M. Harris, "Feminism and Shakespeare's Cressida: *If* I be false. . . ," *Women's Studies* 18 (1990): 65–82. See also Claire M. Tylee, "The Text of Cressida and Every Ticklish Reader: *Troilus and Cressida* and the Greek Camp Scene," *Shakespeare Survey* 41 (1989): 63–76.

2. F actually reads "*Exennt,*" but throughout the chapter I refer to the direction as if spelt correctly.

3. Rowe has the direction "Diomedes leads out Cressida and returns" after Nestor's line "A woman of quick sense." Pope followed Rowe in his first edition, but in his second edition changed the direction to "Diomedes leads Cressida off" and placed it one line earlier.

4. Wells et al., *A Textual Companion,* 435.

5. Taylor, "Bibliography, Performance, Interpretation," 113–14.

6. Peter Alexander first proposed that F was printed from an annotated copy of Q ("*Troilus and Cressida,* 1609," *The Library* 9 [1928], 265–86), but the theory was given more substantial analysis and support by Philip Williams ("Shakespeare's *Troilus and Cressida:* The Relationship of Quarto and Folio," *Studies in Bibliography* 3 [1950]: 130–43). Editors since Baldwin have supported Williams' findings.

7. *Shakespeare Restored* (1726), 136. Quoted in New Variorum, 226.

8. Paul Gaudet, "Playing Father: Q and F versions of *Troilus and Cressida,* 4.5," unpublished paper contributed to the *Troilus and Cressida* seminar at the annual meeting of the Shakespeare Association of America Convention, Albuquerque, New Mexico, 2–3 March 1994.

9. Gaudet, "Playing Father," 4.

10. For reaction to Juliet Stevenson's Cressida, see Claire M. Tylee, "The Text of Cressida and Every Ticklish Reader: *Troilus and Cressida* and the Greek Camp Scene."

11. The Royal Shakespeare Theatre program (1985) has seven pages of the actors, director, and fight choreographer reporting on their research into the Crimean War. The Barbican Theatre program (1986) replaced the company's research with a time line, 1852–1878, and four pages of quotations from the nineteenth century on the topics of "Wars and Heroes" and "Whores and Angels."

12. "Joyfully" is Windeatt's interpretation of Boccaccio's *Il Filostrato,* Parte Quinta, 14/1: "Il padre la raccolse con gran festa." Windeatt, ed., *Troilus and Criseyde,* 456.

13. Windeatt, *Oxford Guides to Chaucer: Troilus and Criseyde* (Oxford: Clarendon, 1992), 86.

14. Ann Thompson, *Shakespeare's Chaucer* (Liverpool: Liverpool University Press, 1978), 139.

15. Bullough, *Narrative and Dramatic Sources,* 202.

16. Bullough, *Narrative and Dramatic Sources,* 203.

17. *The Recuyell of the Historyes of Troye Written in French by Raoul Levevre Translated*

and Printed by William Caxton, edited by H. Oskar Sommer, (London, 1894), 2:604–5. The passage is omitted by Bullough.

18. Bullough, *Narrative and Dramatic Sources,* 203.

19. Ibid.

20. For a comparison of the different versions of Calchas's request, see Robert K. Presson, *Shakespeare's "Troilus and Cressida" & the Legends of Troy* (Madison: University of Wisconsin Press, 1953), 121–22.

21. Taylor offers a middle ground, with Calchas appearing "at the door" (Wells et al., *A Textual Companion,* 435).

22. See *The Works of John Dryden,* 13:516, 560–61; Lewis Moore, "For King and Country: John Dryden's *Troilus and Cressida,*" *CLA Journal* 26 (1982): 98–111; and G. McFadden, *Dryden: The Public Writer, 1660–1685* (Princeton: Princeton University Press 1978), 211–16.

7. "THEY CALL HIM TROILUS"

1. See the "Sources" chapter in *Oxford Guides to Chaucer: Troilus and Criseyde,* by Barry Windeatt. Chaucer refers to Lollius at 1.394, 5.1653, and to a Latin source at 2.14.

2. For a study of the significance of naming in *Troilus and Cressida,* see Elizabeth Freund, "'Ariachne's broken woof': The Rhetoric of Citation in *Troilus and Cressida.*"

3. Benoit's *Le Roman de Troie* offers the first extant portrayal of Troilus as a lover as well as a warrior. In his section describing the main figures in the war, Benoit writes that Troilus

> was much loved, and he himself loved dearly and endured great suffering for that reason. He was the handsomest young knight among the youth of Troy and the most valiant, except for his brother Hector who was the true commander and leader when it came to the conduct of battle, as Dares assures us. (N. R. Havely, ed. and trans., *Chaucer's Boccaccio* [Woodbridge, England: D. S. Brewer, 1980], 168.)

Guido cuts much of the Benoit's version of Dares's description of Troilus, but does write that Troilus is "equal or next to Hector" (Havely, 184). Chaucer has several relevant passages where Troilus is described as "The wise, worthi Ector the secounde" (2.158), "save Ector, most y-dred of any wight" (3.1775), and "withouten any peer, / Save Ector" (5.1803). Windeatt points to sources and departures from sources for all these passages (*Troilus and Criseyde,* edited by Windeatt).

More direct sources for Ulysses' speech have been found in Lydgate and Caxton. Lydgate refers to the descriptions by Dares, Guido, and Chaucer of the main characters in the war, and in his description of Troilus, Lydgate stresses the reported nature of the legend:

> The seconde Ector for his worthynesse
> He called was . . .
> None so named of Famous hardynesse,
> As bokes olde of hym bere wytnesse.
> Except Ector there ne was such another.
> (Lydgate, 2.4871–72, 4893–95; Bullough,
> *Narrative and Dramatic Sources,* 160)

Caxton also offers a version of what "Dares sayeth" about Troilus and other main characters in the war: "he resamblid moche to hector / And was the second after hym of prowesse" (Bullough, *Narrative and Dramatic Sources,* 194).

4. Muir, ed., *Troilus and Cressida*, 155.

5. See Sharon M. Harris, "Feminism and Shakespeare's Cressida: *If* I be false . . . ,"
and Claire M. Tylee, "The Text of Cressida and Every Ticklish Reader: *Troilus and
Cressida* and the Greek Camp Scene." For QF "Why beg then" (4.6.49), Johnson
(1765) writes, "for the sake of rhime, we shold read, 'Why beg two.'" Palmer follows
this, and Walker, Taylor, and Bevington follow Ritson's (1783) conjecture, with various punctuation, "Why beg, too." See New Variorum, 230.

6. Ann Thompson, *Shakespeare's Chaucer*, 139–40. E. Talbot Donaldson notes that
Ulysses' likening Diomedes' spirit to his gait completely misinterprets the "flatly re-
alistic womanizer." *The Swan at the Well* (New Haven: Yale University Press, 1985), 111.

7. *Troilus and Criseyde*, edited by Windeatt, 457.

8. *Lydgate's Troy Book*, edited by Henry Bergen (London, 1906), Book 3, line
4344. These lines are omitted by Bullough.

9. Lydgate, 3. 4362.

10. For Cressida's reunion with Calchas, see Chaucer, 5.190, Lydgate 3.4427 (Bullough, 172), and Caxton (Bullough, 203).

11. Robert Presson, Alice Walker, and Ann Thompson cite Caxton as the primary
source for the scene.

12. Presson, *Shakespeare's "Troilus and Cressida,"* 130.

13. A. P. Rossiter, *Angels With Horns* (London: Longman, 1961), 133.

14. Wells et al., *A Textual Companion*, 435.

15. Quoted in New Variorum, 244.

16. See Dessen, *Elizabethan Stage Conventions and Modern Interpreters*.

17. Kenneth Muir describes the location of the duel scene as "Near the Greek
camp," and notes that "all editors have placed this scene in the Greek camp" (150).
Muir refutes this editorial tradition by citing Aeneas's line, (1.3.275) quoted above.

18. Palmer, 254.

19. Robert Presson gives a summary account of Shakespeare's, Caxton's, Chap-
man's Homer, and Heywood's versions of "The Combat," *Shakespeare's "Troilus and
Cressida,"* 43–50. Relevant passages from Lydgate are given in Bullough, *Narrative and
Dramatic Sources*, 160–162, but Bullough omits Lydgate 3.2122–51, which parallels
Caxton's moralizing about Hector's mercy.

20. Bullough, 198.

21. Ibid.

22. Ibid., 198–99.

23. Lydgate's and Caxton's conclusions about the mercy shown by Hector when
he heeded Ajax's request to withdraw is cited by Palmer (283–84) as a source for the
debate between Troilus and Hector about mercy and fair play (5.3).

24. R. A. Foakes, *Illustrations of the English Stage 1580–1642* (Stanford: Stanford
University Press, 1985), 134–35.

25. Palmer, 254.

26. Wells et al., *A Textual Companion*, 435.

27. Andrew Gurr, ed., *King Richard II*, New Cambridge Shakespeare (Cambridge:
Cambridge University Press, 1984), 37.

28. Hodges's drawing appears in Andrew Gurr, ed., *King Richard II*, 38.

29. Gurr has reconsidered his decisions made in collaboration with Hodges, and
now believes that Richard's "chair of state" would be centrally placed, and not at the
back of the stage. His discussion is relevant to the present consideration of how different stagings would alter the reception of a scene. "The 'State' of Shakespeare's
Audiences," in *Shakespeare and the Sense of Performance*, edited by Marvin and Ruth
Thompson (Newark: University of Delaware Press, 1989), 162–79.

30. See Presson, *Shakespeare's "Troilus and Cressida,"* 43–50.

31. Lydgate, 3.2054 (Bullough, 161).

32. Barry Nass, "'Yet in the trial much opinion dwells': The Combat Between Hector and Ajax in *Troilus and Cressida*," *English Studies* 65 (1984): 1; Reuben A. Brower, *Hero and Saint* (Oxford: Clarendon, 1971), 267.

33. Daniel Seltzer, introduction to Signet Classic (1963), xxix, also printed in *The Complete Signet Classic Shakespeare,* edited by Sylvan Barnet et al. (New York: Harcourt Brace Jovanovich, 1972), 1001. Nass only quotes part of the above.

34. Susan Snyder, "Ourselves Alone: The Challenge to Single Combat in Shakespeare," *Studies in English Literature* 20 (1960): 209.

35. Line numbering is as Taylor, but reading is QF. Taylor has "as asking" for QF "asking."

36. Berry offers the following note: "In John Barton's production (RSC, 1976), Ajax's reiterated commands persistently defeated the trumpeter's timing, so that he raised and lowered his trumpet several times before the opening blast."

37. Berry, *Shakespeare and the Awareness of the Audience,* 123.

38. See New Variorum, 225 for their arguments. Editors since Malone have followed Ritson's conjecture that F's "Dio" is a mistake for Deiphobus in the speech prefix to the F only line "Let us make ready straight" (4.5.144), which precedes Aeneas' scene ending speech.

39. Charles Edelman, *Brawl Ridiculous: Swordfighting in Shakespeare's Plays* (Manchester: Manchester University Press, 1992), 129.

40. Ibid., 121.

41. Ibid., 128; Palmer, 248.

42. Edelman, 128.

43. Ibid., 131.

44. Wells et al., *A Textual Companion,* 435, note to 4.6.94.

45. Taylor, "Bibliography, Performance, Interpretation," 114.

46. Ibid., 115.

47. Ibid., 114.

48. Wells et al., *A Textual Companion,* 435–36.

49. Ibid., p. 436, note to 4.7.41.

50. E. K. Chambers, *William Shakespeare , A Study of Problems and Facts* (Oxford: Clarendon, 1930), 1:440.

51. W. W. Greg, *The Shakespeare First Folio* (Oxford: Clarendon, 1955), 346–47.

52. J. M. Nosworthy, *Shakespeare's Occasional Plays: Their Origin and Transmission* (London: Edward Arnold, 1965), 83.

53. Honigmann, "Shakespeare Suppressed," 121.

54. Ibid.

55. Taylor, "Bibliography, Performance, Interpretation," 101–2.

56. Honigmann, "Shakespeare Suppressed," 229.

57. I quote F here, and follow F's spelling to highlight the fact. Taylor ends the first line after "Priam," creating a full first line, and leaving the second line, "They call him Troilus," as the short line. Other quotations, unless stated, follow the Oxford *Complete Works.*

58. Palmer, 108.

59. Lydgate, 2. 4871, Bullough, 160.

60. Bevington, 416.

61. Taylor, *A Textual Companion,* 435; Foakes, ed., 209.

62. Palmer, 250.

63. Ibid; 250; Taylor, "Bibliography, Performance, Interpretation," 114.

64. *Hamlet* Q2, which has neither of these directions, has "Trumpets / the while" next to the last two lines of Claudius's speech. Taylor interprets the Q2 direction as "Trumpets the while he drinks," having the trumpets more of an accompaniment to the drinking rather than throughout the speech. Is Q2 offering a more specific preparation for the duel, or as Taylor suggests, simply punctuating Claudius' speech?

65. Seltzer, xxix.

66. Bullough, *Narrative and Dramatic Sources,* 201.

67. Muir, 155.

68. The *Richard III* quartos assign the speech to Brakenbury ("Brok."), but F assigns it to the Keeper ("Keep").

69. Dryden's Ajax is not without his fair share of buffoonery, and Dryden does include Thersites' pageant of Ajax (*Truth Found Too Late,* 3.1.70), but in the lines discussed where Ajax requests a trumpet, the opportunity for comic overstatement is excised.

70. The photograph was torn as an unwanted proof copy.

71. Christy, "Five Twentieth-Century Productions," 186–87.

72. Agamemnon's remark about "the combatants being kin . . . begin" (4.6.94) was also cut, further eliminating any pause between Agamemnon's instructions to Diomedes and the commencement of the fight.

73. *Troilus and Cressida,* ed. by Papp and Beckerman, 205.

74. The quotation follows Alice Walker's punctuation, used for the promptbook.

75. Barton interview.

76. Program for 1985 *Troilus and Cressida* at the Royal Shakespeare Theatre.

8. "HENCE BROKER, LACKEY"

1. Barbara E. Bowen, *Gender in the Theater of War* (New York: Garland, 1993), 80.

2. Steevens (1773), quoted in New Variorum, 292–93.

3. The only critics or editors I have found to defend F's repetition is Knight (in his Pictorial edition, 1839–42), who asked, "is not the loathing which Troilus feels towards Pandarus more strongly marked by this repetition?" quoted in New Variorum, 294, and W. L. Godshalk, "The Texts of *Troilus and Cressida,*" *Early Modern Literary Studies* 1, no. 2 (1995): 1–54.

4. Malone (1790), quoted in New Variorum, 293.

5. Steevens (1793), quoted in New Variorum, 313–14.

6. W. S. Walker, *A Critical Examination of the Text of Shakespeare* (London, 1860), 3:203.

7. Ibid., 204.

8. Ibid.

9. See New Variorum "Authorship" appendix, 369–74.

10. *The Henry Irving Shakespeare,* edited by Henry Irving and F. A. Marshall (London, 1888), 4:340.

11. Alfred Thiselton, *Notulae Criticae* (London, 1907), 33.

12. Ibid.

13. Peter Alexander, "*Troilus and Cressida,* 1609," *Library* 9 (1928–29): 274.

14. Ibid., 278.

15. E. K. Chambers, *William Shakespeare* (Oxford: Clarendon, 1930), 1:446.

16. Ibid., 1:446–47. Chambers is paraphrasing R. A. Small, *The Stage Quarrel between Ben Jonson and the So-Called Poetasters* (Breslau, 1899), 148–49.

17. Chambers, *William Shakespeare,* 1:447.

18. Chambers, *William Shakespeare,* 1:440. Nearly all editions number the last scene 5.10 but, as elsewhere in this book, I refer to scene and line numbering in the Oxford *Complete Works.* I refer to F's repeated passage and Pandarus's final appearance as occurring at the end of 5.11, the scene number unique to the Oxford *Complete Works,* though, as detailed below, in the Oxford text the lines are not included in that scene but appear as Additional Passage B.

19. F. G. Fleay, "On the Composition of *Troylus and Cressida,*" *The New Shakspere Society's Transactions* (1874): 312. See also New Variorum "Authorship" appendix, esp. 371.

20. Chambers, *William Shakespeare,* 1:447.

21. Samuel Tannenbaum, "A Critique of the Text of *Troilus and Cressida:* Part 1, The Quarto Text," *Shakespeare Association Bulletin* 9 (1934): 144.

22. Ibid., 139.

23. Ibid. 132.

24. W. W. Greg, *The Shakespeare First Folio* (Oxford: Clarendon, 1953), 346.

25. Alice Walker, *Textual Problems of the First Folio* (Cambridge: Cambridge University Press, 1953), 74.

26. Nevill Coghill, *Shakespeare's Professional Skills* (Cambridge: Cambridge University Press, 1964); J. M. Nosworthy, *Shakespeare's Occasional Plays;* E. A. J. Honigmann, *The Stability of Shakespeare's Text* (London: Edward Arnold, 1965).

27. Nosworthy, *Shakespeare Occasional Plays,* 81.

28. Ibid.

29. Coghill, *Shakespeare's Professional Skills,* 78.

30. *Times Literary Supplement,* 1965, 220, 240; 1967, 52, 136, 167, 202, 226, 274, 296, 340, 384. J. K. Walton, "The Year's Contribution to Shakespearian Study: Textual Studies," *Shakespeare Survey* 19 (1966): 162.

31. *Times Literary Supplement,* 19 January 1967, 52.

32. *Times Literary Supplement,* 16 February 1967, 136.

33. Ibid.

34. *Times Literary Supplement,* 6 April 1967, 296.

35. *Times Literary Supplement,* 4 May 1967, 384.

36. Ibid.

37. Taylor, "*Troilus and Cressida:* Bibliography, Performance, and Interpretation."

38. Ibid., 99–100.

39. Ibid., 103.

40. Ibid.

41. Ibid., 131.

42. In a footnote, Taylor offers the additional argument that "the last page of the promptbook would have contained the approval of the Master of the Revels; the page would therefore certainly have been retained, even if all the dialogue on it were intended for omission."

43. Taylor, "Bibliography, Performance, and Interpretation," 104.

44. Iibd., 128.

45. *The Norton Shakespeare,* ed. Stephen Greenblatt (New York: W. W. Norton, 1997), 75. The quotation is Greenblatt's explanation of *Hamlet* passages, but the comments seem applicable to the indented and italicized *Troilus and Cressida* passages.

46. Stanley Wells and Gary Taylor, "The Oxford Shakespeare Re-viewed by the General Editors" *AEB,* n.s., 4 (1990): 6–20.

47. Ibid., 14–15.

48. Honigmann, *The Stability of Shakespeare's Text,* 6.

49. See *The Division of the Kingdoms*, edited by Gary Taylor and Michael Warren.

50. E. A. J. Honigmann, *Myriad-minded Shakespeare* (New York: St. Martins Press, 1989), 121.

51. New Variorum, 316. W. Hertzberg, ed., *Shakespeare's Dramatische Werke* (Berlin, 1877).

52. Muir, 7–8.

53. R. A. Foakes, "The Ending of *Troilus and Cressida*," in *KM 80: A Birthday Album for Kenneth Muir* (Liverpool: Liverpool University Press, 1987), 51.

54. Wells et al., *A Textual Companion*, 438.

55. Palmer, 21. He also conjectures that "two months hence" fits the time between Epiphany (6 January) and Ash Wednesday in 1602, and Pandarus could have appeared at the Inns as a Lord of Misrule.

56. New Variorum, 317.

57. Jarold W. Ramsey, "The Provenance of *Troilus and Cressida*," *Shakespeare Quarterly* 21 (1970): 232.

58. Foakes, 28.

59. Ibid., 9.

60. The two lines are quoted from Foakes's edition. Foakes and F have "and Pandar," Q has just "Pandar," and Taylor has "pander."

61. Robert Kimbrough, "The Origins of *Troilus and Cressida:* Stage, Quarto, and Folio," *PMLA* 78 (June 1962): 197.

62. David Farley-Hills, *Shakespeare and the Rival Playwrights, 1600–1606* (London: Routledge, 1990), 48.

63. Ibid., 48–49.

64. René Girard, *A Theatre of Envy* (Oxford: Clarendon, 1991), 158–59.

65. Bowen, *"Troilus and Cressida* on the Stage," 270.

66. For Caxton's and Lydgate's version of Troilus's death, see Bullough, *Narrative and Dramatic Sources*, 182–86, 212–15.

67. Joel B. Altman, "The Practice of Shakespeare's Text," *Style: Texts and Pretexts in the English Renaissance* 23 (fall 1989): 484. Altman does not connect his argument about Shakespeare's change of genre to Dryden's play.

68. *The Works of John Dryden*, 13:517.

69. *Shakespeare: A Dramatic Life* (London: Sinclair-Stevenson, 1994), 224. The "present" can be interpreted as either a Shakespearean present (with the references to "Winchester goose"), or any present (with Pandarus directly addressing the audience).

70. *The Works of John Dryden*, 13:565.

71. See James Thorson, "The Dialogue Between the Stage and the Audience: Prologues and Epilogues in the Era of the Popish Plot," in *Compendious Conversations: The Method of Dialogue in the Early Enlightenment*, edited by Kevin L. Cope (Frankfurt: P. Lang, 1992), 331–45.

72. Kemble's copy of Qa is in the Huntington Library.

73. James Boaden, *Memoirs of the Life of John Philip Kemble* (London, 1825), 1:156.

74. Ibid., 2:3.

75. Newlin, "The Darkened Stage: J. P. Kemble and *Troilus and Cressida*," 192.

76. Kemble's promptbook in the Folger Shakespeare Library.

77. "Letter" is the title of the scene in the promptbook made in the 1893 edition. The scene is untitled in the promptbook made in the 1899 edition. The cuts and curtains described above are the same in both promptbooks.

78. R. T. Rundle Milliken, *Stratford-upon-Avon Herald*, 16 May 1913. The remarks are from the review of the 1912 King's Hall, London performance, reprinted on the occasion of the production's revival at the Shakespeare Memorial Theatre.

79. Line reference is to the Oxford *Complete Works,* but the passage is quoted from Poel's promptbook (Cassell's).

80. *Saturday Review,* 14 December 1912.

81. H. M. W., *Pall Mall Gazette,* 11 December 1912.

82. George Bernard Shaw, preface to *Plays Unpleasant,* reprinted in *The Bodley Head Bernard Shaw,* edited by Dan H. Laurence (London: Bodley Head, 1970), 1:29.

83. Interview with Macowan by James Christy. Quoted in Christy, "Five Twentieth-Century Productions of *Troilus and Cressida,*" 128.

84. Christy's appendix is titled "Battle Sequence from Macowan's Production, V.iv through x," 339–44. I have inserted the words that were cut, in brackets.

85. Although not stated by Christy, Macowan presumably supplied Christy with a copy of his performance text, as Christy throughout the thesis selectively notes Macowan's cuts, and thanks Macowan for granting a personal interview. Unfortunately, Christy does not indicate if Pandarus was rejected at the end of 5.3, nor does Christy indicate the edition Macowan used. Although no date is given for the interview, it was presumably more than 30 years after the production.

86. J. G. B., *Evening News,* 22 August 1938.

87. Christy, "Five Twentieth-Century Productions," 129.

88. Ibid.

89. Ibid., 130.

90. Ridley, 119.

91. The braces are Ridley's indication of an F only passage. The braced words were unmarked in Payne's promptbook, and presumably uncut.

92. *Evening Dispatch,* 3 July 1948.

93. *Observer,* 4 July 1948.

94. The direction "tearing the letter" was first added by Rowe, and is substantially followed in nearly all editions. Rowe also added "strikes him" after "ignomy and shame." While the direction was included by editors until Johnson (1765), few have followed it since until Taylor, who explained, "this blow is presumably the 'goodly medicine for my aking bones' that Pandarus refers to" (Wells et al., *A Textual Companion,* 438).

95. Ridley's braces indicating F only.

96. Berry, *Changing Styles in Shakespeare,* 52. Cocteau's play was a great artistic and financial success in London during the two years before Quayle's production.

97. Shaw's promptbook has the first half of Pandarus's speech, through the song, pasted in at the end of 5.3. The line "Good traders in the flesh, set this in your painted cloths" is written in under the pasted passage.

98. "Mustard and Cressida," *Birmingham Mail,* 14 July 1954.

99. *Sunday Times,* 18 July 1954.

100. "Stratford 1954," *Shakespeare Quarterly* 5 (1954): 392.

101. J. C. Trewin, *John O'London's Weekly,* 30 July 1954.

102. Berry, *Changing Styles in Shakespeare,* 52.

103. *Kensington Post,* 13 April 1956.

104. *Truth,* 13 April 1956.

105. Guthrie cut 9 of 21 lines of Troilus's last speech. The cuts were "Let him . . . out of itself" (16–21), and "and, thou great-sized coward . . . frenzy's thoughts" (27–29).

106. Tyrone Guthrie, *New York Herald Tribune,* 23 December 1956.

107. Robert Speaight, "The 1960 Season at Stratford-upon-Avon," *Shakespeare Quarterly* 11 (1960): 451–52.

108. A. Alvarez, *New Statesman,* 30 July 1960. T. C. Worsley thought Adrian's Pan-

darus was "particularly dazzling," *Financial Times*, 27 July 1960. Gareth Lloyd Evans also praised the "consummate playing of Pandarus by Max Adrian," *Guardian*, 28 July 1960.

109. *Times* (London), 27 July 1960.

110. Trewin, *Illustrated London News*, 6 August 1960.

111. Trewin, "The Old Vic and Stratford-upon-Avon 1961–1962," *Shakespeare Quarterly* 12 (1962): 519. Trewin was reviewing the production's revival at the Edinburgh Festival. The cast remained largely intact, including Max Adrian, but Ian Holm replaced Denholm Elliott as Troilus.

112. Christy, "Five Twentieth-Century Productions," 253.

113. Greenwald, *Directions By Indirections*, 66.

114. Barton interview.

115. Irving Wardle, "Sex and Warfare at Stratford," *Times* (London), 9 August 1968; Rosemary Say, "So Thersites Was Right," *Sunday Telegraph*, 11 August 1968.

116. Rodway interview.

117. Greenwald, *Directions By Indirections*, 74–75. The critic quoted is Rosemary Say.

118. Royal Shakespeare Theatre program.

119. Sheila Bannock, "John Barton Brings the Trojan War Right into 20th Century," *Stratford-upon-Avon Herald*, 16 August 1968.

120. Barton interview.

121. Greenwald, *Directions by Indirections*, 75.

122. Ibid., 80.

123. David, *Shakespeare in the Theatre*, 120–21.

124. *Times* (London), 19 August 1976.

125. "The End Crowns All," *Times Educational Supplement*, 14 October 1977, 70.

126. Stage manager's (Louise Horswill) rehearsal notes, in the Shakespeare Centre Library.

127. *Financial Times*, reprinted in *London Theatre Record*, 2–15 July 1981, 340.

128. *Guardian*, 8 July 1981.

129. Henry Fenwick, "The Production," in *Troilus and Cressida*, The BBC TV Shakespeare (London: British Broadcasting Company, 1981), 26–27.

130. Willis, *BBC Shakespeare Plays*, 250.

131. Ibid.

132. *Guardian*, 8 May 1986. Billington was reviewing the production after its transfer to London.

133. Nicholas Shrimpton, "Shakespeare Performances in London and Stratford-upon-Avon, 1984–5," *Shakespeare Survey* 39 (1986): 205.

134. Peter Holland, "Shakespeare Performances in England 1989–1990," *Shakespeare Survey* 44 (1992): 172.

135. Elizabeth Beroud, "Scrutiny of a Mask," *Cahiers Elisabethains* 39 (April 1991): 66.

136. Rodway interview.

137. Mendes interview.

138. Interview by author, Stratford-upon-Avon, 4 January 1999.

139. *Times* (London), 15 November 1998.

140. *Daily Telegraph*, 9 November 1998.

141. I was given a copy of the production's typescript, which I checked both by my attendance at Swan Theatre performances in January 1999, and by comparison to the promptbook on deposit at the Shakespeare Centre Library. The final pages of the script, from the page that has Pandarus's final appearance to the end of the play,

is typed in a different font. The second "I reck . . . today" is preceded by a second, but crossed out, "Fate, here me what I say!" The final line of the production, the third "End my life today," is handwritten under the last line of type. The wording and punctuation of the passage follow the script.

142. The text is derived from my notes taken during previews, in March 1999, and during the last week of the production, July 1999.

143. Alistair Macualay, *Financial Times*, 17 March 1999; Robert Butler, *Independent on Sunday*, 21 March 1999; John Peter, *Sunday Times*, 21 March 1999; John Gross, *Sunday Telegraph*, 21 March 1999; Benedict Nightingale, *Times* (London), 17 March 1999.

Works Cited

All editions of *Troilus and Cressida* are listed in Appendix A, and the source for reviews and review articles are listed in Appendix B, and are therefore not given here. There are several excellent annotated bibliographies of *Troilus and Cressida,* including

"World Shakespeare Bibliography," annually in *Shakespeare Quarterly.*

Shakespeare Index: An Annotated Bibliography of Critical Articles of the Plays, 1959–1983, ed. by Bruce T. Sajdak. Millwood, N.Y.: Kraus, 1992.

Lewis Walker, ed., *Shakespeare and the Classical Tradition.* New York: Garland, 2001.

Adams, Howard, C. "'What Cressid Is.'" In *Sexuality and Politics in Renaissance Drama,* ed. Carole Levin and Karen Robertson, 75–93. Lewiston, N.Y.: Edwin Mellon, 1991.

Adamson, Jane. *Troilus and Cressida.* Harvester New Critical Introductions to Shakespeare. Boston: Twayne Publishers, 1987.

Adelman, Janet. *Suffocating Mothers.* New York: Routledge, 1992.

Alexander, Peter. "*Troilus and Cressida,* 1609." *The Library* 9 (1928): 265–86.

———. "Letters to the Editor." *Times Literary Supplement,* 1965, 220; 1967, 136, 340

Altman, Joel B. "The Practice of Shakespeare's Text." *Style: Texts and Pretexts in the English Renaissance* 23 (1989): 466–500.

Beale, Simon Russell. "Thersites in *Troilus and Cressida.*" In *Players of Shakespeare 3: Further Essays in Shakespearian Performance by Players with the Royal Shakespeare Company,* ed. Russell Jackson and Robert Smallwood, 160–73. Cambridge: Cambridge University Press, 1993.

Berger, Harry, Jr. "*Troilus and Cressida:* The Observer as Basilisk." *Comparative Drama* 2 (1968): 122–36.

Berry, Ralph. *Changing Styles in Shakespeare.* London: George Allen, 1981.

———. *Shakespeare and the Awareness of the Audience.* London: Macmillan, 1985.

Bjelland, Karen. "Cressida and the Renaissance 'Marketplace'—The Role of Binarism and Amphibology in Shakespeare's Articulation of the Troy Legend." In *Ideological Approaches to Shakespeare: The Practice of Theory,* ed. Robert P. Merrix and Nicholas Ranson, 165–85. Lewiston, N.Y.: Edwin Mellen, 1992.

———. "The Cultural Value of Analytical Bibliography and Textual Criticism: The Case of *Troilus and Cressida.*" *Text* 7 (1994): 272–95.

————. "Variants as Epistemological Shifts: A Proposed Methodology for Recovering the Two Texts of Shakespeare's *Troilus and Cressida.*" *Papers of the Bibliographical Society of America* (1994): 53–78.

Boaden, James, *Memoirs of the Life of John Philip Kemble.* London, 1825.

[Boccaccio]. *Chaucer's Boccaccio.* Ed. and trans. N. R. Havely. Woodbridge, England: D. S. Brewer, 1980.

Bowen, Barbara E. "*Troilus and Cressida* on the Stage." In *Troilus and Cressida,* Signet Classic Shakespeare, revised edition, ed. Daniel Seltzer, 265–87. New York: Penguin, 1988.

————. *Gender in the Theater of War: Shakespeare's "Troilus and Cressida."* Gender and Genre in Literature, vol 4. New York: Garland, 1993.

Bower, Reuben A. *Hero and Saint: Shakespeare and the Graeco-Roman Heroic Tradition.* Oxford: Clarendon, 1971.

Bradley, David. *From Text to Performance in the Elizabethan Theatre: Preparing the Play for the Stage.* Cambridge: Cambridge University Press, 1992

Bredbeck, Gregory, W. "Constructing Patroclus: The High and Low Discourses of Renaissance Sodomy." In *The Performance of Power: Theatrical Discourse and Politics,* ed. Sue Ellen Case and Janelle Reinelt, 77–91. Iowa City: University of Iowa Press, 1991.

Bullough, G. "The Lost *Troilus and Cressida.*" *Essays and Studies* 17 (1964): 24–40.

————. *Narrative and Dramatic Sources of Shakespeare.* Vol. 6, *Other "Classical" Plays.* London: Routledge, 1977.

Bulman, James C., ed. *Shakespeare, Theory, and Performance.* London: Routledge, 1996.

Caxton, William, *The Recuyell of the Historyes of Troye Written in French by Raoul Leveure Translated and Printed by William Caxton.* Ed. H. Oskar Sommer. London, 1894.

Chambers, E. K. *The Elizabethan Stage.* Oxford: Clarendon, 1923.

Charnes, Linda. *Materializing the Subject in Shakespeare.* Cambridge: Harvard University Press, 1993.

Chaucer, Geoffrey, *Troilus and Criseyde: A New Edition of "The Book of Troilus."* Ed. B. A. Windeatt. London: Longman, 1984.

Christy, James. "Five Twentieth-Century Productions of *Troilus and Cressida.*" Ph.D. diss., Stanford University, 1972.

Coghill, Nevill. *Shakespeare's Professional Skills.* Cambridge: Cambridge University Press 1964.

————. "Letters to the Editor." *Times Literary Supplement.* 1967, 53, 274, 384

David, Richard. *Shakespeare in the Theatre.* Cambridge: Cambridge University Press, 1978.

de Grazia, Margreta. *Shakespeare Verbatim.* Oxford: Clarendon, 1991.

de Grazia, Margreta, and Peter Stallybrass. "The Materiality of the Shakespearean Text." *Shakespeare Quarterly* 44 (1993): 255–83.

Dessen, Alan. "Shakespeare's Scripts and the Modern Director." *Shakespeare Survey* 36 (1983): 57–64.

————. *Elizabethan Stage Conventions and Modern Interpreters.* Cambridge: Cambridge University Press, 1984.

————. "Modern Productions and the Elizabethan Scholar." *Renaissance Drama* 18 (1987): 205–23

————. *Recovering Shakespeare's Theatrical Vocabulary*. Cambridge: Cambridge University Press, 1995.

Dessen, Alan and Leslie Thomson. *A Dictionary of Stage Directions in English Drama, 1580–1642*. Cambridge: Cambridge University Press, 1999.

Donaldson, E. Talbot. *The Swan at the Well*. New Haven: Yale University Press, 1985.

Dryden, John. *Troilus and Cressida, or Truth Found Too Late*. In *Plays*, vol. 13 of *The Works of John Dryden*, ed. Maximillian E. Novak. Berkeley and Los Angeles: University of California Press, 1984.

Edelman, Charles. *Brawl Ridiculous: Swordfighting in Shakespeare's Plays*. Manchester: Manchester University Press, 1992.

Farley-Hills, David. *Shakespeare and the Rival Playwrights, 1600–1606*. London: Routledge, 1990.

Fleay, F. G. "On the Composition of *Troylus and Cressida*." *The New Shakspere Society's Transactions* (1874): 304–17.

Foakes, R. A. "*Troilus and Cressida* Reconsidered." *University of Toronto Quarterly* 32 (1963): 142–54.

————. *Illustrations of the English Stage 1580–1642*. Stanford: Stanford University Press, 1985.

————. "The Ending of *Troilus and Cressida*." In *KM 80: A Birthday Album for Kenneth Muir, Tuesday, 5 May, 1987*. Liverpool: Liverpool University Press, 1987.

————. "Stage Images in *Troilus and Cressida*." In *Shakespeare and the Sense of Performance*, ed. Marvin and Ruth Thompson, 150–61. Newark: University of Delaware Press, 1989.

Freund, Elizabeth. "'Ariachne's broken woof': the Rhetoric of Citation in *Troilus and Cressida*." In *Shakespeare and the Question of Theory*, ed. Patricia Parker and Geoffrey Hartman, 19–36. New York: Methuen, 1985.

Frey, Charles H. *Experiencing Shakespeare: Essays on Text, Classroom, and Performance*. Columbia: University of Missouri Press, 1988.

Gaudet, Paul. "Playing Father: Q and F versions of *Troilus and Cressida*, 4.5." Paper contributed to Thomas Berger's *Troilus and Cressida* seminar at the annual meeting of the Shakespeare Association of America, Albuquerque, New Mexico, 1994.

Girard, René. "The Politics of Desire in *Troilus and Cressida*." In *Shakespeare and the Question of Theory*, edited by Patricia Parker and Geoffrey Hartman, 188–209. New York: Methuen, 1985.

————. *A Theatre of Envy*. Oxford: Clarendon, 1991.

Greenwald. Michael. *Directions By Indirections: John Barton of the Royal Shakespeare Company*. Newark: University of Delaware Press, 1985.

Greg, W. W. *Dramatic Documents from the Elizabethan Playhouses*. Oxford: Clarendon, 1931.

————. *The Shakespeare First Folio*. Oxford: Clarendon, 1953.

Gurr, Andrew. "The 'State' of Shakespeare's Audiences." In *Shakespeare and the Sense of Performance*, ed. Marvin and Ruth Thompson, 162–79. Newark: University of Delaware Press, 1989.

————, ed. *King Richard II*. New Cambridge Shakespeare. Cambridge: Cambridge University Press, 1984.

Guthrie, Tyrone. "This is Shakespeare?" *New York Herald Tribune*, 23 December 1956.

A typescript of the article, with cuts and corrections by Guthrie, is in the Lincoln Center Performing Arts Library, New York City.

Harris, Sharon M. "Feminism and Shakespeare's Cressida: *If* I be false . . . " *Women's Studies* 18 (1990): 65–82.

Hattaway, Michael. *Elizabethan Popular Theatre.* London: Routledge, 1982.

Hawkes, Terence. *That Shakespeherian Rag.* London: Methuen, 1986.

Heywood, Thomas. *The Iron Age.* Ed. Arlene W. Weiner. London: Garland, 1979.

————. *The Second Part of The Iron Age.* London, 1623.

Hodgdon, Barbara. "He Do Cressida in Different Voices." *English Literary Renaissance* 20 (1990): 254–86.

Holland, Peter. "*Troilus and Cressida* and the Rate of Exchange." In *Surprised by Scenes: Essays in Honour of Professor Yasunari Takahashi,* ed. Yasunari Takada, 86–104. Tokyo: Keyusha, 1994.

Holland, Peter. *English Shakespeares: Shakespeare on the English Stage in the 1990s.* Cambridge: Cambridge University Press, 1997.

Honigmann, E. A. J. *The Stability of Shakespeare's Text.* London: Edward Arnold, 1965.

————. "Re-enter the Stage Direction." *Shakespeare Survey* 29 (1976): 117–25.

————. *Myriad-minded Shakespeare.* New York: St. Martins Press, 1989.

Hosley, Richard. "Shakespeare's Use of a Gallery Over the Stage." *Shakespeare Survey* 10 (1957): 77–89.

Ide, Richard S. *Possessed With Greatness: The Heroic Tragedies of Chapman and Shakespeare.* Chapel Hill: University of North Carolina Press, 1980.

Jones, John. *Shakespeare at Work.* Oxford: Clarendon, 1995.

Kimbrough, Robert. "The Origins of *Troilus and Cressida:* Stage, Quarto, and Folio." *PMLA* 78 (1962): 194–99.

————. *Shakespeare's Troilus and Cressida and its Setting.* (Cambridge: Harvard University Press, 1964.

Leech, Clifford. "Shakespeare's Prologues and Epilogues." In *Studies in Honor of T. W. Baldwin,* ed. Don Cameron Allen, 150–64. Urbana: University of Illinois Press, 1958.

Lydgate's Troy Book. ed. Henry Bergen (1906–35), Early English Text Society, extra series, 97, 103, 106, 126.

McDonald, Russ. ed., *Shakespeare Reread.* Ithaca, N. Y.: Cornell University Press, 1994.

McFadden, G. *Dryden: The Public Writer, 1660–1685.* Princeton: Princeton University Press, 1978.

McGann, Jerome J. *A Critique of Modern Textual Criticism.* Chicago: University of Chicago Press, 1983.

————. *The Textual Condition.* Princeton: Princeton University Press, 1991.

McKenzie, D. F. "Printers of the Mind: Some Notes on Bibliographical Theories and Printing House Practices." *Studies in Bibliography* 22 (1969): 1–77.

Mallin, Eric S. *Shakespeare and the End of Elizabethan England.* Berkeley and Los Angeles: University of California Press, 1995.

Maguire, Laurie. *Shakespearean Suspect Texts: The "Bad" Quartoes and their Contexts.* Cambridge: Cambridge University Press, 1996.

Marcus, Leah. *Puzzling Shakespeare.* Berkeley and Los Angeles: University of California Press, 1988.

————. "The Shakespearean Editor as Shrew-Tamer." *English Literary Renaissance* 22 (1992): 177–200.

Martin, Priscilla, ed. *Troilus and Cressida: A Casebook.* London: Macmillan, 1976.

Maxwell, J. C. "Letters to the Editor." *Times Literary Supplement,* 1967, 296.

Moore, E. M. "William Poel." *Shakespeare Quarterly* 23 (1972): 21–36.

Moore, Lewis. "For King and Country: John Dryden's *Troilus and Cressida.*" *CLA Journal* 26 (1982): 98–111.

Nass, Barry. "'Yet in the trial much opinion dwells': The Combat Between Hector and Ajax in *Troilus and Cressida.*" *English Studies* 65 (1984): 1–11.

Newlin, Jeanne T. "The Modernity of *Troilus and Cressida:* The Case for Theatrical Criticism." *Harvard Library Bulletin* 17 (1969): 353–73.

————. "The Darkened Stage: J. P. Kemble and *Troilus and Cressida.*" In *The Triple Bond,* ed. Joseph Price, 190–202. University Park: Pennsylvania State University Press, 1975.

Nicoll, Allardyce. "Passing Over the Stage." *Shakespeare Survey* 12 (1959): 47–55.

Nosworthy, J. M. *Shakespeare's Occasional Plays.* London: Edward Arnold, 1965.

Orgel, Stephen. "The Authentic Shakespeare." *Representations* 21 (1988): 1–26.

O'Rourke, James. "'Rule in Unity' and Otherwise: Love and Sex in Troilus and Cressida." *Shakespeare Quarterly* 43 (1992): 139–58.

Osborne, Laurie E. "The Texts of *Twelfth Night.*" *English Literary History* (1990): 37–61.

————. "Rethinking the Performance Editions: Theatrical and Textual Productions of Shakespeare." In *Shakespeare, Theory, and Performance,* ed. James Bulman, 168–86. London: Routledge, 1996.

Parker, Patricia and Geoffrey Hartman, eds. *Shakespeare and the Question of Theory.* New York: Methuen, 1985.

Pechter, Edward, ed. *Textual and Theatrical Shakespeare: Questions of Evidence.* Iowa City: University of Iowa Press, 1996.

Poel, William, "Shakespeare's *Troilus and Cressida.*" "Shakespeare and Ben Jonson." *New Age,* 28 November 1912, 82–83; "Shakespeare and Essex." *New Age,* 5 December 1912, 106–7.

————. *Shakespeare in the Theatre.* London: Sidgwick and Jackson, 1913.

Presson, Robert K. *Shakespeare's "Troilus and Cressida" and the Legends of Troy.* Madison: University of Wisconsin Press, 1953.

Ramsey, Jarold W. "The Provenance of *Troilus and Cressida.*" *Shakespeare Quarterly* 21 (1970): 223–39.

Rossiter, A. P. *Angels With Horns.* London: Longman, 1961.

Sinden, Donald. "Playing *King Lear:* Donald Sinden Talks to J. W. R. Meadowcroft." *Shakespeare Survey* 33 (1980): 81–89.

Snyder, Susan. "Ourselves Alone: The Challenge to Single Combat in Shakespeare." *Studies in English Literature* 20 (1960): 200–216.

Spevak, Marvin, ed. *A New Variorum Edition of Shakespeare: Antony and Cleopatra.* New York: Modern Language Association, 1990.

Sternfeld, F. W. *Music in Shakespearean Tragedy.* London: Routledge, 1963.

Tannenbaum, Samuel. "A Critique of the Text of *Troilus and Cressida:* Part 1, The Quarto Text." *Shakespeare Association Bulletin* 9 (1934): 125–44.

Tatlock, John S. P. "The Siege of Troy in Elizabethan Literature, Especially in Shakespeare and Heywood." *PMLA* 30 (1915): 673–770.

Taylor, Gary. "*Troilus and Cressida:* Bibliography, Performance, and Interpretation." *Shakespeare Studies* 15 (1982): 99–136.

Taylor, Gary, and Michael Warren, eds. *The Division of the Kingdoms.* Oxford: Clarendon, 1983.

Thiselton, Alfred. *Notulae Criticae.* London, 1907.

Thomas, Vivian. *The Moral Universe of Shakespeare's Problem Plays.* London: Routledge, 1987.

Thompson, Ann. *Shakespeare's Chaucer.* Liverpool: University of Liverpool Press, 1978.

Thompson, Peter. *Shakespeare's Theatre.* London: Routledge, 1983.

Thomson, Leslie. "'Enter Above': The Staging of *Women Beware Women.*" *Studies in English Literature* 26 (1986): 331–44.

———. "Broken Brackets and 'Mended Texts.'" *Renaissance Drama* 19 (1988) 175–93.

Thorson, James. "The Dialogue Between the Stage and the Audience: Prologues and Epilogues in the Era of the Popish Plot." In *Compendious Conversations: The Method of Dialogue in the Early Enlightenment,* ed. Kevin L. Cope, 331–45. Frankfurt: P. Lang, 1992.

Tompkins, Jane, ed. *Reader-Response Criticism: From Formalism to Post-Structuralism.* Baltimore: Johns Hopkins University Press, 1980

Trewin, J. C. *Going To Shakespeare.* London: G. Allen & Unwin, 1978.

Trousdale, Marion. "Diachronic and Synchronic: Critical Bibliography and the Acting of Plays." In *Shakespeare: Text, Language, Criticism: Essays in Honor of Marvin Spevack,* ed. Bernhard Fabian and Kurt Tetzeli von Rosador, 307–14. Hildesheim: Olms-Weidmann, 1987.

———. "A Second Look at Critical Bibliography and the Acting of Plays." *Shakespeare Quarterly* 41 (1990): 87–96.

Tylee, Claire M. "The Text of Cressida and Every Ticklish Reader: *Troilus and Cressida* and the Greek Camp Scene." *Shakespeare Survey* 41 (1989): 63–76.

Waith, Eugene, M., ed. *Titus Andronicus,* Oxford Shakespeare. Oxford: Clarendon, 1984.

Walker, Alice. *Textual Problems of the First Folio.* Cambridge: Cambridge University Press, 1953.

Walker, W. S. *A Critical Examination of the Text of Shakespeare.* Ed. W. N. Lettsom. London, 1860.

Warren, Michael. "Textual Problems, Editorial Assertions in Editions of Shakespeare." In *Textual Criticism and Literary Interpretation,* ed. Jerome J. McGann, 23–37. Chicago: University of Chicago Press, 1985.

Wells, Stanley. "Introduction: The Once and Future *King Lear.*" In *The Division of the Kingdoms,* ed. Gary Taylor and Michael Warren. Oxford: Clarendon, 1983.

———. *Re-editing Shakespeare for the Modern Reader.* Oxford: Clarendon, 1984.

———. *Shakespeare: A Dramatic Life.* London: Sinclair-Stevenson, 1994.

Wells, Stanley, and Gary Taylor. "The Oxford Shakespeare Re-viewed by the General Editors" *AEB,* n.s., 4 (1990): 6–20.

Wells, Stanley, and Gary Taylor, with John Jowett and William Montgomery. *A Textual Companion.* Oxford: Clarendon, 1987.

Werstine, Paul. "'Foul Papers' and 'Promptbooks': Printer's Copy for Shakespeare's *Comedy of Errors.*" *Studies in Bibliography* 41 (1988): 232–46.

———. "Narratives about Printed Shakespearean Texts: 'Foul Papers' and 'Bad' Quartos." *Shakespeare Quarterly* 41 (1990): 65–86.

Williams, Philip. "The 'Second Issue' of Shakespeare's *Troilus and Cressida, 1609.*" *Studies in Bibliography* 2 (1949): 25–33.

———. "Shakespeare's *Troilus and Cressida:* The Relationship of Quarto and Folio." *Studies in Bibliography* 3 (1950): 130–43.

Willis, Susan. *The BBC Shakespeare Plays.* Chapel Hill: University of North Carolina Press, 1991.

Wilson, F. P. *Shakespeare and the New Bibliography.* Revised by Helen Gardner. Oxford: Clarendon, 1970.

Windeatt, Barry. *Oxford Guides to Chaucer: Troilus and Criseyde.* Oxford: Clarendon, 1992.

Index

Note: Pages for illustrations are indicated in italics.